The British Library Studies in the

BRITISH BOOK P
AS A BUSINESS SINCE THE 1960s

ERIC DE BELLAIGUE

BRITISH BOOK PUBLISHING AS A BUSINESS SINCE THE 1960s

SELECTED ESSAYS

THE BRITISH LIBRARY

2004

© 2004 Eric de Bellaigue

First published 2004 by
The British Library
96 Euston Road
London NW1 2DB

British Library Cataloguing in Publication Data
A CIP record for this volume is available
from The British Library

ISBN 0 7123 4836 0

Designed by John Trevitt
Typeset by
Norman Tilley Graphics, Northampton
Printed in England by
St Edmundsbury Press, Bury St Edmunds

CONTENTS

FOREWORD

Professor Paul Richardson

In his classic text, *The Truth About Publishing*, Sir Stanley Unwin quotes with approbation Raymond Mortimer's characterization of publishing not as a profession but 'at once an art, a craft, and a business'. That three-way distinction between those whose skills lay respectively with the creation of intellectual properties, the publication processes, and the commercial performance of publishing companies has been apparent from the earliest days of moveable type. Gutenberg was an inspired craftsman, but he was a terrible businessman who forfeited all his best machinery to his financial backer. Caxton, by way of contrast, had no great technical skills but was a true businessman, who moved among the opinion-formers of his day and identified a market niche: books in English for merchants and educated women who could read but not in Latin. In more recent times the distinction between the art and business of publishing is most finely depicted in Diana Athill's *Stet*, which contrasts her own approach to publishing as a consummate editor and nurturer of creative talent and that of her infuriating, adored publisher boss, André Deutsch, who was more, and equally, concerned with the latest rights deal and the installation of 40-watt bulbs throughout the office.

Many of the great publishing innovators of the twentieth century, Sir Allen Lane, Sir Stanley Unwin, Lord Hamlyn, for instance, were not, on the whole, bookish people. They were less interested in the idea in the book than the idea of books – as objects for deals and trading, as building blocks in the creation of businesses. That is not to say they published without principle - far from it. Allen Lane was a hero (albeit, rather unwilling) in the defence of *Lady Chatterley's Lover*; Sir Stanley told his son, Rayner, he could lose £1000 on the first edition of the *Lord of the Rings* if he thought it was a work of genius; and Hamlyn, who made millions from the inspired publishing of high-quality mass-market illustrated ephemera and the judicious buying and selling of publishing companies, faced down Margaret Thatcher over publication in Australia of *Spycatcher*. But at the end of the day, they were in it for the business.

Yet strangely, although book publishing has an on-going fascination for the other media – witness the coverage of the Man Booker Prize spats or the latest Harry Potter sales figures – serious consideration of book publishing as a business is sadly thin on the ground. The company histories and the personal

vii

FOREWORD

publishing memoirs are mostly self-serving and unenlightening about the real commercial issues behind the literary anecdotes.

However, over recent decades there has been at least one observer of the book publishing scene who has applied a cool, detached, deeply informed critical analysis to the passing events from the point of view of financial performance. First as a professional City analyst and latterly as the most elegant of contributors in *The Bookseller, LOGOS,* and elsewhere, Eric de Bellaigue has been the pre-eminent source of informed commentary on what is going on in British publishing and why from a business point of view. And, while his eye never strays far from the bottom line, he also displays a profound understanding of the non-commercial motivations and issues of culture and quality which are relevant not uniquely, but unusually powerfully, to the book trade. In *British Book Publishing as a Business since the 1960s* he brings together in a revised form much of his most fascinating earlier material and adds a wealth of new analyses and perspectives.

As a director of Heinemann shortly before that eminent house fell into the hands of BTR, Collins Publishers at the time of the first, unsuccessful, assault by Rupert Murdoch, and Octopus/Reed International Books during Paul Hamlyn's astoundingly brilliant sale of Octopus to Reed weeks before the Stock Exchange crash of 1987, I have been, if not a major player, at least a ring-side observer of a number of the key events described in this book. Not only are Eric de Bellaigue's analyses extraordinarily accurate, they have extended my own understanding of events in which I was intimately involved.

There is no other book which explains so perceptively what on earth has been going on in British publishing in business terms over the last half century. It should surely become essential reading for aspirant entrants to the publishing industry, beleaguered publishing CEOs, beguiled venture capitalists, and acquisitive and self-deluding media moguls alike.

Oxford International Centre for Publishing Studies
Oxford Brookes University

ACKNOWLEDGEMENTS

I wish to thank numerous book men and book women for their help and suggestions over the years. One of the most engaging features of the book trade is the readiness with which its participants are prepared to discuss trading matters and practices, not only among themselves, but also with outsiders. My writing on the business has involved me in numerous interviews – some might say interrogations – and I have benefited greatly from such remarkable openness.

This book derives in part from articles written for *LOGOS* (chiefly chapters 3 [2001] and 4 [1994] and *The Bookseller* (chapters 2 [1995], 5 [1996], 6 [1999], 7 [1999], 8 [1998], 9 [1997]). I am most appreciative of the opportunity to see them republished and wish to record my thanks to *LOGOS* and *The Bookseller*. More particularly, I am especially indebted to Penny Mountain, for many years deputy editor of *The Bookseller*, without whose persistent encouragement their conversion into book format would never have occurred.

INTRODUCTION

EVER SINCE 'Communications' was designated a growth industry in the aftermath of the Second World War, book publishing has attracted a high level of investor attention. This goes far to explain the part played by mergers and acquisitions in the history of book publishing, as entrepreneurs, business groups, and investors have sought to share in and contribute to the development of such growth. That much of this activity should have been concentrated in the UK and the USA is attributable in the first instance to the international dominance that English has progressively acquired in so many fields, some previously shared with French and German. This has been reinforced by the role of New York and London as the two outstanding international centres of financial expertise and more generally the position the two countries enjoy in the dissemination of information.

With growth has come transformation. Today's publishing structures carry only faint echoes of the prewar period. In the present work many of the changes that have taken place are traced, sometimes directly as with the analysis of mergers and acquisitions across all types of publishing, sometimes more obliquely through the accounts of individual groups, including Penguin, Associated Book Publishers, Octopus, Reed International, Chatto Bodley Head & Jonathan Cape, and William Collins. For the most part, these chapters relate to the business experience of publishing houses up to their absorption into larger units. The emphasis is on the experience of UK trade publishers, in all their diversity; this leads to attention being paid to some of the colourful and idiosyncratic individuals whose personalities have so often determined the character of their lists.

The concluding section, the lengthiest in the book, concerns itself with trends and issues currently affecting publishing. In some cases, it involves a more timely assessment of subjects touched on in the earlier chapters, such as the effect of conglomeration on literary standards and the part played by literary agents. A spotlight is thrown on the trading experience of the large publishing businesses in a market freed from the price restraints of the Net Book Agreement, while the section on independent trade publishers provides an opportunity to draw attention to vitality in publishing outside the big media groups.

I

INTRODUCTION

Three unrelated subjects concern the outlook for the Chinese market in a context of greater copyright enforcement, the implications for publishing of digital printing, and the scope for self-publishing. In the two concluding sections – broadened once again to encompass all types of publishing – a return is made to the financial considerations that have been a recurrent theme throughout this book. There is first of all a look at the greatly expanded role of venture capital in the financing of industry, including that of publishing. The book concludes with a consideration of valuations accorded publishing businesses up to the present, which illustrate in some sectors extreme consistency and in others fluctuations in the image of a roller-coaster.

There remains the conundrum: How is it that a business so lacking in scale should have been home to so much financial activity? Judged by such statistical measures as sales, employment, and invested capital, book publishing is an industrial minnow. A key lies in the central role played by copyright. By recognizing the uniqueness of any title, copyright has imparted to publishers' lists certain monopoly characteristics. Although the commercial consequences can be exaggerated, since within different subject ranges the degree of substitution between titles can be considerable, it has permitted, at the very least, the creation of literary properties resistant to direct competition. More emphatically, *Animal Farm*, the *Lord of the Rings*, and the *Oxford English Dictionary* are three instances – out of many possible examples – of enduring sales phenomena achieved under the protection of copyright.

So long as the productivity of publishers remains buttressed by the laws of copyright, investment interest – whether at the level of the individual title, the publishing list, the publishing division or the company as a whole – promises to remain a feature of the industry. This should give to financial events of the past a degree of relevance to the present.

Chapter 1

POST-WAR MERGERS
AND ACQUISITIONS

MERGERS, ACQUISITIONS, AND TAKEOVERS have at various times shaped many an industry. What makes publishing's experience distinctive is the way the process has been sustained, starting in the 1960s, accelerating through the 1980s and thereafter being maintained at a rapid, albeit less frantic, pace. This is a pattern that shows few signs of changing.

The history of the book illustrates generously the paradox – by no means confined to this industry, however – whereby strategies that dominate one period are replaced by others, which can go all the way to representing a total reversal of policy. In publishing one can observe several broad phases of agglomeration followed by diffusion.

The first, which occurred in the late 1960s, extending into the early 1970s, reflected the theory that the combination of communications groups and publishing companies spelled prosperity. This argument was swallowed by numerous major US broadcasting and electronically-based corporations. Xerox acquired Ginn, a venerable school publisher, and R. R. Bowker, which, through *Publishers Weekly* and *Books in Print* had become an institution at the heart of US book publishing. CBS bought Holt, Rinehart & Winston, a collection of distinguished college textbook houses; Raytheon, best known as a major supplier to the defence industry, bought the schoolbook publisher D. C. Heath; and RCA acquired Random House. Parallels in the UK included the acquisition of Hutchinson by London Weekend Television and Granada's purchases of MacGibbon & Kee, Rupert Hart-Davis, and Panther. Subsequent disenchantment turned out to be profound, with the anticipated mutual benefits proving elusive to non-existent. The gulf in management styles between broadcasting executives and hardware manufacturers on the one hand and the creators of intellectual properties on the other proved unbridgeable. In all these cases, the publishing houses were later disgorged.

A second phase in this period had much to do with US firms' initiatives in the UK, predominantly those with existing media interests. It was a case of companies seeking to take advantage of purchase opportunities in a country with which many had cultural affinities, plus a language in common, and doing so using the dollar for payment, the one fully convertible world currency. US purchases included André Deutsch (40% stake by Time Inc.), Phaidon Press

3

(Frederick Praeger), and Geoffrey Chapman and Cassells (Crowell Collier Macmillan). At the same time, the Canadian Thomson Organization, as it was then known, acquired Thomas Nelson, Michael Joseph, and Hamish Hamilton.

The US purchase attempts that were foiled or failed were in fact more noteworthy than those that were realized. Crowell Collier Macmillan lost out to the International Publishing Corporation (IPC) in its attempt to buy the legal publisher, Butterworths, and Litton Industries and Famous Artists failed in their attempts to take over George Harrap and Sir Isaac Pitman respectively. Leasco's celebrated bid for Robert Maxwell's Pergamon came to nothing, while McGraw-Hill was a disappointed bidder for Penguin, which went to Pearson, and for Heinemann. Undoubtedly, the limited American success owed something to chauvinistic sentiment. Pearson and IPC were regarded as 'good citizens' in thwarting north American ambitions.

The third phase, dating from the mid-1970s, which saw a reversal of capital flows between the USA and the UK, was linked to the easing of currency controls and progressive deregulation of markets. The single most important instance of deregulation directly affecting publishing occurred in the USA, not the UK: this was the break-up of the 'Traditional Markets Agreement', an informal arrangement reached in 1947 by British and American publishers. Under the Anti-Trust suit of 1975, they were charged with dividing up world markets in restraint of trade. Its demise led directly to Penguin's acquisition that year of Viking Inc. Other UK purchases around that time included those of World Publishing by William Collins and David McKay by Morgan Grampian. Meanwhile, some of the US purchases of the 1960s were being unwound, with for example ownership of André Deutsch, Weidenfeld & Nicolson, Phaidon, and W. H. Allen repatriated to the UK.

By the late 1980s, the effects of deregulation on the international character of publishing transactions was being amply demonstrated. Predators included German, French, Australian, Canadian as well as British and American companies. Much of the activity was centred on US targets. For example, in the five years 1985-9, Bertelsmann bought Doubleday for $475m; Pearson bought Addison-Wesley for $283m; Hachette bought Grolier for $450m; Rupert Murdoch's News Corporation paid $300m for Harper & Row, which it later united with William Collins into HarperCollins; the Thomson Corporation's subsidiary, International Thomson, paid $810m Lawyers Cooperative; Harcourt Brace Jovanovich acquired Holt Rinehart & Winston and W. B. Saunders for $586m; Maxwell Communications paid $2.6bn for Macmillan Inc. In contrast with the 1960s, all the acquisitors were in publishing. At no stage were hardware manufacturers involved.

In the 1990s through to the end of 2000, the buying and selling of publishing houses on both sides of the Atlantic continued, at a somewhat less rapid pace. On the international front, continental European firms played particularly prominent roles, with Holtzbrinck buying control of Macmillan in the UK in 1995, Bertelsmann paying $1.3bn for Random House in 1998, and

4

Elsevier and Reed International merging to form a group having a market capitalization of over £6bn. In October 2000, Reed Elsevier acquired Harcourt General for $5.7bn (including Harcourt debt); Thomson for its part consolidated at the same time its position in higher education with its purchase from Reed Elsevier of the Harcourt higher education and professional division.

The most recent phase has coincided with the collapse of financial markets leading first to a much reduced level of merger activity between publishing groups and second to the emergence of financial buyers – venture capital groups – as substitutes for trade buyers. The international character of such transactions has also become much more fluid, it being often impossible to attach to them national labels: US venture capital funds are increasingly raising funds for European investment, while European based funds will also combine forces with their US counterparts on a particular purchase. This development is discussed in Chapter 10.

The emergence of the financial buyer has also coincided with the dismantling of a number of media groups, notably Vivendi and AOL Time Warner, created in the late 1990s and the early years of this century in the midst of the enthusiasm over the global promise of electronic communication. Their decline provides another example of how strategies adopted one day can be reversed the next – almost literally true of Houghton Mifflin, bought and sold by Vivendi within the space of 18 months. At AOL Time Warner, the book division has had a reprieve; but even if a bid acceptable to the vendor (over $400m) had been forthcoming, this would have represented only a modest step in the company's debt-reduction programme. This is a humbling reminder of the low profile that book publishing cuts within some of the large communications groups.

There are several themes that underlie the more important transactions of the last fifteen years or so:

GEOGRAPHIC DIVERSIFICATION

Under various guises, geographic diversification has been behind numerous publishing decisions. From a postwar UK base, it started by being a means of escaping the limitations of an economy which for many years was held to be the sick man of Europe. This was achieved initially through exports – in the 1970s over 35% of UK publishing turnover was accounted for by exports – and subsequently increasingly by the development of local publishing branches and subsidiaries, primarily in the former colonial territories. The emphasis tended to be on the educational markets, where Longman, Macmillan, Oxford University Press, Cambridge University Press, and Heinemann held prime position. These are also the publishers whose development of English Language Teaching has given the British publishing industry the dominant position in this massive world-wide market.

For US publishers, the most enduring pursuit of geographic diversification has been in the college textbook market. From an early date, companies such as McGraw-Hill, John Wiley, and Prentice Hall created international offices, particularly strong in science, technology, and medicine (subjects in which they had displaced German prewar leaders) and also in economics and business. Among trade publishers, however, the existence of a huge domestic market readily to hand has often deflected US firms from the pursuit of geographic diversification. One outstanding exception is the supremely international Readers Digest Company.

From the perspective of some continental publishers, an important spur to geographic diversification was initially linguistic. The desirability of diversification out of French language publishing was undoubtedly a factor behind Hachette's acquisition of the US encyclopaedia publishers, Grolier, in 1988 (subsequently sold to Scholastic in 2000) and the more recent purchases of Orion (70%) in 1998 and Octopus (the management buy-out from Reed) in 2001.

In contrast to the situation in the USA, the Dutch publishers, Elsevier and Wolters Samson (later Wolters Kluwer) recognized early on the limitations in terms of scale of their domestic market. This led them to set up branches and make acquisitions in the UK and USA. Language was no obstacle. Indeed, in 1986, Wolters Kluwer became one of the first non-English speaking publishers to establish English as the company's official language.

Bertelsmann's purchases in 1977 of Bantam and in 1986 of Doubleday are other early instances of a continental European publisher diversifying into an English-speaking market. Holtzbrinck dates its entry into English language publishing to its purchase fifteen years ago of the textbook publishers W. H. Freeman and Scientific American.

Market share is perhaps the most cited justification in company acquisitions. In trade publishing, the importance attached to market share has risen in tandem with the huge statistical advances in sales measurement and the much greater concentration in retailing. Nielsen BookScan's calculation for the UK of the total consumer market (£1.98bn in 2002), the most comprehensive and detailed source of retail sales information for books, is essential to the lives of retailers and publishers alike. In descending order of importance, the principal shares in 2002 were: Random House Group 12.7%; Penguin Group 11.3%; HarperCollins 9.5%; Hodder Headline 6.9%; Hachette Group 5.9%; Pan Macmillan 4.4%; Time Warner 2.9%.

The story of Penguin's expansion of its American interests is that of a sustained effort at broadening its base, laboriously pushing up its market share; this culminated in the purchase of Putnam Berkley in 1996 when its share doubled overnight to 12%. Two years later, Bertelsmann's US market share went from 10% to 20%–23% on its purchase of Random House.

On a more modest scale, there is the simple quest for size within trade publishing. The UK provides three striking examples of sprats catching mackerels: Century Publishing, Headline, and Orion buying Hutchinson, Hodder & Stoughton, and Weidenfeld & Nicolson respectively. This forms the basis of Chapter 4.

In many areas of professional publishing, the emphasis placed on market share has much to do with increasing development costs. This is nowhere more evident than in schoolbook publishing, the economics of which have changed dramatically, requiring the publisher to finance increasingly lumpy investments, for which a number one or number two position – conceivably number three – is needed to be confident of spreading the costs sufficiently widely. In US school publishing, the cost of a multi- component core curriculum reading program was estimated at $50m in 1997. Not surprisingly, there has been a bewildering jockeying for position. At one point, the arch-rivals, Macmillan Inc. and McGraw-Hill, halted hostilities and united their schoolbook publishing interests in a joint company. In October 1995 Houghton Mifflin bought D. C. Heath, thus moving from being the fourth largest elementary/high school publisher to being number three at the elementary level and number two at the secondary level. In February 1996 HarperCollins sold to Pearson (already owner of Addison-Wesley) its school textbook interests, Pearson thereby displacing Houghton Mifflin from the slot it had enjoyed for three months. In the UK, one spur to Wolters Kluwer's purchase of Thomas Nelson in 2000 was that it had the effect of lifting it to the number two position in the UK educational market.

Much the same motivation has governed changes of ownership in the US college textbook market. The Los Angeles Times Mirror Group bought Richard D. Irwin, leading college publisher in management and economics in 1988. By 1996, the Times Mirror higher education division (including Irwin) had sales of $228m, making it the fifth largest college publisher in the country. But operating profits were a meagre $15m. Times Mirror decided it did not want to be a college publisher after all and did a swap with McGraw-Hill, who then became number one in college sales, having previously been number four, displacing Thomson Corporation, which had achieved that position only a few months earlier as a side-effect of its purchase of the legal publisher West Publishing (see below).

The other side of the swap involved the sale by McGraw-Hill to Times Mirror of Shepard's Citations, a highly profitable small legal publisher, which fitted in well with the Times Mirror's Matthew Bender. Legal publishing has in fact been home for some of the largest transactions governed by market share ambitions. Thomson Corporation, having acquired over the years a number of medium-sized legal imprints in the USA, purchased in 1996 West Publishing, the largest, most powerful and for long impregnable privately owned legal publisher in the USA, famed for its online research services and its database of primary sources. Thomson paid $3.5bn. This may have been

7

somewhat in reaction to Wolters Kluwer's acquisition of Commerce Clearing House, the USA's leading tax publisher, in 1995, at a price of $1.9bn. And both Thomson and Wolters Kluwer were very conscious of Reed Elsevier's acquisition in 1994 for $1.5bn of the US online legal research service Lexis/Nexis from the Mead Corporation. It is worth noting that all three of these huge targets were American, while the acquirers were Canadian, Dutch, and Anglo-Dutch. And when in 1998 Times Mirror decided that after all US legal publishing was not an essential part of their portfolio, Reed Elsevier helped them out by taking full possession of Shepard and Matthew Bender.

So far, market share has been essentially domestic in its application. Among instances that are international in scope, scientific journal publishing provides a shining example. The market ignores national boundaries; publishing economics favours the creation of portfolios of titles; and for many years demand was on a sustained upwards trend. In March 1991, Elsevier, the world market leader, bought what was probably the number two publisher, Pergamon Press, for £440m. Given the dubious stable from which Pergamon came, i.e. Maxwell Communications Corporation, justifying the price presented Elsevier with a special problem. In order to sidestep dependence on the normal due diligence exercises, they took three sets of data whose objectivity was incontrovertible: the list of titles, their recent circulation patterns, and their recent pricing history. With these they built a model of the business, to which they attached a value.

In medical publishing, while logic demands that it should be international, in practice there is often a significant localized element even in countries that share the same climate. This has a lot to do with ingrained historical attitudes. Coverage of liver complaints in a French medical publication, for example, needs to be much more extensive than in, say, a British title, to reflect the French obsession with that organ. Nonetheless, stimulated in part by mergers of global pharmaceutical companies, there has been considerable consolidation among medical publishers. Reed Elsevier, following the Harcourt General purchase in October 2000, is in number one position. Wolters Kluwer's purchase from News Corporation of J. B. Lippincott in 1990 arose out of their strategy of developing in all forms of professional publishing, and this meant expanding in non-Dutch markets. It did not reflect any marked trans-national medical aspirations. Having thus bought the number three medical publisher in the USA, it then added Williams & Wilkins, fourth in size, plus the nursing publisher Springhouse.

That said, one important consequence of technological advance is the opportunity it gives to publishers to spread applications from one market to another, even where the publishing may be characteristically local in character. In the legal market, Thomson launched Westlaw UK in March 2000, since when Westlaw services have been introduced to Australia, Canada, and Germany.

MEDIA GROUP AMBITIONS

Beneath the surface of many of these transactions cited as instances of geographic diversification and the pursuit of market share lies the wider goal: that of the creation of media groups. At its broadest, there is the case of News Corporation where book publishing sits alongside newspaper, film, and television interests, distributed across several continents. Bertelsmann, with its strong trans-Atlantic bias, now combines books with television, magazines, music, and printing.

At the same time, certain media groups have been pursuing a policy of refinement: Pearson, for example, has shed its provincial newspaper and television interests, while pursuing a two-fold strategy in books: (a) diversification into US education; (b) extension of its trade publishing in both the USA and the UK.

The Thomson Organization is now single-minded in its concentration on professional and college publishing, having disposed of its travel business and its north American newspaper interests.

Reed Elsevier, after abandoning trade book publishing in 1997/98, nurtures a major trans-Atlantic portfolio of educational, legal, scientific, and medical publishing interests.

HarperCollins, by contrast, having sold its north American medical and educational publishing, has largely devoted itself to trade publishing.

SPECIALIZATIONS

Refinement within media groups, if carried far enough, converts into the goal of 'focus'. This can deny merit to the multi-market and the multi-product approach to publishing and in general casts doubt on many types of diversification. At the time of writing, the achievement of 'greater focus around core activities' occupies a prominent position in many chief executives' reports to shareholders across numerous industries. Strange, though, how quickly yesterday's 'core' business can become today's surplus-to-requirements business.

In publishing, this accounts for numerous cases of disposals from the larger groups of units and lists which, on fresh examination, are seen to be taking up too much management time, while giving unacceptable returns. Among the more important recent divestments, in October 2002 Wolters Kluwer sold its academic publishing division and in May 2003 Bertelsmann sold its scientific and professional publishing division. A more specialized approach may also stimulate management buy-outs and they can provide the paradoxical sight of the scorned asset turning into a prized business. Thomson's sale of Routledge is one example.

GLOBALIZATION

Globalization has been given a bad name, not least by some of its most vocal proponents. After Time Inc. bought Warner Communications in 1990, the joint chairmen revealed to shareholders that 'in the 1980s we witnessed the most profound political and economic changes since the end of the Second World War. As these changes unfolded, Time Inc. and Warner Communications Inc. came independently to the same fundamental conclusion: globalization was rapidly evolving from a prophecy to a fact of life. No serious competitors could hope for any long-term success, unless, building on a secure home base, it achieved a major presence in all the world's important markets.' Nine years later, when it was absorbed into America On Line, the prospective chief executive let it be known that 'the internet, unlike anything that has existed before, is instantly world-wide. We have got hold of something that is not an American institution, it is a global phenomenon.' But unlike the situation in the 1960s when the electronic groups were clamouring to get into publishing, books are an insignificant part of this type of vision.

It is in the more mundane ambition of trade publishers wishing to exploit world rights that globalization means most to the book trade. This goal has a long history, extending back, for instance, to when Penguin acquired in Viking a US arm in 1975. It also was oversold as a concept. Belatedly, however, and in the teeth of opposition from most literary agents, the exploitation of world rights by a number of leading trade publishing groups is of growing relevance. This is not confined to the large multi-nationals: a medium-sized firm such as Bloomsbury and a small company such as Canongate both endeavour to retain world rights. Among the major groups, Penguin and HarperCollins are particularly well positioned given their powerful trans-Atlantic and Australasian presences. Jane Friedman, chief executive of HarperCollins, is explicit in her aim to have HarperCollins seek to operate as a single global company with simultaneous publication occurring in New York, London, Sydney ... rather than as one having a portfolio of autonomous outposts. The realization of this objective should be helped by HarperCollins's presence within News Corporation, a group whose overwhelming emphasis is on mass entertainment spread across the globe. What more supportive corporate environment can one conceive of for the publication in 2003 of the 'autobiography' of the internationally acclaimed football icon, David Beckham?

CONCLUSION

This rapid survey of postwar publishing mergers and acquisitions may have served to illustrate the diversity of reasons behind such transactions and the lack of consistency that has governed many publishing strategies. As for valuations, in addition to considerations such as the degree to which a publishing business is sensitive to the business cycle, plus whether or not it generates cash or absorbs it, what its underlying pattern of growth may be, to mention the most obvious, the element of fashion has undoubtedly also played a role. All of this is reflected in the prices paid at different times for different publishing businesses. In the final chapter, a number of transactions are studied and the valuations broken down between broad publishing sectors, covering the years since the early 1980s.

What of the future?

A reasonably safe prediction is that the merits of diversification, variously defined, will come back in favour. This could extend all the way from product diversification to a mere broadening of a spring publishing programme.

Related to this, the present emphasis many place on front-list publishing will give way to renewed respect for the reassurance provided by backlist strengths.

While in a number of professional sectors it is difficult to see where the opportunities lie for more amalgamations, under-performing assets wherever they exist will always remain a focus for predatorial attention.

Publishing demographers have long been exercised over the possibility of declining birth-rates. For businesses with clearly defined profiles, this is likely to remain a worry rather than a reality.

Finally, a racing certainty. Once equity markets achieve a measure of health, merger and takeover activity will pick up. The financial purchasers of today, whether they are merely warehousing publishing assets or actively melding them into more desirable properties, will be looking for an exit. This might take the form of stock market flotations or trade sales – at which time the strategies that underlie many of the transactions of the last twenty years will be re-examined and in some cases re-enacted.

Chapter 2

IMPRINTS UNDER CONGLOMERATION

'POLARIZATION IS ALSO taking place in the lists themselves. Only Dependable Best Sellers Need Apply' (Hilary Rubinstein, the *Author*, autumn 1992).

'Editors are there to produce in the shortest time and at the least cost books that will sell. There's no room for sentiment' (Michael Pountney, the *Author*, spring 1991).

'There is an increasingly autonomic and savourless quality to all this publishing activity' (Gerald Howard of W. W. Norton, the *Author*, summer 1994).

As the bellman intoned, 'I have said it thrice: What I tell you three times is true' (Fit the First, 'The Hunting of the Snark'). Is this really the end of the story?

Following a survey which has involved discussions with publishers, retailers, literary editors and agents, charitable organizations, and authors, the answer is a resounding 'No'. Strongly differing views are held in the book business on the question of publishing homogenization.

This enquiry (largely undertaken in 1994) has centred on adult trade publishing, with a bias towards literary imprints, and has concerned itself primarily with trends over the last fifteen to twenty years.

First of all, a feel for the variety of opinions to the question: 'Has there been a loss of distinctiveness in the major British adult trade imprints over this period?'

Martin Lee (W. H. Smith) 'I think there has been a loss of distinctiveness, but I'm not interested in the debate so long as our customers are themselves not worried.'

Alastair Niven (Arts Council) 'This is a question on which I reserve judgement at present. We are getting an increasing number of books published and there is some very good new writing.'

Charles Elliott (Knopf) 'The levelling process is a reflection of the degree of understanding of the chartered accountant acting on his return on capital brief.'

Richard Charkin (Reed) 'There has been increased homogeneity in the packaging of books, rather than in the books themselves.'

Mark Le Fanu (Society of Authors) 'Imprints are now quite a lot less distinctive than when they were all separately run by eccentric individuals with unpredictable tastes.'

Penelope Lively (author) 'There's quite a high retention of identity among imprints. It's not so much a loss of distinctiveness as a loss of viability among small independent publishers.'

Harriet Harvey-Wood (lately of the British Council) 'Publishers are playing for safety and rely on old formulas too much.'

Martyn Goff (Booker Prize) 'Yes, I think there has been some loss of distinctiveness, but not to the extent that many believe.'

Simon Master (Random House) 'Some of the older-established literary imprints have benefited from conglomerization because their lists are subject to better-muscled scrutiny and better support.'

Brian Perman (Book Trust and formerly Heinemann and Hutchinson) 'There has certainly been a loss of distinctive profile. Old-style publishing autocracy actually has a lot to recommend it.'

Tom Rosenthal (André Deutsch) 'What an impossible subject.'

In *The Publishing Game*, Anthony Blond provided vignettes of 43 London publishers, chosen in 1971 'for their size, significance, and sometimes oddity'. The great majority were engaged wholly or partly in trade publishing; 27 were defined as being independent and 16 formed part of larger groups. Twenty-four years later, 10 of the independents have lost their independence, several of them more than once so to speak, and of the others eight have changed owners at least once.

The *Bookseller* published in March 1990 a supplement entitled *Who Owns Whom*, which dealt with corporate developments in book publishing and retailing in the years 1980 to 1989. The picture that emerges is one of frenetic activity. It notes the entry into the trade of such names as Headline, Bloomsbury, Pavilion Books, and Sinclair-Stevenson. But most of all it records what was the phenomenon of the 1980s, namely the gradual emergence of publishing combines. This has brought about a concentration of editorial skills in general publishing within the hands of seven large groups, the bookish equivalent of the oil industry's seven sisters: HarperCollins, Hodder Headline, Macmillan, Penguin, Random House, Reed Consumer Books, and Transworld.

In the 1920s and 1930s, when many of the imprints we know today had their origins, the publishing scene was characterized by vigorous entrepreneurs whose despotic rule was elegantly illustrated in Michael Howard's account of *Jonathan Cape, Publisher.* Jonathan Cape's own attitude to authors was proprietorial, and he expected them to show him loyalty, since it was his money that bore the risks of publication and it was on his shrewd knowledge of the trade that they depended.

The firm's style of business was spelled out by Howard. Writing in 1971, he recorded that, while a publishing coup or a bestseller was uplifting to the spirit and to turnover, 'what gives the Cape list its strength is the great range of books published for reasons unconnected with the balance sheet'. He went on to explain that while smaller sums of money might be spent on the less commercial titles than on the bestsellers, the time, energy, and thought were identical.

In the same vein, Anthony Blond in 1971 recognized that the publisher-owner would frequently 'produce a book which he *knows* will lose money. If he doesn't do this he forfeits his own self-respect and the esteem of the professional literati who expect the occasional obvious sacrifice.'

Book publishing, however, has always been an absorber of capital; it is also sensitive to the ups and downs of the economy. This is a cocktail that more or less guarantees periodic financial crises for small undercapitalized firms, of which publishing in the pre-war and immediate post-war years provided numerous examples. Fresh capital injections, often from non-publishing sources, led to more diffused ownership, and this in turn was accompanied by the rise of the salaried editor, thereby weakening the links between the publisher-owner and the author.

The requirements of the new capital providers, and the greater emancipation of authors, served at the same time to give to publishing objectives a flavour that has become more and more explicitly financial. This is epitomized in Richard Charkin's own job description: 'I'm a commercial publisher. Publishing – not scholarship and research – is the end for me: my job is to find good books and sell the hell out of them' (profile by Michael Geare in the *Author*, spring 1991). We might spare a thought for today's editor at Reed Books who is caught following Michael Howard's precepts, democratically dividing his or her time between money-spinners and also-rans.

The cuckoo in the independent publisher's nest has been the paperback.

Picture the joy in the hearts of the publisher-owner in the late 1930s when offered by Penguin a new trickle or stream of revenue. The paperback licences granted were for a limited duration; the part of the consumer market that was being targeted was new to the joys of book purchasing, and there remained the original hardback side to exploit in the normal way.

In the post-war years, other specialist paperback houses emerged, some free-standing like Pan and Corgi, some captive such as Fontana and Panther, but all on the lookout for reprint rights. Little wonder that advances on paperback licences started to build up to become the determining factor in hardback publishing decisions. At the time, there was a 50:50 split between the hardback publisher and the author. For the publisher whose finances were stretched, the cash flow benefits, furthermore, loomed almost as large as the profit share.

It was indeed fortunate for the hardback publisher that paperbacks were buoyant, since public library demand for hardbacks was being eroded. At the same time, the consumer was developing a taste for paperbacks at the expense of hardbacks.

The next stage in this lightning tour of the changing economics of trade publishing was marked by the dawning realization that paperbacks held the key to financial soundness. This meant that hardback publishers came under strong pressure to acquire or develop their own paperback imprints, while the stand-alone paperback imprints such as Penguin and Corgi reasoned that they should protect their future by securing hardcover resources of their own and at the same time develop further the skills that enabled them to publish originals in paperback format.

Where has this left the independent hardback house? 'With limited scope' is the quick answer. First of all, little help is coming from the institutional market, the traditional support for adult trade hardbacks. As far as paperback revenues are concerned, the stand-alone houses have ceased to exist and the appetite of the integrated houses for outside purchases is greatly reduced by their inhouse supplies. And there is the little matter of the author's shares of royalties: how can the independent hardback publisher afford to match the vertically integrated group's ability to grant 100% royalties on the paperback as well as the hardback editions?

In the case of the more successful authors, co-publishing arrangements with a captive paperback house are an option – but this calls for a capital commitment that the independent publisher may have difficulty contemplating, whereas previously its share of paperback royalties represented a precious cash injection.

The paperback phenomenon, far from proving a saviour, has pushed some independent hardback publishers out of the nest and has left many others severely weakened. This must rank as one of the most important influences for concentration and is behind Richard Charkin's pithy judgement, 'Hardbacks are not a business, they're a hobby.' It is also at the heart of the debate concerning homogenization in trade publishing.

IMPRINTS AND BRANDS

Within the big publishing groups there are two schools, whose members may be termed very loosely the minimalists and the maximalists. The minimalists are the great respecters of individual imprints, the maximalists are the great admirers of the collective strengths provided by single branding. Within particular firms, intermediate positions can also be held.

The chief example of an overt move towards maximalist principles is provided by HarperCollins, the bulk of whose trade publishing is now carried out under the HarperCollins imprint. This has involved the eclipse of such well-known trade publishing names as Unwin, Grafton, and Fontana, and may be stimulating Christopher MacLehose in his efforts to effect a buyout of the Harvill Press. As Iain Burns of Macmillan commented, 'I believe this branding has helped their profile. They have established a very strong image for HarperCollins books and I'm sure it helps their presentation to the retail trade.'

With such an endorsement, it comes as little surprise that last summer Macmillan started to introduce a new corporate identity through the development of a 'common visual link which will work alongside and unite our divisions, enhancing general understanding and perceptions of the group as a whole'. Individual imprints that nestle in the shade of the double 'M' comprise Macmillan, Pan, Papermac, St Martin's Press, Picador, and Sidgwick & Jackson.

The reverse strategy has been pursued by Penguin, which paradoxically provides the outstanding instance of branding among the major adult trade houses. What other publishing imprint has entered the language as a transitive verb? But this has not meant that management has sought to have it absorb its cousins. Hence the development and preservation of Viking, Hamish Hamilton, and Michael Joseph. In Trevor Glover's words, this had enabled Penguin to avoid 'getting into an amorphous conglomerate situation'.

The other large publishing groups have had the retention of separate imprints as a specific goal. Occasionally a programme of rationalization has involved some names falling into a publishing limbo; on the other hand new names have also been launched.

The case of Reed is interesting. When Macmillan exercised its option to acquire Reed's half interest in Pan in 1987, Reed was left in the vulnerable position of having lost its vertical publishing arm. The solution was to invest heavily in a new paperback imprint, Mandarin, to feed off Heinemann, Secker, Methuen, and, later, Sinclair-Stevenson.

At Random House, Century, Hutchinson, Arrow, Cape, Chatto, and Vintage flourish, but the Bodley Head is now confined to children's titles. Hodder & Stoughton, Headline, Coronet, New English Library, and Sceptre retain their separate identities within Hodder Headline.

Transworld, for its part, has made a business out of creating imprints, both hardback and paperback: to the original Bantam and Corgi have been added Bantam Press, Black Swan, Partridge Press, and Doubleday. This owes much to management's preference for organic growth, thereby earning for Transworld the publishing trade's unofficial environmental prize.

The virtues of a single brand over those of multiple imprints can be debated indefinitely. John Coldstream, literary editor of the *Daily Telegraph*, is an outsider, but very much in trade publishers' sights. He is impressed by the monthly receipt from HarperCollins of fatter and fatter boxes of books, whose packaging poses an increasing challenge to the recipient. Far from introducing

Table 1: *Total number of titles published*

	1971-73	% change	1981-83	% change	1991-93
Total	*33,643*	*+41*	*47,487*	*+61*	*76,287*
Biography	1043	+50	1568	+59	2499
Fiction	3863	+29	4964	+61	7980
History	1500	+4	1558	+104	3174
Literature	1060	+56	1650	+30	2151

Note: three-year averages: includes revised and new editions and translations.

a strong character throughout a large list, he finds the effect is to suggest a swallowing of character. He concedes, however, that this is a highly personal view and he is far from believing that the simple act of preserving the name of an imprint guarantees distinctiveness.

TITLES EXPLOSION

Any investigation into the distinctiveness or otherwise of trade imprints has to confront the phenomenon of the explosion in titles published. On the one hand it is an encouraging sign of creative vitality. On the other it threatens the whole trade with submersion. Over the two ten-year periods (see table 1: 1971-73 to 1981-83 and 1981-83 to 1991-93), there was a marked acceleration in total titles published, and the experience was repeated within the main trade classifications. This occurred notwithstanding a widely held view in publishing and bookselling circles that, even in the 1970s, the flow was becoming oppressive.

A more detailed breakdown of fiction and historical titles, which is available for the period since the start of 1990, shows some slowdown in romance titles, westerns, and world war books, but continued growth in the major fiction and historical categories.

One puzzle is that the large publishing groups have had a policy for some time of holding or reducing their title output. This is epitomized in David Young's goal at HarperCollins of 'selling more of less'.

The one exception is Hodder Headline, whose push for market share is backed by a one-third rise in titles planned for 1995.

The evidence from literary agents also points in the direction of greater selectivity, notwithstanding the high standards and the wide range of choice that many applaud in current British writing. In the experience of Rivers Scott and Gloria Ferris, of Scott Ferris Associates, many a mid-list book that fifteen years ago might have been placed if an agent had given it his or her sustained backing will now be unlikely to be accepted. Such opportunities as do exist for the title lie with small-scale firms, but that means all the disadvantages of limited promotional backing, reduced chances of a paperback edition, and weak ties with the retail chains.

Under these circumstances it is hard to explain the unremitting increases in

17

titles. It cannot surely all be vanity publishing. Freedom of entry into the industry will have contributed something, but not on such a scale as to explain the bulk of the rise. Whatever the other reasons, growth in titles has posed problems for many in the trade.

At the *Daily Telegraph*, John Coldstream calculates that he receives for review about one-tenth of the trade books published in any one year. Each week some 25 titles are mentioned in reviews of one kind or another in the paper, making a total of about 1300 titles over 12 months. The level of reviewing has been maintained by and large from one year to the next, so this means a declining percentage of the annual book intake is covered and hence an increasingly severe winnowing exercise.

Explaining the process of selection, John Coldstream emphasizes that under no circumstances will they neglect an author of distinction. Secondly, when the curiosity of the public is tickled it is absolutely right that some kind of authoritative voice (that of the outside reviewer, not that of the literary editor) should discuss the merits of the book. A recent light-hearted case in point is the current fad for 3-D books. There is in addition the gut feel of the literary editor and his staff, with their whims, predilections, and enthusiasms. Taking the *Telegraph*'s experience as a proxy for literary reviewing, the bases of selection would seem to lend a fair degree of support to imprints seeking to maintain their individual character.

An enquiry into the distinctiveness of publishing imprints has a tendency to vere off into a study of the distinction of imprints. This is an important aspect of the subject. The difficulty lies in the subjectivity of all critical judgements. One way of sidestepping this problem is to make the Booker Prize judges arbiters of excellence in the matter of fiction, covering a period of 26 years.

Table 2 records the occasions that individual imprints have had titles in the shortlist (and within that the prize winners). This is done over two 5-year and two 13-year periods, and the imprints are presented under their present ownership umbrellas.

Table 2 is confined to the seven large trade publishing groups. Three form part of quoted conglomerates (HarperCollins, Penguin, Reed), three are part of diversified unquoted groups (Macmillan, Random House, Transworld) while Hodder Headline is a large quoted independent publisher. This means that they are not necessarily subject simultaneously to the same commercial pressures. What they do have in common is that they have all emerged in their present form since the late 1980s.

The striking feature of the table is the consistency of many of the imprints over a period of 26 years, regardless of ownership.

Among the other publishing houses, Faber is the strongest Booker performer over the whole period with Duckworth and Deutsch not far behind, while Bloomsbury takes the honours for the impact it had achieved during its brief life up to the start of 1994.

Table 2: *Booker Prize showings 1969-1994*

	13 years to 1981	13 years to 1994	5 years to 1973	5 years to 1994
HarperCollins	3 (1)	2 (–)	–	1 (–)
Collins	3 (1)	2 (–)	–	1 (–)
HodderHeadline	2 (–)	2 (2)	–	–
Hodder & Stoughton	2 (–)	2 (2)	–	–
Macmillan	4 (–)	3 (–)	1 (–)	2 (–)
Macmillan	4 (–)	2 (–)	1 (–)	1 (–)
Picador	–	1 (–)	–	1 (–)
Penguin	10 (–)	12 (1)	2 (–)	3 (–)
Hamish Hamilton	3 (–)	7 (1)	1 (–)	2 (–)
Michael Joseph	5 (–)	–	1 (–)	–
Allen Lane	2 (–)	–	–	–
Viking	–	5 (–)	–	1 (–)
Random House	22 (5)	24 (4)	8 (–)	10 (2)
Cape	11 (3)	11 (2)	3 (–)	3 (1)
Chatto & Windus	5 (1)	10 (1)	4 (–)	6 (1)
Bodley Head	3 (–)	–	1 (–)	–
Hutchinson	3 (1)	2 (1)	–	–
Virago	–	1 (–)	–	1 (–)
Reed	5 (1)	15 (3)	2 (–)	3 (2)
Heinemann	4 (1)	5 (–)	1 (–)	–
Secker & Warburg	1 (–)	9 (3)	1 (–)	3 (2)
Methuen	–	1 (–)	–	–
Transworld	–	–	–	–

Note: brackets relate to titles that received the Booker Prize: they have been included in the unbracketed figures of shortlisted titles.

A prize which has a more limited range is the David Higham Prize. This is given to a first published work of adult fiction. In 1994 it went to *The Longest Memory* by Fred D'Aguiar, published by Chatto; at the same time, the judges commended books published by Michael Joseph, Cape, and Macmillan.

Conglomerates are evidently continuing to be sources of literary excellence and are thereby sustaining the character of a number of those literary imprints that form part of their portfolios. Within Reed and Random House, the view is also strongly held that such imprints are now better able to fulfil their destiny since they have fewer distractions and are relieved of the need to publish for the popular end of the market. It has to be said that there is a counter-argument, along the lines that they are now burdened with a share of central overheads.

One further point that emerges from the analysis is that, notwithstanding the dominant position of the 'seven sisters', this does not appear so far to have had the effect of crowding out the less financially endowed independent publishers.

The importance of the seven major trade houses has already been amply demonstrated. The way they publish and sell books is clearly relevant to the issue of homogenization in trade publishing.

Vertical publishing. Full integration of hardback and paperback publishing can be said to come about when the same commissioning editor covers all formats. This is broadly speaking the case today at HarperCollins, Hodder Headline, Macmillan, Random House, and Reed, and is seen as a logical outcome of the blurring of the old distinctions between formats.

At Penguin and Transworld, on the other hand, the main hardback and paperback imprints still have their separate editors; co-ordination is achieved through frequent consultation, including attendance at the same commissioning meetings. In the view of Paul Scherer, 'by integrating hardbacks and paperbacks, we believe you can lose something in terms of focus on an imprint. Corgi, for instance, is a very distinct imprint with a real focus and a great character running it.' Penguin and Corgi started life as free-standing specialist paperback houses, and this may have given them a greater degree of robust self-confidence.

Commissioning editors. The role a commissioning editor plays is naturally enough a reflection of his or her standing in a firm. It is also powerfully influenced by the structure within which the person in question operates. It would be necessary to be present at editorial meetings to assess the influence an editor wields and to see the extent to which editorial convictions are tempered – or perhaps overturned – by the judgements of the other participants. Suffice it so say that commissioning editors have star billing and some undoubtedly have considerable pull.

For evidence of that one need look no further than Richard Cohen, formerly publishing director at Hutchinson and Hodder Headline, who has just set up his own eponymous publishing house, with the financial backing of eight authors. Greater love hath no man. ... And yet there have been occasions when prominent editors have moved from one house to another, often in the wake of company takeovers, and their ability to bring with them major authors has proved less than they had hoped (setting aside contractual commitments). In a self-defeating way, this may owe something to their own increased mobility and the unsettling effect it creates. More importantly it is a measure of the strengths that long-established publishing houses enjoy in their own right.

Production. Among the most predictable decisions within a conglomerate, the sharing of a central production department is second only to the use of a common warehouse. And yet it carries with it high homogenization risks. Within the major trade houses, centralized production and design is the rule, though at Hodder Headline the two constituents have retained their separate production departments. The practical effect, however, may have been muted following the promotion of Headline's production director to the equivalent post at Hodder.

The lament that one hears is that, while covers may still retain distinctiveness, once inside the book a sameness of paper and typographic arrangement takes over. How often does one now read a review that concludes 'the book is beautifully edited, produced, and illustrated'? The answer is all too infrequently, unless it were to come from under Ion Trewin's vigilant eye at Weidenfeld. The book in question is *My Mistress the Queen: the Letters of Frieda Arnold, Dresser to Queen Victoria 1854-9*, edited by Benita Stoney and Heinrich C. Weltzien, translated from the German by Sheila de Bellaigue. As Gill Davies points out in her eminently sensible *Book Commissioning and Acquisition*, the bookshop manager who recognizes a Cape book 'has a certain level of expectation about it. That level of expectation, unless it is a negative one, is actually valuable to the publisher. ... So disturb that at your peril.'

Sales. Vertical publishing with editors handling both hardbacks and paperbacks might be expected to have its counterpart in the fusion of hardback and paperback sales. This is indeed the case at Reed, Random House, Macmillan, Hodder Headline, and HarperCollins. Transworld also has a sales force that handles both hardbacks and paperbacks, notwithstanding the fact that at the editorial level management has retained the divisions according to format. Penguin, which has also maintained such editorial divisions, is the one group to have preserved separate hardback and paperback sales teams as well.

The vision of monolithic trade sales forces needs some qualification. Random House has two, one for the commercial division (Century, Hutchinson, Arrow), and one for the literary division (Cape, Chatto, Vintage). At Hodder Headline there are two sales forces corresponding to the Hodder division and the Headline division. HarperCollins has one sales team for its adult trade side (which also carries Thorsons and the religious list), and another for the children's, general reference, dictionary, cartographic, audiobooks, and products. It is therefore only at Reed, Macmillan, and Transworld that all-encompassing sales forces exist.

An initiative by HarperCollins has involved the creation of product managers, who act as a conduit for information and views between editorial and sales; this has the effect of tempering the impact of a single adult trade sales unit. Hodder Headline's approach has been simpler. In the first instance, management has maintained separate trade sales forces for the two constituent companies. It also has the avowed aim of creating additional sales teams as and when justified by turnover growth; in the light of its general expansionary ambitions, this is a practical rather than a theoretical objective. As Tim Hely

Hutchinson emphasizes, 'Some publishers have believed in putting all sales together – we believe strongly the contrary.'

In relation to the distinctiveness of trade imprints, this section has touched on three highly sensitive areas: in editorial, in production, and in sales, the tidy, head-office conglomerate mind is handed opportunities for rationalization and consolidation which pose a threat to publishing individuality. As we have seen, a variety of actions have been taken by publishing managements, quite often with the result that one move has skilfully neutralized another. Looking ahead, the time of greatest risk will come when publishers have to submit their budgets in the middle of the next major business downturn.

AUTHORS

Where do authors stand in the debate about conglomeration and the homo-genization – or otherwise – of publishing imprints? The answer is that they stand in need of reassurance. As Mark Le Fanu of the Society of Authors constantly emphasizes, their natural conservatism leads them to abhor change, and in a publishing world of great fluidity they find comfort increasingly in the arms of their agents.

Fortunately for literature, supply has risen to meet demand: the population of literary agencies increased from 34 in 1946 to 55 in 1966 and to some 120 in 1994. In recent experience, their numbers have been swelled by the inclusion of several prominent commissioning editors who have been attracted to 'a better life, albeit a less decent living' (Hilary Rubinstein's assessment).

Writers' experiences of publishing houses are infinitely varied, as any reader of the *Author* will be aware. This makes impossible any generalizations. Additional light can be cast, however, on some of the issues that have arisen in the course of this exploration by considering the particular experience of an author such as Penelope Lively.

For fourteen years Penelope Lively was published by Heinemann in hard-back. In the mid-1980s she was attracted to André Deutsch, where she had Anthony Thwaite as editor. Another consideration at the time was that Heinemann had by then been acquired by Octopus, and she found the prospect of being with an independent house rather than a conglomerate appealing. In 1987 Deutsch published *Moon Tiger*, which won the Booker Prize.

Some three years later, however, having become uncertain about the future of Deutsch, Penelope Lively made her second move, this time to Viking. It was a difficult decision for her to take, but made somewhat easier by the fact that Penguin was already her paperback publisher.

In addition, she and her literary agent, Murray Pollinger, recognized more and more the merits of a vertically integrated publisher, one argument being that if a publisher owns the whole of an author, that publisher is likely to work all the harder. Furthermore, at Viking Claire Alexander was an editor with whom she was thoroughly happy.

From this account, a number of points arise:

– Within a publishing house, Penelope Lively has looked for 'constructive hands-on editing'. Indeed, the importance given to this editorial relationship was behind much of the earlier attraction of Deutsch. At the same time, increasing disenchantment with the emerging conglomerate character of Heinemann gave added impetus to the move.

– The editorial relationship subsequently proved weaker than the economic argument.

– Financial stability had become increasingly associated with size, and that in turn meant a hardback/paperback capability.

– An instinctive antipathy to bigness was, therefore, suppressed, with the decision to move back to a conglomerate.

– Throughout this writing career, one enduring ingredient has been Murray Pollinger, the agent whom Penelope Lively approached 22 years ago with her first manuscript.

All of which leads to the conclusion that the foremost attribute of a publishing firm which an author of Penelope Lively's standing must look for has to be viability.

A further point to emerge from this 'case study' is that the advantages of an author putting herself/himself into the hands of one publishing group did not become transatlantic in scope. Viking Penguin might logically have been expected to become Penelope Lively's US publisher in the wake of her move in the UK. In the event, having been published in the US for several years by Grove Press, when that company ran into difficulties she switched to HarperCollins, which was already her US paperback publisher. This also represented a move towards financial stability.

FATAL FLAW?

'No amount of juggling with trade paperbacks or discounting or desktop publishing will conceal the fatal flaw in the book industry. It is an industry which was once dominated by the major publishing groups and is now in the hands of the bookselling chains.' Christopher Sinclair-Stevenson's comment in the 1991 winter issue of the *Author* serves to highlight the debate that continues over the changing patterns in book retailing.

The background to the debate centres on statistics whose consistency sadly leaves much to be desired. The broad outlines are clear enough, however.

The retail value of consumer book sales in the UK at current prices has risen from £1048m in 1985 to £1845m in 1993, representing a compound rate of growth of 7.3%. Adjusted for inflation, the annual increase has been of the order of 1.7%, not in itself a statistic that sets the pulse pounding. By contrast, Sir Malcolm Field has revealed that over the same period W. H. Smith's share of the UK book market has risen from 12% in the 1980s to 23% (W.H.S.' 14% plus Waterstones' 9%). This near-doubling in market share has reflected an annual growth rate of around 16% (or close to 4% in real terms).

Between 1985 and 1993, Dillons' turnover rose from £31.6m to £138.7m, a 20% compound rate of growth. It now lays claim to a 12% market share. While this indicates a different definition to the one favoured by W. H. Smith, the message remains the same, namely of a chain that has been expanding at speed.

This characteristic of growth is shared by other chains. The names of James Thin, John Smith, Ottakars, and Books Etc come to mind, to mention but a few. While some of the expansion has been of a corporate nature, reflecting changes of ownership when existing businesses or outlets are absorbed into the larger groups, much has been organic.

DISPLACEMENT OR GROWTH?

This brings one up against a conundrum: how much of these organic sales advances reflects the creation of new demand stemming from the attractions of the shops and their offerings and how much simply results from the displacement of sales at other outlets. essentially independents? The monitoring carried out by the Booksellers Association suggests a net drop of about 3% over the past three years in the numbers of independent bookshops. Its own membership, which stands at 3340, has in fact been rising as a result of improved coverage. The point is also made that the rate of bookshop births remains high. Nonetheless, most people can cite their personal disappointments, as does Tom Rosenthal in typically robust terms: 'The Hampstead Waterstones is one of the best in the country, but I don't half miss the High Hill Bookshop. What have the Hampstead residents gained? B****r all!'

Fortunately for the purposes of this article, the riddle does not have to be unlocked. The critical issue is the end result, the rise in what economists might call the countervailing power of the chains, and others their commercial clout.

This requires a further look at market share, but related to adult trade books rather than to the UK book market as a whole.

In the Headline/Hodder merger document, the proportion of total group sales accounted for by W. H. Smith and its subsidiaries (Waterstones and Heathcote) came for Headline to 29% and for Hodder to 23%; the inclusion of academic business depressed Hodder's percentage. The six other large publishing groups currently estimate that the W. H. Smith group takes between 25% and 35% of their adult trade output, usefully ahead of the figure of 23% that W. H. Smith gives for its share of the UK book market. Pentos for its part is typically credited with shares ranging from 8% to 10%. W. H. Smith and Pentos together account, therefore, for some two fifths of adult trade sales.

If the list is broadened to cover publishers' top 10 book selling customers, HarperCollins estimates the percentage at over 50%; taking the top 20, this rises to over 65%. Transworld's estimate for the top 10 is closer to 70%, while Hodder Headline suggests 80% for the top 20.

While these figures are approximations and the bases on which they are calculated not necessarily identical (whether or not book clubs and trade wholesalers are included being one variable), they all point to a considerable concentration at the retail level.

A further refinement to the analysis can be made if one distinguishes between hardbacks and paperbacks. As a percentage of publishers' total sales, paperbacks represented some 30% in the early 1970s, rising to 35% in the mid-1980s and to in excess of 40% currently. With W. H. Smith emerging in a number of surveys as the preferred source for paperback purchases, this has clearly provided impetus to W. H. Smith's growth.

In terms of trade publishing, notably fiction, the sales of which are now nearly 60% paperback, it is easy to see how the role played by W. H. Smith in respect of individual titles can be much greater than any 30% market share average. When Mark Le Fanu comments that power has moved into the paperback imprint which now dominates editorial decision-making, he is also drawing attention to W. H. Smith's pivotal position in the industry.

What impact the chains have on the distinctiveness or otherwise of imprints must be visible in the way they buy. At W. H. Smith itself, subject-based buying has been a long standing feature, but whereas in Michael Pountney's day in the late 1970s and early 1980s there were three subject divisions, Martin Lee, until recently product group manager, has six.

This increase has been in response to a 60% plus rise in titles published and the consequent need for more decisions and greater selectivity. Each year some 12,000 to 15,000 titles are subscribed to; this level has been maintained for the past five years, indicating therefore a declining percentage take-up of an increasing number of new titles.

In Martin Lee's view, there are 'far too many books being presented to W. H. Smith that should have been strangled at birth'. Presentations to W. H. Smith by major publishers, which were already a feature in the 1970s and 1980s, have become more organized. The consultation over covers, which has taken place for many years, has also become more systematic. W. H. Smith sees some 90 publishers on a regular monthly basis and has 2000 accounts with individual publishing firms.

While this indicates a catholic approach, inevitably the impression made by the major houses reflects their size and their financial strength. Whenever the question of promotional support comes up in discussions with W. H. Smith buyers, the experience of a literary agent such as Sonia Land of Sheil Land is that a title that originates with a large publishing house has an immediate advantage.

Waterstones for its part remains wedded to decentralization. 'We are committed to stocking and displaying a wider range than any other competitor,' declares Alan Giles. This involves having 10,000 suppliers and giving each of Waterstones' 90 outlets responsibility for purchases, with individual stores stocking on average 60,000 titles.

This does not free the shops from the effects of such central decisions as last year's inventory reduction exercise. Also last year, a central function was created covering such matters as the quality of stock space planning and the positioning of merchandise. At Dillons, decentralized buying is being qualified following the creation last November of a central merchandising and buying position.

Within other chains, a variety of practices is followed. Thins combines decentralized buying, which is typical of its general shops, and centralized buying at the twenty Volume One outlets, where, however, considerable freedom exists for weightings to be adjusted to local needs.

BY AUTHOR NOT IMPRINT

While generalizations are hard to make, the increasing size of the book chains sets in train a search for efficiencies. One that is widespread is in the display of books in the shops, where segmentation according to imprints has long been replaced by classification according to authors. As John Lauder of Austicks points out, where an author is published by several houses, few customers would want to search through shelves dedicated to two or more imprints before finding the desired edition. To Ainsley Thin, imprint differentiation was 'designed solely for the convenience of the staff and completely ignores the convenience of the customer'.

While there is widespread agreement that the individual book-buyer is largely unconscious of the publishers whose books she or he buys, the abandonment of imprint segmentation will have served to reinforce this condition. It equates to a small nail in the coffin marked 'Imprint Awareness Within the General Public'.

The single most important development in retailing efficiency is doubtless EPOS, whose measure of acceptance in book retailing is symbolized by the fact that Waterstones now has it installed in all but half a dozen of its 90 shops. At W. H. Smith itself, the introduction of EPOS was completed in 1989. The reduction of the shelf life of books has been striking, illustrated in the chilling statistic that for 90% of the books purchased, the first week is the biggest week in terms of sales.

The sales data monitoring facility that EPOS gives individual shops and chains stands to be widened through, for instance, Book Track, whose objective is to monitor on a continuous basis book sales throughout the country. EPOS and EPOS-related developments stand to expose empty hype, to undermine tired reputations, to create new ones and to reduce some sales staff and some publishers to total silence. The traditional role of the publisher's representative looks as if it will suffer, and the arguments for more centralized buying by the bookshop chains seem likely to increase. These are influences that point in the direction of less diversity in publishing and greater uniformity in retailing.

A key issue concerns publishers' responses to the increased concentration of book sales in a smaller number of retail groups, accompanied by greatly improved market information at the selling end. Were these trends to persist, might this lead publishers to concentrate their attention on what a handful of retailers want to sell *today*, with a consequent impoverishment of the editorial role? Iain Burns of Macmillan recognizes that 'the retail influence of the big chains on what and how we publish is significant'. Trevor Glover of Penguin concedes, 'Commercial pressures have made publishers embrace books they wouldn't have twenty years ago.'

The nightmare precedent is the domination exercised on new fiction by Mudie's Circulating Library in the second half of the 19th century: not only did Mudie's decree the format ('three-deckers' which helped the profits of a lending business based on volumes lent rather than titles), but also the plots, covered by what was known as 'the young girl standard', and the cover prices set at levels that converted book buyers into borrowers.

Fortunately circumstances today differ markedly. But still, the question posed at editorial meetings, 'Will W.H.S. like this?', gains significance at every advance in W. H. Smith's overall market share.

In reviewing the ebb and flow of arguments in this article the results must be judged inconclusive. While many *a priori* judgements assume homogenization, these are not supported by much of the available evidence. What have emerged as threads running through the discussion are the advantages of scale and a build-up of pressures on both publishing and retailing that could well pose a threat to diversity and individuality in publishing in the next few years. This in turn would make the retention of distinctiveness in publishing imprints all the harder.

The key to the future rests on the results of a continuous census of good bookmen and women whose chief characteristic is 'Love of literature, because without that the writing and handling of books becomes at best mechanical, at worst cynical, and either quality is pregnant with the seeds of failure' (Basil Blackwell, 1931).

Chapter 3

PENGUIN

'VERY FEW GREAT ENTERPRISES like this survive their founder.' The speaker was Allen Lane, the founder of Penguin, the year before his death in 1970. Thirty-one years later (in 2001), this prediction invites investigation.

When Penguin Books was floated on the Stock Exchange in April 1961, it already had twenty-five profitable years behind it. The first ten Penguin reprints, spearheaded by André Maurois' *Ariel* and Ernest Hemingway's *Farewell to Arms*, came out in 1935 under the imprint of the Bodley Head, but with Allen Lane and his two brothers underwriting the venture. In 1936, Penguin Books Ltd was incorporated, the Bodley Head having been placed into voluntary receivership.

The story goes that the choice of the cover price was determined by Woolworth's slogan 'Nothing over sixpence'. Woolworths did indeed stock the first ten titles, but Allen Lane attributed his selection of sixpence as equivalent to a packet of cigarettes, an expenditure that imposed little strain on the average person's decision-making processes.

Penguin's immediate success brought a rapid build-up of new titles, all of them fiction, as more and more hardback publishers came to view Penguin as a useful source of supplementary income.

By the spring of 1937, more than a hundred titles had been 'Penguinized'. Having discovered a successful formula, Lane swiftly looked for ways to extend it. He entered the non-fiction market with the launch of Pelican Books, which included works by such writers as Clive Bell, Julian Huxley, and Bernard Shaw. Also in 1937, Penguin became an original publisher when it commissioned books on subjects of topical interest, Geneviève Tabouis' *Blackmail or War?* being an early instance. Many of these Penguin specials, which eventually ran to more than 150, sold in excess of a quarter of a million copies. Such sales led to a substantial allocation of paper during the war years, which enabled Penguin to meet a huge demand from the armed forces. The war years turned out, therefore, to be a period of considerable development for Penguin – under the continued direction of Allen Lane, it having been agreed among the brothers that he should be the one to stay in a 'reserved occupation' and manage the business. Four new series were launched: King Penguins, in colour and hardback; Puffin children's books; Penguin Modern Painters; and, in 1946, the Penguin Classics, the first volume being E. V. Rieu's translation of the Odyssey. The emphasis in the Pelican list shifted decisively from reprints to original titles.

By the mid-1950s, Penguin's unit sales had reached ten million, more than half of which were new titles 'which in one way or another are animated by the explicit intention of providing the public with the varied pleasures and discoveries of the mind'. A casual glance at the *Pelican History of Art*, edited by Nikolaus Pevsner, shows that this noble objective was grounded on reality.

Of the ten million units, a little over half were exported, and of these, one million went to the United States. Two hundred and fifty new titles were published each year, and the warehouse held a thousand titles in stock. Turnover in 1956 amounted to £1.1 million, on which profits before tax were £123,000, a profit margin of 11.2%. The mid-1950s were a golden age for Penguin. They were a shining example of what the whole of British industry was being exhorted to do – bolster the country's foreign exchange reserves through exports. While other publishers were paying it the compliment of imitation – Pan Books was launched in 1946, Fontana in 1952, Panther by two Air Force men on their gratuities after the war – Penguin remained the towering figure. In *The Penguin Story*, to mark the company's twenty-first birthday, it was claimed that 'the struggles for admission to the Penguin list are increasingly difficult. Books which have done well for two or three printings, and would doubtless do as well in another couple of editions, have to be abandoned in favour of untried titles which are standing in the unpublished queue. Publishers who used to be dubious about releasing their reprint rights are now more than anxious to get titles into Penguin editions, and often have to be reluctantly refused admission into the list, or asked to defer their hopes for several years – by which time, of course, the claimants will be more numerous than ever.' A number of literary hardback publishers (Heinemann, Hamish Hamilton, Faber, Chatto & Windus, and Michael Joseph) sought to sidestep this congestion by agreeing in 1948 to give Penguin first call on all paperbound editions from their lists. Within Penguin, they became known as 'The Group'.

The complacency with which Penguin described its market position in 1956 is at odds with the way in which it was shortly to respond to a more competitive environment. Natural justice alone seemed to call for an immediate and humiliating fall from grace. But Allen Lane did not believe his own publicity: in October 1958 he wrote: 'One must appreciate how much change there has been in publishing during the last ten years. When we started Penguins we had no competition. ... The situation today is that we are, whether we like it or not, in a tough, highly competitive industry, and we have to fight every inch of the way, from the facing of colossal advances if we are to keep books away from Pan, Corgi, Ace, Panther, etc. to the real struggle to retain space at the retail outlet.' (Quoted by J. E. Morpurgo in *Allen Lane: King Penguin*, Hutchinson, 1979.)

The company's financial performance for these years confirmed Lane's assessment, with competitive pressures visible in 1958 and 1959 (see table 3).

Table 3: *Penguin results 1956-1960*

	1956	1957	1958	1959	1960
Turnover (£000)	1100	1150	1264	1436	1965
Pre-tax profits (£000)	123	154	128	133	364
Profit margins	11.2%	13.4%	10.1%	9.3%	18.5%

The year 1960, however, witnessed a dramatic advance, with pre-tax profits rising nearly three-fold and profit margins doubling. Publication that August of *Lady Chatterley's Lover* by D. H. Lawrence had been followed two months later by Penguin being arraigned on a charge of having published 'an obscene article'. The 'not guilty' verdict, delivered on 2 November, clarified the law of obscenity for all time. *Lady Chatterley's Lover* sold two million copies and lifted Penguin's pre-tax profits for 1960 by £62,000.

The Chatterley effect persisted into 1961 and brought to a head a decision to secure a stock market listing. Firms such as Butterworths, Cassells, Collins, and Longman had had quotations for many years. In all cases, the motivation was the same: to facilitate the payment of death duties by having an objective basis of valuation. At the same time, these companies usually tried to lessen the possible impact of the payment of death duties through the creation of two classes of shares, one fully voting and one voteless (or with limited enfranchisement). The voteless shares, it was hoped, could be sold to pay the death duties.

Penguin's stated objective was to meet immediate family needs, as well as to help cope with death duties. Most of the shares to be issued were held by Allen Lane's younger brother, Richard, who retired at this time from running the firm's Australian subsidiary. No attempt was made to list more than one class of shares; differential voting rights were increasingly frowned upon by the Stock Exchange and by investors. However, it was indicated that, following the issue, Allen Lane would himself hold 51% of the capital and family interests a further 19%.

While previous listings had been through introductions, where no shares are disposed of, or placings, where the issuing house finds buyers among its clients, the Penguin shares were offered for sale to the public. The timing of the issue was influenced by the continued sales of *Lady Chatterley's Lover*, which, it was estimated, would add a further £50,000 to profits in 1961.

Allen Lane denied this. 'I should hate people to think that we were going public on the strength of *Lady Chatterley's Lover*, as if this were our one and only chance.' It is certain, however, that the Chatterley phenomenon, not forgetting the advantageous publicity this generated, would have been in the forefront of Lane's banking advisers' minds. At the same time, the brokers to the issue, Cazenove & Company, will have drawn attention to the happy coincidence of a well-received national budget, lifting the UK stock market index to a new peak. Wall Street was also at a new high. Some sparkling price movements had occurred in the wake of new listings in a climate which the *Financial Times* Lex column termed 'a new issue bid fever'.

The offer for sale of 750,000 shares (30% of the equity) at a price of twelve shillings a share was over-subscribed about 150 times – indicating buyers for over 112 million shares. Of the 150,000 applications, 3450 were selected by ballot to receive 200 shares each. On the first day of dealings, the shares closed at seventeen shillings and three pence, 44% up on the issue price.

Allen Lane became a paper millionaire and the stock market had its first 'hot' book-publishing stock. The next one to emerge was in April 1983, when Paul Hamlyn's Octopus Publishing Group went public.

In the postwar history of British book publishing, the two names that spring most readily to the public mind are Allen Lane and Paul Hamlyn. Together they changed the bookish landscape. Although their achievements in the long run differed widely, curiously they had much in common, both at a trivial level and more fundamentally:

– Both men had changed their names. Allen Williams had become Allen Lane in 1919 at the request of the chairman of the Bodley Head, a distant relative on his mother's side, who had no heirs and who saw Allen as his successor. Paul Hamburger switched to Paul Hamlyn with a view to distancing himself from the comestible of that name.

– Both were ennobled, Lane receiving his knighthood in 1951, Hamlyn his peerage in 1998.

– Neither was a literary man. As W. E. Williams recalls in his *Personal Portrait*, Lane read very little for personal or business motives and knew virtually nothing about literature. Hamlyn roundly stated in an interview with the *Financial Times*, shortly after the launch of Octopus, 'I am in no way a literary person.'

– Both had strong social consciences, were supporters of the Labour Party and rejoiced in the role of popular educators, whether, in Lane's case, this meant making available good reading to a wide audience by way of the Penguin Classics, or, in Hamlyn's case, of introducing the less affluent to the delights of opera by subsidizing Covent Garden tickets.

– They both had an appetite for risk-taking, were fiercely competitive and were great salesmen. But neither man laid claim to having much in the way of administrative skills.

– Both believed that the demand for books was much greater than the existing market, and they shared in the excitement of supplying this need through finely produced books which most people could afford.

– But most of all, single-minded determination was the trait that governed their business lives.

On the financial front, there were also some arresting similarities:

– Penguin and Octopus were brought to the market at times of investor euphoria, and this enabled both to begin their lives as publicly quoted companies in a joyful financial environment.

– At the issue prices, the modesty of the market capitalizations – £1.5m for Penguin and £55m for Octopus – alerted the investment community to the fact that, notwithstanding household name labelling, book publishing shares were at that time for connoisseurs, not for general investment.

– The scarcity value of the shares was further exaggerated by the controlling shareholdings of Lane (70%) and Hamlyn (67%). Moreover, both encouraged employee share ownership by giving staff a preferential allocation of shares.

Differences between the two men related to their motivations. Hamlyn's intentions were expansionary and financial. Little more than four years after the Octopus listing, Hamlyn had used his highly valued shares to make several major acquisitions. In July 1987 Octopus was sold to Reed International for £535m, nearly ten times the value at flotation. A shareholder in April 1983 would have seen his investment grow more than five-fold.

Lane, on the other hand, was prompted by defensive considerations, anticipating the demands of the tax man. The idea of using his own highly valued shares to expand his business was foreign to his thinking. Indeed, in the nine years between the flotation and his death, Lane spent much time considering the hereafter: at one level, who would be his successor as chief executive and, at another, who would own the company after his retirement or death.

The anointment of Allen Lane's successor became a much-repeated ceremony, and the courting of acquisitors took many a turn. Hamlyn remembered being told by Lane that if he ever sold he would sell to him, personally, but he would not sell to Paul's employer at that time, the International Publishing Corporation. Hamlyn, having got an assurance from IPC's chairman, Cecil King, that he would be released should the situation arise, sat back in mild anticipation of a telephone call. This never came. So he went on to found Octopus.

One of the more surprising possibilities explored by Allen Lane involved placing Penguin into the protective custody of a number of universities, to whom Lane was prepared to sell his shares at two-thirds of their market value. Nothing came of it, one rock on which it foundered being the need to make provision for future capital needs. Richard Hoggart, who was asked for his advice at the time, feels on reflection that 'the proposal indicated both Allen Lane's innocence of the ways of universities and his high and, at bottom, non-commercial vision of Penguin'.

Although Penguin did not use its shares to raise money or to buy companies, it undertook three significant expansionary initiatives in the 1960s:

1. Starting in 1957, Penguin promoted the establishment of Penguin Bookshops, most of which were specific areas set aside in existing bookshops. Retailers planning to refit the paperback sections of their shops would be offered half the cost of racking, designed by Penguin and dedicated to Penguin

titles. The evidence that these Penguin shops within shops both stimulated sales of Penguin titles and increased traffic through the rest of the shop was persuasive. By 1968, there were 83 Penguin Bookshops. Two years later, the total was 100, of which nearly 20 were overseas. This merchandizing initiative illustrates Penguin's ability to capitalize on its UK market share – then standing at about 28% – and to exploit its outstanding brand strengths.

2. In 1965, Penguin moved tentatively into hardback publishing with the formation of Allen Lane the Penguin Press. From the outset, there was no intention that it should publish fiction. Patrick Wright, whose first job when he joined Penguin in 1968 was to be *the* Allen Lane sales representative, was made to understand that it was a feed for Penguin and Pelican titles. As such, it was a facility for non-fiction authors who wished their books to be published in hardcover, thereby enhancing review prospects and widening their appeal to the library market. In 1968, thirty-seven titles were published and in the next few years an annual rate of forty to fifty titles was achieved. In common with all Penguin publishing, careful attention was paid to production and design. Pre-tax losses in the first three years amounted to £47,000, £83,000, and £35,000. By 1969, turnover had risen to £154,000 and at the trading level losses had been almost eliminated. However, Allen Lane told *The Times* in April 1969 that he didn't think 'we should keep it going for more than three or four years if it doesn't break even'.

Tony Godwin, who was then editor-in-chief of Penguin, had envisaged a more active role for Allen Lane the Penguin Press. He had not, however, gone so far as to call into question the self-imposed prohibition on original fiction publishing, anchored in Penguin's origins as a fiction paperback reprint house. This reprint role had been reinforced in 1948 by the exclusive understanding on paperback rights with the five leading literary publishers known as 'The Group'. The effectiveness of this agreement was monitored closely. Dieter Pevsner, who had joined Penguin in 1958, recalls that in the 1960s some of the hardback publishers had started withholding titles for their own paperback imprints. The Rubicon of Penguin fiction originals had not yet been crossed, but the Penguin management were alert to the inherent insecurity of their position, based on five-year licences which might or might not be renewed.

Indeed, by the late 1960s, Penguin had plenty of competition and had become the only independent paperback house (see table 4). All the other imprints had their hardback affiliations – including several that were members of 'The Group'.

3. Penguin entered the school textbook field in 1964. Its educational credentials were such that this was almost pre-ordained. Pelicans had grown into a library of modern knowledge. Richard Hoggart, in his tribute to Allen Lane at the service of thanksgiving in 1970, declared himself to have been one of the many thousands of graduates from Penguin's citizens' university, whose ranks he first joined during the war by sheltering these handy volumes in his back pocket and his kitbag.

Table 4: *Paperback sales*

Imprint	Affiliation	Unit sales (m)	
		1969	1972
Penguin	Independent	27	35
Pan	Macmillan; Heinemann; Collins	17	22.5
Fontana	William Collins	13	21
Corgi	Bantam; Grosset & Dunlap	13	15
Hodder, Coronet	Hodder & Stoughton	6	9
Panther	Granada	9	11.5
(including in 1972 Mayflower)			
Sphere	Michael Joseph, Int. Thomson	4	4.5
New English Library	New American Library	3	8
(including in 1972 Ace and Four Square)			
Mills & Boon	Harlequin (from 1972)	4.5	7
Arrow	Hutchinson	4	6.5

Penguins, and especially Pelicans, had become ancillaries in courses at universities and institutions of higher education. By the mid-1950s, more than half of Penguin's new books were 'designed in various ways to provide the public with the pleasures and discoveries of the mind'. About half of the one million Penguins sold in the USA were supplied to campus bookstores.

Pre-ordained or not, the way Penguin got involved in school textbooks was characteristic of these more reflective times. Charles Clark, who was in charge of Penguin Education, recalls that the initial impetus came via Jack Morpurgo, who put Penguin in touch with the Nuffield Foundation at a time when they were looking for a non-traditional publisher to become involved in US-style 'child-centred education'. Tony Godwin became convinced; Allen Lane was also converted, influenced by the prestige of the Nuffield link, and attracted to the idea that Penguin, a pioneer in trade publishing, should also be innovative in education publishing.

An auspicious start was made with Penguin and Longman co-publishing, on a commission basis, the Nuffield O-level science and combined science projects. Later, Penguin secured the sole appointment (in competition with Longman) for the Nuffield A-level sciences course on a royalty basis. Penguin Education was built up first by Christopher Dolley, who had joined Penguin from Unilever in 1962, initially as export manager, and, from 1966, by Charles Clark, at the time Penguin's deputy chief editor.

Fifty titles were published in 1968, 75 in 1969, and 100 in 1970. By that time, the Nuffield titles were also building up – 150 for the O-level science course alone. Other projects included the New Penguin Shakespeare; *Voices*, a three-volume anthology of poetry and pictures for secondary schools; *Success with English*, a course teaching English as a foreign language; and *Connexions*, a series of liberal-studies topic books in magazine style.

34

Table 5: *Penguin results 1961-1970*

	Turnover (£000)	Pre-tax profits (£000)	Margins (%)
1961	2102	221	10.5
1962	2404	289	12.0
1963	2681	445	16.6
1964	3119	573	18.4
1965	3564	540	15.2
1966	4131	533	12.9
1967	4469	477	10.7
1968	5319	512	9.6
1969	5927	609	10.3
1970	7036	966	13.7

By entering into school publishing, Penguin was no longer fighting off competitors from a position of marked dominance. It was entering a field which was unfamiliar to it and was already well supplied by publishers of long standing. School publishing is a national business. Penguin was no longer catering for a world market and was committing itself to financing its own development in a notoriously capital-hungry segment of the publishing industry.

In the period from the flotation in 1961 to 1970, the year of Allen Lane's death, turnover rose at a remarkable annual compound rate of 14.4% and pre-tax profits at an even more rapid, but jagged, rate of 17.8%. The impact of development expenditure and start-up losses at the hardback subsidiary and particularly at the educational division are visible in the flat profits from 1965 to 1968. The rebounds in 1969 and in 1970 reflect an easing of these pressures (see table 5).

What these statistics fail to convey is the creative excitement within Penguin during this period. One of Allen Lane's great strengths was his ability to attract talented men and women, whether as advisers or colleagues, to whom he gave a loose rein – though occasionally the rein got converted into a hangman's rope.

Throughout the early years, the fiction list was presided over by Eunice Frost, who had begun life as Allen Lane's personal assistant. The non-fiction side included such figures as Jack Morpurgo, who was to become professor of American Literature at Leeds University; Krishna Menon, the radical Indian barrister; W. E. Williams, the future secretary-general of the Arts Council; and Alan Glover, the remarkable polymath, whose detailed criticisms of Pelican titles published during the war led to his being invited to exercise his critical faculties from within the organization.

In the late 1950s, some of the spark may have gone out of Penguin's editorial side, but, as Dieter Pevsner amusingly expresses it, 'after the decline of the 1950s he [Allen Lane] succeeded yet again in brewing up a cauldron of people who gave Penguin another renaissance as fruitful as its early peaks'. The recruits included Tom Maschler, fiction editor in 1958 (he left to join Jonathan Cape two years later); Tony Godwin in 1960, who, to a great extent, fashioned Penguin's editorial stance in the 1960s until his dismissal in May 1967; Dieter Pevsner in 1958; Charles Clark in 1960; and Kaye Webb, also in 1960, an inspired appointment by Tony Godwin to run the Puffin lists.

Tony Godwin's dismissal draws attention to Allen Lane's innate suspicion of heirs apparent. Godwin had been made editor-in-chief and main board director in 1964. His fall from grace was precipitated by his espousal of cover designs and promotional initiatives that Allen Lane regarded as vulgar, plus the publication of a book by the French cartoonist Siné, which Foyle's refused to stock. Lane also thought it sacrilegious and had it pulped within weeks of its release. Two years after Godwin's dismissal, Christopher Dolley was made joint managing director with Harry Paroissien, a long-serving Penguin director and colleague of Lane's. There was no doubt about Dolley's ability to manage and direct. But those who knew the erratic history of the claims to succession suspected (in the words of Jack Morpurgo) that 'he owed his inheritance to the accident that Allen Lane had not been given time to change his mind yet again'.

Allen Lane's death on 7 July 1970 had been preceded by a major operation for cancer in 1968. As his health declined, a bright light was directed at what should happen to the business once the controlling shareholder was no more. The announcement on 8 July of an agreed merger with Longman demonstrated the ultimate in advance financial planning.

Conversations had taken place with Longman at a fairly early stage and were sustained after Longman's sale in 1968 to the Pearson Group. This choice of acquisitor had had Allen Lane's ultimate blessing.

In a reverse takeover formula, Penguin issued 6.25m new shares to Pearson Longman in payment for Longman. Penguin's issued capital was raised to 10m shares, in which Pearson Longman had consequently a 62.5% stake. While this gave the Pearson interests control of the Penguin-Longman businesses, Penguin's shareholders still held the balance of 37.5%. Penguin Publishing's stock market quotation was retained. On the stock exchange, the market valued the combined Group at £22.5m, £14.1m being attributable to Longman and £8.4m to Penguin. The latter figure represented a near-six-fold advance on the valuation placed on Penguin at the 1961 flotation.

The reason for the haste with which the old king's successor was announced became clear when the president of the McGraw-Hill Book Company, Edward E. Booher, expressed great surprise at the news, pointing out that McGraw-Hill had a holding of 17.3% and had 'always hoped to offer for the rest'. Gordon Graham, who was then managing director of McGraw-Hill in the UK, recalls attending a meeting between Shelton Fisher, chairman of McGraw Inc., and Allen Lane in 1968. At that time, McGraw-Hill's share in Penguin was 10%. Fisher inquired how Lane would view an increase in McGraw-Hill's holding. Lane replied 'You are most welcome'.

Subsequent contacts with Penguin, usually involving Christopher Dolley, did nothing to dispel the cordial atmosphere, thereby encouraging further purchases of Penguin shares and even prompting the creation of an organization chart in anticipation of full ownership. McGraw-Hill appointed Morgan Grenfell to handle its bid. Harcourt Brace Jovanovich, which had a 65% stake in Longmans Canada, promptly offered Penguin its services with a view to thwarting any McGraw-Hill bid. Serious discussions were held with the Penguin board and the trustees of the Lane trust, leading to McGraw-Hill making a cash offer for a controlling interest. This was rejected. At the same time, Edward Boyle, Penguin's acting chairman, made a speech opposing a foreign takeover. Being unwilling to pursue a hostile bid, McGraw-Hill withdrew from the scene, with Booher thoroughly aggrieved and firmly convinced that he had been led up the garden path.

As Mark Longman told *Publishers Weekly*, 'this is the outcome of years of quiet talks between Sir Allen and me. We had reached a tacit understanding that this was the only way for certain survival of the two companies.' He also went out of his way to thank Gordon Graham for McGraw-Hill's 'gentlemanly behaviour'.

The so-called merger of Penguin and Longman lasted for a relatively short time. In August 1971, the Pearson Group paid £13m for the 37.5% minority in Penguin Publishing. Longman and Penguin thereby became two wholly-owned – and separate – subsidiaries within Pearson Longman.

For many people, whether Penguin employees, investors, or authors, the attractions of the sale to Pearson included assurances of editorial and to a great extent managerial independence; inclusion in a group which had little in the way of trade publishing and therefore no immediate call for rationalization and integration; a British address at a time of considerable US takeover activity in the UK which was stirring chauvinistic reaction; and, on a longer time scale, the prospect of access to capital on an inebriating scale.

IN PEARSON'S OWNERSHIP

As happens frequently in the aftermath of a change of ownership, Penguin's early years with Pearson were marked by a number of prominent departures. Charles Clark left in 1972 to join Hutchinson, of which he later became chief executive. Dieter Pevsner and Oliver Caldecott departed in July that year to set up Wildwood House, with backing from Random House. Christopher Dolley, who had joined the Pearson Longman board shortly after the 1970 merger, left abruptly in February 1973, 'to be free to move into a wider field of business activity'.

New appointments included Peter Calvocoressi, Reader in International Relations at Sussex University, as editorial director. Earlier he had been

Table 6: *Interest rates and inflation*

| | Minimum lending rate and inflation rate | | |
	three-year average 1970-1972	four-year average 1973-1976	four-year average 1977-1980
MLR	6.9%	11.0%	11.9%
Inflation	7.7%	11.0%	14.2%

partner/director at Chatto & Windus for eleven years. Under his terms of appointment in January 1972, Calvocoressi made it a condition that he would retire on reaching the age of sixty-five in about five years' time. In January 1973, Peter Carson, who was later to become editorial director, joined Penguin as senior editor of the hardback subsidiary. In March 1973, in the wake of Christopher Dolley's departure, Jim Rose, sixty-three years old, became chairman of Penguin Books – in a non-executive capacity. He had been editorial director of Pearson's provincial newspaper subsidiary, the *Westminster Press*. Peter Calvocoressi was then appointed publisher and chief executive. He had turned down the position of executive chairman so that Pearson should be strongly represented on the Penguin board (in the event by Jim Rose).

The new management team inherited from the start a turbulent economic scene, bracketed, as it turned out, by the two oil shocks in 1973 and 1979 and the cyclical recessions of 1974/75 and 1980/81. The deterioration in the economic climate is encapsulated in table 6, which links the annual rates of domestic inflation and the level of interest rates as represented by the Bank of England's minimum lending rate (MLR). The use of averages in the table masks peaks and troughs – such as an annualized inflation rate that hit 27% in August 1975 and 22% in May 1980.

For an industry that, for the most part, is an absorber of capital, rather than a generator of cash, with stocks and trade debtors exceeding trade creditors by a substantial margin, the consequences of accelerating rates of inflation and interest are hugely negative. Many a book publisher unwillingly illustrated the operation of the 'Inflationary Doomsday Machine', under which companies need more working capital – just to keep going, let alone meeting any expansionary targets – than their profits can provide. For publishing as a whole, the result is little real growth, albeit frequently disguised by powerful nominal growth (see table 7).

Penguin's experience was to see total volume sales fall from 44m in 1974 to 39m in 1979, a soft domestic market more than offsetting strength overseas. A prominent victim of the economic situation was Penguin Education. The announcement of its closure in March 1974 was linked by the Penguin chairman, Jim Rose, to financial pressures stemming from the budgeted capital needs for the ensuing three years. High among these was the Penguin English

Table 7: *UK book publishing turnover 1972-1982*

	1972	1973	1974	1975	1976	1977	1978	1979	1980	1981	1982
Nominal (£m)	288	314	384	469	563	653	751	844	976	1077	1100
Inflation adj.*	100.0	104.4	108.7	106.2	109.0	104.6	104.4	106.0	104.4	98.0	88.8

*Adjusted by the Book Price Index. *Source:* Publishers Association.

Project for secondary schools, launched in 1970. While Peter Calvocoressi recalls that it had been well received by the more progressive and articulate elements in the teaching profession, initial sales had been poor and it promised to absorb a lot of money over a period of years.

The Times Education Supplement (TES) editorial on the subject pointed to a deteriorating economic environment for school publishing generally: high interest rates, stringency in public spending, the incipient threat of subsidized publishing by some local education authorities, rocketing paper prices, the downward floating pound. What they were unable to predict was the imminent onset of the three-day working week. More contentiously, management indicated that Penguin Education had in effect been a non-profit trust within the Group for its eight-year life. This was swiftly rebutted by Charles Clark in a letter to the TES pointing out that the imprint had shown an operating profit each year from 1970 onwards. The after-interest figures, however, were not quoted.

The closure of Penguin Education also prompted a letter to the TES deploring the decision, signed by eighty Penguin Education writers and sympathizers. They further suggested that 'decisions which affect the cultural life of a country should not he taken secretly in board rooms, and when they are taken in this way they should be publicly examined'. (One wonders what might have been their response had Jim Rose expressed himself as did Rick Wagoner, chief executive of General Motors, when announcing in December 2000 the closure of the Luton car plant in the UK and the whole of the Oldsmobile line in the USA: 'We surgically have to go after the fat in the system.') In the 1970s, the phrasing was perhaps gentler, but the end result much the same. Economics and finance apart, a small, upstart Penguin Education and a massive, venerable Longman Holdings were always going to find it difficult to share the same roof. No prizes as to who would prevail in the long run.

Closure of the hardback side of Penguin was seriously contemplated. Following the merger with Longman, Allen Lane the Penguin Press had migrated to Longman where it was allied to Longman's general hardback list. This somewhat bizarre arrangement was later reversed, and in 1973 the two were transferred back to Penguin where they found in Peter Calvocoressi a powerful advocate who championed a more central role for Allen Lane within the group. But the 1974 economic crisis dealt harshly with Allen Lane, which was subjected to some of the company's most severe cost-cutting measures and only just survived the recommendations of those who thought that Penguin should fall back on what it knew best – paperback reprints – and avoid diversions into the world of original hardbacks.

It would be wrong to assume that management was wholly preoccupied with immediate problems. The year 1975 saw an initiative of capital importance to Penguin's future development: Penguin's role in the USA. As early as 1939, Penguin Inc. had been set up in New York City as a sales office, managed by Ian Ballantine, a recent college graduate. Once again, Penguin was ahead of its time. The umbilical cord linking Harmondsworth to New York was in practical terms severed, however, during the war, leaving Penguin Inc. to develop into a small and, in effect, independent publishing company. This was not altogether to Allen Lane's satisfaction, and in 1945 Ian Ballantine left to set up Bantam Books, with the backing of Curtis Publishing and Grosset & Dunlap. Kurt Enoch took over in a caretaker capacity, and in 1946, Victor Weybright was appointed chairman. He initiated a vigorous publishing programme and, predictably, there was a parting of ways. In 1948, Weybright and Enoch bought Penguin's US assets, which were injected into a newly formed company, whose sonorous title The New American Library of World Literature Inc. was later to be shortened to New American Library Inc. Some twelve years on, in 1960, having developed such imprints as Signet, inspired by Penguin Classics, and Mentor, in the Pelican tradition, it was acquired by The Times Mirror Company for $13.5m.

What was left of the Penguin business in the USA reverted to sales and distribution, based in Baltimore, a city unremarkable for its publishing links. For four years in the 1960s, it was 49% owned by Houghton Mifflin, which at the time carried the Penguin list. During the 1960s, there were some half-hearted attempts at re-establishing a publishing presence in New York, but only with the arrival of Peter Calvocoressi was the issue firmly faced. He saw the need either to close the Baltimore operation or for it to be strengthened and relocated to New York City. The latter policy was adopted. A hiccup occurred with the appointment of a chief executive whose alleged links with the underworld rendered him unsuitable for long-term employment. John Hitchin was seconded to New York and presided over a gratifying increase in sales. Calvocoressi then campaigned for the purchase of a US imprint. This received Pearson's blessing and, after a number of false starts, the purchase of Viking Press Inc. was announced in November 1975.

As Peter Calvocoressi recently reiterated, 'my basic belief was that Penguin's constituency was not Britain (plus the Commonwealth) but the English-speaking world'. On the announcement, Jim Rose had explained that the aim was 'to create a united publishing house offering authors worldwide publication, in both hardcover and paperbound forms, under imprints occupying pre-eminent positions in the English speaking world'.

The purchase was given a degree of urgency by the 1975 Anti-Trust suit, which charged 21 American publishers (Penguin Inc. being one of these) with conspiring with British publishers to divide up world markets in restraint of trade. This heralded the break-up of the British 'traditional markets agreement' and prompted a number of other British houses to take advantage of a coincidental relaxation of exchange controls to buy US publishing businesses – not always with happy long-term consequences. These included such purchases as World Publishing by William Collins; David McKay by Morgan Grampian; and west coast education publisher Fearon by Pitman.

The Penguin purchase appeared to satisfy several key company objectives. Viking Press Inc., a privately-owned publishing house founded in 1925 by Harold K. Guinzburg, was a highly respected trade publisher, whose authors included John Steinbeck, Arthur Miller, James Joyce, Iris Murdoch, Graham Greene, Lawrence Durrell, and Frederick Forsyth. With sales of some $15m, Viking Press was three times as large as Penguin Inc. Through Viking, Penguin acquired, crucially, a significant position in hardback publishing. This made up three-quarters of Viking's business, the remaining 25% being accounted for by its comparatively weak paperback line, Compass; from the start, Compass was destined to be absorbed into the Penguin imprint and Viking's juvenile Seafarers titles were to be transformed into Puffins.

Viking became available because of a liquidity squeeze. With ownership vested in a foundation, further capital was not forthcoming. Fortuitously, the S. Pearson oil production and servicing company, Midhurst Corporation, was at the time cash rich, and Pearson was looking for an investment home for these US funds. Under the terms of the purchase, an initial 66% controlling interest in the Viking Press was acquired by Penguin, in conjunction with its ultimate parent, S. Pearson. Assuming the exercise of an option granted in respect of the minority 34%, the overall cost was estimated at $9m. Part was payable on completion of the transaction and part after four years, based on an earnings formula; $3m of additional working capital was also immediately forthcoming from Pearson. Thomas H. Guinzburg, son of the founder and since 1961 president of Viking Press, was named president and chief executive of the merged firm, Viking Penguin Inc., with tenure for 'at least the next seven years'.

Pearson management was in no doubt about the significance of this initiative. The 1975 report and accounts conveyed to shareholders a ringing declaration: 'This purchase establishes in New York a means of increasing substantially the sale of Penguins in the US and should create in four or five years a publishing base there comparable to the Penguin operation in the United Kingdom. The old rigid distinctions between hardcover and paperback publishing are becoming obsolete. Penguin and Viking will be able to publish every kind of book for their markets in any appropriate form or shape, for sale virtually throughout the world.'

Penguin during the 1970s had roller coaster results (see table 8), starting

Table 8: *Penguin results 1971-1980*

	1971	1972	1973	1974	1975	1976	1977	1978	1979	1980
Turnover (£000)	8162	8741	10,872	13,604	17,227	18,698	18,935	22,673	27,725	36,127
Pre-tax profits (£000)	1118	1003	749	917	1843	2776	1409	1525	319*	242
Margins	13.7%	11.5%	6.9%	6.7%	10.7%	14.8%	7.4%	6.7%	1.2%	0.7%

* Excluding exceptional relocation charges of £700,000

with a margin of 13.7%, then succumbing to the domestic recession in the mid-1970s. This was followed by a vigorous recovery, leading to a margin as high as 14.8% in 1976, only to be followed by a plunge into negligible profits in 1979 and 1980. This unhappy sequence was accompanied by industrial unrest at the national level, union dissatisfaction within the company, and repeated, painful rationalization decisions taken by management. At the end of the decade, a free-floating sterling was accorded petro-currency status, thereby inflicting severe damage on export sales and eroding, in sterling terms, the earnings of overseas subsidiaries.

Turbulence in profit and loss was accompanied by boardroom changes. Links between the two, however, are not proven. After all, the appointments of Jim Rose and Peter Calvocoressi as chairman and chief executive in 1973 carried the stamp of an interregnum. It was not simply a question of the two men's ages – 63 and 61 respectively – but there was Peter Calvocoressi's precise stipulation that he would not serve beyond his sixty-fifth birthday. In the event, he was replaced in July 1976, shortly before his sixty-fourth birthday.

Early in 1974 Pat Gibson, chairman of Pearson Longman, had abruptly altered Jim Rose's position from that of Penguin's non-executive chairman, as had been originally agreed, to that of executive chairman. This change of role proved, in many ways, unsettling. As Calvocoressi pointed out two years later in a sharply worded memorandum to Rose, its effect had been to confuse lines of responsibility. To the question 'Who runs Penguin?', he gave the answer 'Nobody knows'. He went on to point out that Pearson's representation on the Penguin board had stopped being in the interests of communication and instead had become an aspect of management. Given what he saw as 'the owner's alarming incomprehension of publishing in general and Penguin publishing in particular', this could serve only to fuel a growing disenchantment. Calvocoressi's dismissal in July 1976 can be linked to an irretrievable breakdown, as the divorce courts express it. It cannot be tied directly to the performance of the company, which in 1976 was to achieve record profits – albeit not destined to be sustained, nor adjusted for inflation – of £2.8m.

Following his departure, the editorial responsibilities were transferred to Tony Mott. At the age of 42, he certainly had the advantage of youth, but his previous experience had been in sales and marketing. His tenure turned out to be short. In October 1978, Penguin recruited a new chief executive. Also aged 42, he came steeped in US publishing experience, having transformed Avon

Books over a period of thirteen years from a small firm into a major US paper-back house. Penguin's opportunity was to have found Peter Mayer unhappy in his current position as president and publisher of Pocket Books, part of Simon & Schuster.

PETER MAYER

The Peter Mayer 'reign', from his coronation in October 1978 to his abdication in December 1996, saw Penguin transformed from sales and operating profits of £22.7m and £2.0m to sales nearly seventeen times greater of £380m and operating profits fifteen and a half times greater of £31.0m. If the base year is taken as being 1979, the improvement in operating profits is from £688,000 and works out at forty-five times.

But a statistical exercise of this kind is far too crude an assessment of Mayer's period at the head of Penguin; elaboration is required. As a starting-point, one can perhaps do worse than turn to the notes of a meeting on 9 March 1979, less than five months after his appointment.

His mind was at the time concentrated on domestic issues. The unification of the editorial responsibilities covering both hardbacks and paperbacks had been marked by the recent appointment of Peter Carson, editorial director of the Allen Lane hardback imprint, to the position of editor-in-chief of all adult non-fiction, whatever the format. At the same time, Philippa Harrison, recruited from Hutchinson, was made editorial director of all adult fiction, while Kaye Webb was confirmed as children's editorial director, encompassing the Kestrel hardback imprint, as well as the Puffin and related paperback lines.

Given the vulnerability of an independent reprint paperback house to erosion in its portfolio of licences, the desirability of paperbacks cuddling up to hardbacks editorially was seen as the important first step. The threat had been recognized by Tony Godwin, Christopher Dolley, and Peter Calvocoressi. A vigorous expansion of the hardback publishing programme from some 65 new titles a year – plus the publication of more paperback originals – was Mayer's immediate goal. Copyright control was the governing consideration.

Peter Mayer had a rule of thumb that a new title had to earn its corn in its home market. This was at odds with quite a few publishing decisions which seemed to make economic sense only when credit was taken for prospective overseas sales. Application of this more rigorous test, particularly relevant to non-fiction, was to lead to the increasing use of the trade ('B' format) paper-back. Trade paperbacks had become a major area of growth in the USA, but were still at an early stage in the UK. By attaching significantly higher prices to the 'B' format titles than to the average paperback, the sums for what were quite often minority interest titles stood to be transformed for the better. Furthermore, the 'B' format also permitted the reissue of backlist titles on an economic footing.

As far as fiction was concerned, Mayer's priority was to correct what he saw as a serious neglect of new publishing. More effective front-list publishing would in turn support and nourish the backlist. From Peter Carson's perspective, there was also limited scope for Penguin's paperback business to expand at the quality end, particularly with other publishers moving into the market. Hence the need for Penguin to spread into more popular latitudes.

This was soon to be given physical impetus with the relocation in 1979 of those engaged in acquisition, production, and selling of titles into a single building in Chelsea. As on other similar occasions, the administrative challenges of this reorganization were smoothed over by Ron Blass; his death at the early age of 61 five years later was to deprive Peter Mayer of an experienced vice chairman, who had long served as an invaluable 'Man Friday' to Penguin chief executives with his unique feel for Penguin's past.

One spectacular benefit emerged shortly with the publication of M. M. Kaye's *The Far Pavilions*:

It was in the then distinctive 'B' format.

It was aggressively priced ('the highest retail price for a mass-market paperback in publishing history').

It was strongly promoted and achieved volume sales of 400,000 within six months.

It illustrated the virtues of a vertical structure, having been successfully published two years previously by Allen Lane as a hardback – an infrequent instance of original fiction publishing under that imprint.

It started by offending retailers whose racks accommodated 'A' format rather than the larger 'B' format books – their sense of outrage diminishing, however, in line with the rising sales curve.

Finally, breaking all known publishing rules, the promotional budget was largely paid for by the author's acceptance of reduced royalty in exchange for an enhanced marketing budget. She and her agent accepted the argument that, notwithstanding this 'sacrifice', her overall revenues stood to be enhanced, as indeed proved to be the case.

Peter Mayer also expressed reservations about the value in the future of the automatic territorial advantage that Penguin had enjoyed for so long in bookshops, from being the largest-selling paperback house. As John Hitchin, Penguin marketing director, recalls, there was growing evidence at the time that the sales benefits of the Penguin shops-within-shops programme were fading. Furthermore, the role of wholesalers supplying non-conventional outlets stood to increase in importance for Penguin as its involvement in bestseller titles rose. The competition for shelf space in such outlets was much freer and the display was by author rather than imprint. Any inclination that Penguin might have to rest on its laurels as a retail brand looked, therefore, increasingly questionable.

More generally, in March 1979 Peter Mayer saw as his first task the need 'to sell his ideas within Penguin and then this will provide the highly talented Penguin editors and executives ... with the confidence and enthusiasm to sell and market effectively throughout the world'. These admirable sentiments tally with the recollection of Patrick Wright, group director of sales and marketing: '... when Peter came, the idea was to add to Penguin's strengths – not to destroy and start again'.

Additions to Penguin's strengths, starting in 1983, included acquisitions. The first of these was the purchase of Frederick Warne for £6m. The Beatrix Potter copyrights then had no more than ten years to run, which may go some way to explain the startling fact that no other publisher participated in the Frederick Warne auction. (The subsequent extension of copyright from fifty years to seventy years proved a considerable unanticipated bonus.) Of the two under-bidders, believed to have been the printing group McCorquodale and the commodities group Booker McConnell, the latter was reported to have offered £4m. Penguin's bid – equivalent to twenty times Warne's latest pre-tax profits of £297,000 – looked to many wildly improvident. In the event, Penguin recovered its purchase price within two to three years. Costs were slashed with the virtual closure of the company, which had had a staff of seventy; assets, aside from the Beatrix Potter interests, were sold off; Sally Floyer, recruited from Kestrel, orchestrated the aggressive exploitation of merchandizing rights – and then there was the build-up of unit sales from the pre-acquisition level of two million to over seven million by 1986. Penguin's purchase of Warne provided the world of publishing with a business-school model of international marketing at its most effective. In April 1987, the books were republished in a new edition, incorporating new plates, to great acclaim.

Two years after the Warne acquisition, Penguin bought two literary hardback houses, Hamish Hamilton and Michael Joseph; the paperback imprint, Sphere; and the specialist packager, Rainbird – all from Thomson. Their sale followed a Thomson management decision to concentrate their book-publishing activities in the professional, reference, and educational areas. This was the most important domestic purchase made under the Mayer regime. The consideration was £20.66m cash, satisfied by the issue of 5.8m Pearson shares placed with institutions. The purchase price represented an apparently undemanding 0.8 times turnover. On pre-tax profits of £0.6m, however, Penguin appeared to be paying thirty-four times profits. The significance of the transaction lay more in the balance sheet than in the profit and loss account.

Through the acquisition of Hamish Hamilton and Michael Joseph, Mayer was decisively dispelling any lingering suspicion that Penguin was at heart a paperback reprint house. Instead it was presenting itself as a vertically integrated book publisher that had in one transaction massively increased its UK hardback capacity well beyond anything that the Allen Lane imprint had been able to achieve through organic growth. Both Hamish Hamilton and Michael Joseph had been members of the 'Group' formed in 1948 to give Penguin first refusal on their new titles for paperbacking. Despite some subsequent weakening of ties, Penguin was still paperbacking one in two of every Hamish Hamilton titles and paying out to Michael Joseph some £400,000 a year in paperback royalties. The possibility that a rival, vertically integrated publisher might acquire control of these businesses acted as a powerful incentive to Penguin.

The initial cost was high, although reduced in 1989 by the sale of Sphere to Maxwell Communications for £13.75m. Honouring the generous redundancy terms of the Thomson house agreements proved an expensive business. The cheques were of a size that 40% of the staff of Michael Joseph, 60% of Sphere, and just under half of Hamish Hamilton seized the opportunity provided for voluntary redundancy. But, as earlier indicated, these purchases had more to do with protecting the asset base than enlivening near-term profits.

For the second half of Peter Mayer's years at Penguin, the US side was destined to become the most absorbing of his responsibilities. Penguin's US operations had received a considerable amount of management attention during Peter Calvocoressi's period as chief executive, leading to the merger of Penguin and Viking. The first corporate development involved the tying of loose ends, with the Pearson interests exercising their option on the minority shareholdings, thereby lifting their stake in Viking Penguin to 100% in September 1979. A year before that, at the same time as Peter Mayer took over as Penguin's chief executive, the resignation of Thomas H. Guinzburg was announced – well before the expiry of his contractual seven years. In his stead, Irving Goodman, previously publisher of Holt Rinehart & Winston, was selected – with Peter Mayer's blessing.

On arrival at Penguin, Mayer had found in Viking Penguin a company that had signally failed to match the high expectations voiced in the Pearson statement to shareholders in the 1975 accounts. By 1979/80, it was supposed to have developed a publishing base comparable to Penguin's UK operation and to be at the heart of a global English language publishing enterprise. The reality was very different. It had 'a disappointing first year' in 1976. A small profit had been achieved in 1977. In 1978, there had been 'a modest overall improvement'. In 1979, it had moved into loss – estimated at $900,000. That year, however, contained the seeds of eventual recovery: Viking Penguin signed up a new author, Stephen King, on a three-book contract. New American Library had acquired volume rights and needed a reputable hardback publisher to front for it. Viking Penguin was happy to oblige.

In December 1986 a major change of pace occurred with the acquisition – no less – of New American Library (NAL). Quite apart from the Stephen King link, Penguin had had a star role in NAL's genesis, when it agreed in 1948 to sell its US assets to Victor Weybright. On the announcement, Peter Mayer pointed to the need for Penguin in the USA to be a full service publisher. 'Penguin in the USA is a trade paperback house, selling mainly through bookstores. What we didn't have in the USA was an ability to massmarket, i.e. to produce, warehouse, and distribute books for such outlets as newsstands, pharmacies, and supermarket racks. I wanted, for instance, to be able to repackage a successful trade paperback in a rack size suitable for mass-market outlets, or simply to publish the book as a rack product in the first place if that format suited it best.'

With NAL said to be among the top five US paperback houses, 70% of whose business was in mass-market publishing, these ambitions now looked readily achievable. Other benefits included the combination in children's book publishing of the hardcover Dutton and Dial imprints with the paperback Puffin imprints.

The financial aspects of the NAL acquisition also looked to be favourable to Penguin. The purchase price of $65.5m cash was an undemanding 0.6 times 1985 sales of $107.7m, 6.2 times 1985 operating profits of $10.6m, and 8.7 times estimated 1986 operating profits of $7.5m. Pearson raised the money by way of a placing of 8.5m shares. The vendors, nine in all, were a group of investors, led by Odyssey Partners plus several NAL executives, who had bought NAL from the Times Mirror in 1983 for $50m and had acquired E. P. Dutton in 1985 for $6.25m, financing these purchases very largely with debt. When the business required additional finance in 1986, they were unable/ unwilling to put up the capital. Penguin was not alone in coveting the business: Harcourt Brace was ready to pay $85m as long as the vendors provided warranties in regard to future profits. This presented them with difficulties. Penguin, once it had secured the comfort it needed from a thorough due diligence, waived the warranties and secured the prize.

Penguin's US interests were thereby transformed into a diversified publishing group with combined sales in 1986 that amounted to $170m, making it the USA's fifth largest general trade publisher. Over two-fifths of its business was accounted for by mass-market paperbacks; ironically, thirty years earlier, Allen Lane in *The Penguin Story* had pronounced that 'the Penguin market, despite its ten million sales, is not a mass market, and the firm never intends to seek a truly mass market'. Penguin Group sales were as a result lifted to some $300m, with the US interests contributing fractionally more than the non-US. Pearson's 1975 ambition had at last been achieved.

When Peter Mayer was being courted by Pearson, Munroe Pofcher, who was to the UK publishing industry as a consultant what Arnold Goodman was to it as a legal adviser, admonished Peter not to be fooled by appearances of amateurishness in the aristocratic family management structure: 'You had better make it on the bottom line or you'll have an early ticket home.' The early years of Mayer's period showed evidence of a healthy respect for this advice.

The period 1979 to 1984 presents a remarkable picture, with operating profits rising from £688,000 to £11.3m and pre-tax profits moving from a loss of £381,000 to a profit of £10m. Operating margins in 1984 were five times those achieved in 1979 (see table 9).

Writing in 1982 in the *Financial Times*, Christian Tyler attributed the turnaround at that stage to a programme of 'major reorganization and cost cutting within and aggressive marketing without'. Significant redundancies in 1980

Table 9: *Penguin's results 1979–1986*

	1979	1980	1981	1982	1983	1984	1985	1986
Turnover (£m)	27.73	36.13	47.25	56.20	72.20	90.00	113.30	133.30
Operating profits (£m)	0.69	1.79	5.17	6.30	9.10	11.30	10.80	9.30
Operating margins	2.5%	5.0%	10.9%	11.2%	12.6%	12.6%	9.5%	7.0%
Pre-tax profits (£m)	(0.38)*	0.24	4.00	5.64	8.00	10.00†	NA	NA

* After exceptional relocation costs of £700,000
† Partially estimated. Thereafter no figures are available for Penguin's pre-tax results.

achieved against strong union opposition; a cut-back in the back list from 4700 titles to 4300; a severe trimming of the new titles published; and consolidation of previously dispersed editorial, sales, and marketing departments were some of the outward signs of new management at work. Penguin's borrowings were halved from £11.6m in 1980 to £5.8m in 1982.

Less tangible or measurable was the personal impact of the new chief executive. As a foreigner, he found himself in the sensitive position of being in charge of a British publishing institution that had recently fallen on hard times. He came to the task with experience of the less structured, more overtly competitive and much larger US market, characteristics that might be calculated to endear him to his employers (Pearson) but not necessarily to his Penguin colleagues. Crucially, however, he was a rare example of a US publisher for whom the overseas, and notably the European, scene, held few terrors; fluency in German, Spanish, French; a year at Christ Church, Oxford; and a Fulbright award at the Free University of Berlin being elements in his curriculum vitae. He came to the task as a young man, at that time still single, with energy reserves that seemed to know no limit and a great talent for generating a sense of tension and excitement. One can almost hear the champagne corks popping when in 1980 Penguin moved instantly to acquire the paperback rights of five out of the seven titles short listed that year for the Booker Prize and then had them printed and into the shops a week before the prize ceremony. What is more, to quote Christopher Sinclair-Stevenson, 'Peter has always had a great nose for a book.'

A certain impatience with the establishment ethos of Penguin was inevitable, however. Explaining his appointment of Alan Wherry, whom he recruited from Corgi, as UK sales manager, Peter Mayer told Christian Tyler, 'we have tried to get people from outside who didn't have "a priori" notions about Penguin'. But many of the publishing decisions which struck a novel note were, so to speak, at the margin, albeit a critically important and profitable one. For example, Mayer, after meeting Audrey Eyton, author of the diet book *The F-Plan*, backed her – influenced by the glint of commitment in the eye of an author of a book on fibre, as a subject an improbable spell-binder and an unlikely entrant into the Penguin list. Penguin sold over one and a half million copies, as well as negotiating in July 1982 its biggest US rights deal to date.

This did not alter the fact that 75% of Penguin's sales were still accounted for by the backlist of literary classics, serious fiction, and reference works.

In his first few years at Penguin, it has to be said that Peter Mayer also had luck on his side. Joining Penguin at the nadir of its fortunes, his timing was perfect. This also meant that his freedom of action was enhanced.

His arrival came two years ahead of a cyclical recovery, which saw UK economic activity start picking up in 1982 after contracting in 1980 and 1981. Inflation, from averaging 18.4% in 1980, was down to 4.7% in 1983.

The unwinding of sterling over-valuation can be dated from the third quarter of 1980 when the average rate was $2.39 to the £; during the same quarter a year later, it had fallen to $1.81 and by 1984 it averaged $1.34 over the whole year.

Mayer had capped this with the 1983 acquisition of Warne – not a case of luck but of lively opportunism, which helped the figures in 1983 and much more so those of 1984.

After the strategic acquisitions of 1985 and 1986, which had endowed the Penguin paperback interests with a major UK hardback arm and Viking Penguin with a full service US paperback facility, came the task of realizing their potential. The next few years were to be so occupied.

In March 1987, Trevor Glover was appointed managing director of Penguin UK, which permitted Peter Mayer to move his base to New York City. Glover had been UK sales and marketing director in the early 1970s. In 1976, he had moved to Australia and had presided over Penguin Australia's profitable growth from a turnover of A$8m in 1976 to one of A$8om in 1986. In that year, sales of Australian titles of A$12m made it a substantial trade publishing house by international standards.

On arrival in England, Glover inherited the task of pursuing the integration of the Thomson companies, bought in May 1985. The extent of the financial challenge is illustrated in table 10.

All three companies achieved pre-interest operating profits in 1988, two of them moving into the black at the pre-tax level. A significant contributor to this trend was a near halving of staff across the three companies, from an average of 226 in 1985 to 127 in 1988. The overall performance in 1988, however, still fell far short of what could be regarded as acceptable to Pearson – or for that matter to Penguin.

In June 1989, Christopher Sinclair-Stevenson, managing director of Hamish Hamilton, decided to leave Penguin, marking the end of the attempt to 'integrate' the hardback companies and the start of what might more properly be called their 'assimilation'. Sinclair-Stevenson had difficulty in accepting the vertical concept of publishing within Penguin and loss of control over such matters as print numbers and remainder decisions. His resignation (followed closely by that of Alan Brooke, managing director of Michael Joseph) was seen by some as the failure of a gallant attempt at achieving that elusive

Table 10: *Results of the Thomson companies*

	1985	1986	1987	1988
Michael Joseph				
Turnover (£000)	7549	8269	9557	11,604
Operating profits (£000)	(178)	(589)	(97)	491
Operating margins	–	–	–	4.2%
Pre-tax profits (£000)	(448)	(1142)	(522)	73
Hamish Hamilton				
Turnover (£000)	5739	5025	5443	5774
Operating profits (£000)	344	(588)	63	309
Operating margins	6.0%	–	1.2%	5.4%
Pre-tax profits (£000)	222	(817)	(159)	100
Sphere Books				
Turnover (£000)	8251	8036	9612	9909
Operating profits (£000)	(2542)	(1486)	409	460
Operating margins	–	–	4.3%	4.6%
Pre-tax profits (£000)	(3105)	(2507)	(437)	(375)

Note: After 1988, the companies ceased to report their results separately.

balance between corporate needs and creative independence. At the same time, a thoughtful article in *Publishing News* drew attention to the elapse of four years since the Penguin purchase and the measure of management tolerance shown to Hamish Hamilton and Michael Joseph that this demonstrated.

An unforeseeable challenge confronted Penguin's management following publication in 1989 of Salman Rushdie's *The Satanic Verses*, leading to Ayatollah Khomeini's sentence of death on the author and those involved in its publication or sale. This was a traumatic experience for many in the company. As the book was published globally by Penguin, the disruption to management was huge. Trevor Glover recalls months on end when he and Patrick Wright would devote every morning to Rushdie matters. The security costs for Penguin in the first year alone came to £1.8m; the following year some £900,000 was charged against group profits.

In the USA, the management issues were of a different kind. Sales of the newly acquired NAL/Dutton amounted to $120m, dwarfing Penguin Viking's sales of $50m. Much the same comparative situation had occurred in 1975 when Viking was acquired with sales of $15m, three times larger than Penguin Inc's sales of $5m. Such revenue imbalances between purchaser and purchased can usually be relied upon to create difficulties in integration and assimilation. In 1975, Pearson had used existing Viking management with, as it turned out, indifferent results. In 1986, there was no wish to have NAL manage the merged group. Given the importance of this purchase to Penguin and bearing in mind Peter Mayer's own background in US publishing, it made eminent sense for Pearson to have made the acquisition conditional on Peter taking direct responsibility for the US business 'for the next two to three years at least'. Nor was it the first time that Mayer had taken day-to-day control: in the autumn of 1983, on the departure of Irving Goodman, he had moved to New York as an interim measure pending the appointment of Alan Kellock as Goodman's successor.

The management challenge in the USA was at two levels – nuts and bolts on the one hand and editorial and sales on the other. Under the first heading came such familiar post-acquisition items as coping with incompatible computer systems, standardizing financial and service operations across the group, combining warehouse and distribution systems – three of them – in one centre and merging three editorial offices in New York City. The finance and service functions were brought together at Bergenfield, New Jersey in 1989; the new warehouse and distribution centre at Newbern, Tennessee, was opened also in 1989, while the editorial office moves, together with sales and administration, took place in April 1990. In 1993, Donnelley's opened a printing plant at Newbern dedicated to Penguin, and two years later, this was supplemented by a dedicated paperback cover printing facility. An indication of the difficulties is discernible in the colourless reference in the 1989 Pearson accounts to 'additional costs connected with the integration of warehouses and service operations in the USA'. Severe distribution problems were in fact experienced that year, causing considerable disruption.

In editorial and sales, the late 1980s and early 1990s witnessed a steady process of integration which included: combining in December 1988 the field sales forces of NAL, Dutton, Viking Penguin; converting in November 1989 the previously separate Dutton adult trade publishing division into an imprint within Penguin USA; consolidation in 1991 of children's paperback editions of Viking, Dutton, and Dial Books for Young Readers under the Puffin imprint.

In the wake of the NAL acquisition, a Penguin USA board was formed, with Peter Mayer as executive chairman. In November 1989, Morton Mint was appointed chief executive officer. He had spent the previous six years running Penguin Canada, whose turnover had quadrupled to $35m during this period. This might have heralded the gradual disengagement of Peter Mayer. However, less than a year later, Mint resigned over differences of opinion on his role.

In December 1991 John Moore, whose background was in the toy industry, was appointed chief operating officer. He assumed responsibility for administration, strategic planning, and sales. This left Peter Mayer and Marvin Brown – one of the great survivors going back to NAL's early days of independence – 'free to concentrate on acquiring and publishing good books that sell well'. It marked the end of what Peter referred to as the complicated process of the executive reorganization of Penguin USA. It also meant that he was destined

PENGUIN

Table 11: *Penguin results 1987–1996*

	1987	1988	1989	1990	1991	1992	1993	1994	1995	1996
Turnover (£m)	217.4	234.0	295.9	292.0	293.5	330.0*	365.9	371.8	369.0	380.2
Operating profits (£m)	20.7	20.7	18.8	15.0	13.1	26.3	32.3	40.0	33.6	31.0†
Operating margins	9.5%	8.8%	6.4%	5.1%	4.5%	8.0%*	8.8%	10.8%	9.1%	8.2%†

* Partly estimated.   † In the 1997 accounts shown as £25.5m (margins of 6.7%).

to remain based in New York for the next five years.

Penguin USA had indeed become a large company. Sales in 1990, at $237m, had grown at a compound rate of 8.7% in the previous four years. Within the 1990 total, mass-market paperbacks accounted for 35%, trade paperbacks 25%, children's 22%, and adult hardcover 18%. But 1990 was not a banner year for profitability in the USA – nor indeed in the UK. On both sides of the Atlantic the economies were in recession, leading to difficult trading conditions that persisted for two years. The 1991 results were further burdened by trading losses incurred by Smithmark (a US promotional book company, purchased in September 1989 and sold in July 1991 at a capital loss), plus provisions made against unlet New York offices, totalling together £7m (see table 11).

While the 1990/91 recession proved both deeper and more prolonged in the UK than in the USA, during the ensuing five years there was little to choose between the two economies as they grew in step with each other. UK book publishers, however, had to cope with a number of local difficulties, one being the widespread destocking at the largest chains in the mid-1990s, reflecting in part the introduction of EPOS systems, another being the unsettling effects of the end of retail price maintenance. Book publishers in the UK found themselves in a microclimate where the chill of winter persisted at a time when the sun shone on much of the rest of British industry.

As the figures demonstrate, Penguin as a whole experienced a marked recovery in the period through 1994, when operating profits of £40m were achieved, three times the £13.1m recorded for 1991 (or twice as large if the £7m of exceptional losses in 1991 are added back). However, a major divergence in the trading experience of Penguin USA and Penguin UK emerges in 1994, with the UK company failing to match a good result the previous year, whereas Penguin USA enjoyed strong results – as did the Australian, Canadian, New Zealand, and Indian companies. In 1995, the pattern was unchanged, disappointing figures from Penguin UK contrasting with strong or encouraging results reported for the other companies. The UK problems had been flagged by 40 redundancies in the summer of 1995 and 75 the following November. While other publishers were also announcing job losses, those at Penguin were accompanied by senior resignations. Trevor Glover himself resigned in November. *The Bookseller* carried the headline 'Penguin – a house in disorder'.

In seeking to understand the special circumstances affecting Penguin UK, the issue of 'verticality' in Penguin's hardback/paperback publishing is frequently invoked. Peter Mayer set the tone early in 1986 when explaining the previous year's purchase of the Thomson hardback imprints: 'We are aiming for as much autonomy as possible and rather more than some people have suggested or feared.' Three years later, Andrew Franklin, Christopher Sinclair-Stevenson's successor as publishing director of Hamish Hamilton, was clear in his own mind: 'You have to buy vertically from the start; you can't go it alone as a hardback house any longer.' Two years later, Clare Alexander, publishing director of Viking (as Allen Lane became known in 1984), recognized that 'as a vertical publisher I have to carry Penguin with me 90% of the time'. But Penguin still found it necessary in July 1995 to undertake a major restructuring whose stated objective was to integrate hardcover and softcover publishing as fully as possible. As Peter Mayer expressed it, 'doing hardback publishing in a disconnected way from the paperback engine which drives the whole company may not be the best way of going about things'. This was ten years after the strategic purchase of the Thomson trade hardback houses. Little wonder that, in the opinion of Tony Lacey, appointed in July 1995 publishing director of the Penguin General Division fiction and nonfiction, 'we came very late to serious verticalization. My own feeling is that Peter didn't get to grips quickly enough with the Thomson imprints and their different cultures.'

Lacey was in a good position to judge because of his very different experience in children's books in the late 1970s and early 1980s. As Liz Attenborough recalls, after she had taken over the hardback Kestrel imprint from Lacey and he had taken over Puffin from Kaye Webb, they swiftly made a practice of working together, buying jointly and using their combined strengths to secure authors. 'Pure verticality' was achieved when Liz, having been appointed chief editor of Puffin in 1983, later assumed (once again) responsibility for Kestrel.

The departure of Peter Mayer to New York in 1987 was originally presented as being a temporary arrangement. It became permanent de facto, but the formal recognition of a shift in the Penguin headquarters is hard to pinpoint. Disarmingly, Mayer concedes that the HQ of Penguin was wherever he was. Initially, this converted into one week in London for every three weeks in New York or thereabouts, lubricated by extensive telephone contact. At one stage he kept two secretaries in London and three in New York well occupied.

All of this made for a punishing schedule. Aside from the complexities inherent in an intricate international business, Peter's workload reflected two aspects of his character. One is his passionate enthusiasm for almost all sides of publishing (warehousing excepted), which led him to get involved one moment in the negotiation of a multimillion pound book deal and the next in passing judgment on the font sizes chosen for a Penguin cover. The other trait, attested by many colleagues, is the difficulty he had at bringing himself to delegate – particularly in areas that interested him, which meant most areas.

Editorially, Peter was quickly missed. 'It was best to have him at the end of the corridor,' as Tony Lacey puts it. Similarly, the absence of his characteristically energizing impact on sales was keenly felt. But this goes only a little way towards explaining the deteriorating morale in Penguin UK in 1994/95. There were other factors.

– Psychologically, Wrights Lane had gradually to accept that it was no longer the centre of the Penguin universe – in itself a painful process.

– The seeming under-performance relative to other parts of the Group earned it critical fusillades from New York – directed in the first instance at Trevor Glover.

– At the same time, Pearson started requiring increased budgetary information in ever changing formats, an additional source of anxiety to people already feeling on the defensive and still bruised by the Rushdie experience.

– There having been little significant recruitment (or promotion) for some time of young executives at a senior level, fresh thinking was in short supply. Instead, economies leading to staff retrenchment had been the order of the day.

– The existing executive team, composed of long-serving employees, became increasingly fractious.

By the end of November, Peter Mayer was back in London in day-to-day charge. The gods were on his side. Within weeks of his return, Penguin author Pat Barker won the Booker Prize with the third volume of her Great War trilogy. He was also able to announce a publishing first with Stephen King's next novel to be published by Penguin simultaneously around the world in six parts; for Penguin UK this was also a first to have him on their list.

But his main task was recruitment. He had already privately indicated to Pearson his wish to relinquish his responsibilities to devote himself totally to the small family publishing company, Overlook Press. A first step was the appointment of Andrew Welham as director of sales, as well as marketing, to fill the gap created by the departure of the sales director, Patrick Hutchinson. And in April 1996, Mayer chose Anthony Forbes-Watson, then head of Ladybird, as managing director of Penguin UK; he was subsequently appointed CEO.

The conclusion of the Peter Mayer era was marked by the acquisition – the largest in the company's history – of the US trade publishing house Putnam Berkley from MCA, the media group controlled by Seagram. The price paid in December 1996, following several months of negotiations, was $336m: a multiple of 1.2 times turnover of $276m and 9.9 times operating profits of $34m. With Penguin USA's sales at over $300m, the combined US publishing turnover was lifted to some $600m, thereby giving Penguin Putnam a 12% share of the US trade publishing market, against a little less than 6% previously. Children's book turnover alone amounted to $150m. The purchase had Peter's enthusiastic endorsement.

Aside from the attractions of scale, the acquisition was seen as having much else to recommend it:

– Putnam Berkley's great strength lay in commercial front list publishing, featuring such names as Tom Clancy, Patricia Cornwell, Dick Francis, Robin Cook, Amy Tan, and Kurt Vonnegut. Penguin USA for its part was hugely dependent on Stephen King. The special mention accorded Stephen King in the narrative accompanying the Pearson annual accounts in every year but three since the link was established in 1979 is in itself a telling commentary on Penguin's potential vulnerability.

– Penguin's backlist strengths complemented admirably Putnam's massive front-list presence.

– The Penguin Group's international reach was in stark contrast to Putnam's US orientation and raised the prospect of improved exploitation of export markets.

– With Putnam lacking any UK affiliate and with its authors agented in that market, the prospect of gradually adding names to Penguin UK's list was a realistic expectation.

– Penguin was acquiring a business that was healthily profitable, with operating margins in the latest year of 12.3%.

– But one of the most important considerations, from Pearson's point of view, was that the gap to be created by the imminent departure of Peter Mayer, in his capacity as executive chairman of Penguin USA, would be filled by Phyllis Grann. Her impressive track record was that of a highly commercial front-list publisher – in contrast to which the trade side of Penguin USA, which was being entrusted to her care, was publishing of a very different stamp.

For the second time in Penguin's history, the management of its US business was being sub-contracted to that of a recently acquired US company. The first occasion saw Penguin Inc. become the responsibility of Viking Inc., with which it shared a similar publishing profile. This second instance saw Putnam Berkley take charge of Penguin USA, a case where the publishing profiles were very different – some might say antipathetic.

Peter Mayer's successor in the wider role as chief executive of the Penguin Group had already been assured with the appointment of Michael Lynton. This was to take formal effect at the end of 1996. His selection was heavily influenced by Mayer, with whom he had quite a lot in common, notably a strong international bent, Lynton having been born in the UK and brought up in the Netherlands and the USA. His youth (36 years old) was no drawback. His business experience had included responsibility for Disney's book and magazine publishing division, followed by the presidency of Hollywood Pictures.

The revelation in mid-February 1997 that Pearson needed to provide for a £100m charge against profits because of unauthorized discounts given to customers of Penguin USA, and that this was behind an alleged fraud by an employee of at least $1.4m, was a startlingly unhappy note on which the merged Penguin Putnam had to start trading. The fact that these accounting irregularities had gone undetected for five years added to the general embarrassment and did little for the credibility of earlier profit figures. It also cast a new light on the comparative performance during those years of Penguin UK versus Penguin USA. The provision against Pearson profits, which, as things turned out, proved to have been accurately estimated, covered the costs of the investigation and rebates to retailers who were not offered discounts, in addition to the value of the discounts actually granted.

One inevitable consequence was that, in the allocation of jobs in the merged group, former Penguin USA executives had even greater difficulty fighting their corner than might normally have been anticipated. The culture within the combined US company received, therefore, an extra Putnam Berkley stamp, while that of Penguin USA was correspondingly weakened.

PEARSON'S EXPOSURE TO BOOKS

In this whole account, the attitude of Pearson to Penguin and, more generally, to book publishing has up to now gone by default. It is time to make amends.

Pearson's original book interests were in professional and educational publishing. Two medical imprints, E. & S. Livingstone and J. & A. Churchill, had been acquired in 1960 and 1962 respectively, and the primary-school textbook publisher, Oliver & Boyd, was also bought in 1962. They formed part of a holding company which encompassed, in addition to the book-publishing interests, one national newspaper (the *Financial Times*) and a portfolio of provincial newspapers (Westminster Press). When Longman was bought in 1968, this represented a major extension of Pearson's educational/professional book publishing. Pearson had thereby established a sizeable presence in what was familiarly called 'the knowledge industry', which was being given at the time the accolade of 'the biggest growth sector of them all'.

The purchase in 1970/71 of a major trade book publisher, such as Penguin, might seem to have been in conflict with the Pearson strategy. One should, however, bear in mind the educational character of much of Penguin's mainstream publishing, quite apart from the presence of an embryonic Penguin Education Division. Furthermore, Longman and Penguin had contemplated marriage as independent companies.

On the financial front, the capital-hungry nature of book publishing, whether educational or trade, may not have appeared that great a drawback. For one reason, the scourge of inflation had yet to descend on Britain, and in any event, these interests were lodged in the same holding company as the strongly cash-generative newspaper divisions.

The 1970s proved a taxing time for the publishing businesses within Pearson Longman, the one exception being the Longman division, which largely bucked the trend. Penguin, as we have seen, shared fully in the decade's vicissitudes. But, when it needed funds to buy Viking Inc., most of the money

Table 12: *Sector operating margins (%)*

	1985	1986	1987	1988	1989
Penguin	9.5	7.0	9.5	8.8	6.4
Longman	10.7	9.1	11.0	9.2	13.5
Addison-Wesley*	[9.6]	[11.3]	[11.4]	11.0	12.9
Elsevier†	[12.6]	[13.8]	[18.0]	20.2	20.9
FT Newspaper	13.7	20.6	19.5	22.2	21.5
Westminster Press	7.1	9.4	16.5	17.8	14.2
Tussauds	31.2	30.0	26.7	26.4	20.4
Fine china	11.8	10.6	8.9	9.6	11.5
Oil services	14.7	5.9	5.8	9.0	10.3

* Acquired in March 1988.
† Pre-tax margins. In September 1988, following a share exchange, Pearson acquired a minority stake in Elsevier and was able to consolidate its share in that company's profits.

was found from Pearson's interests outside of Pearson Longman. This was a telling illustration of the proprietor's commitment. It also put in context the scale of personal disquiet that the Pearson directors were periodically experiencing as evidence of Penguin's radical tradition surfaced. Somewhat to their surprise, they had found E. V. Rieu's translation of the Odyssey rubbing shoulders with Marxist apologia and a work that touched on the manufacture of bombs.

The total absorption of Pearson Longman into the Pearson Group in 1982, when the latter bought out the 36% minority holders in Pearson Longman, simplified a somewhat complicated share structure. It also meant that, with the disappearance of Pearson Longman as a separately quoted company, the publishing divisions achieved sibling status with the Pearson Group's engineering, banking, oil, and other commercial interests. The Pearson board was henceforth in a much better position to judge and respond to the perceived merits of different sectors that made up their portfolio of assets. So long as the board wore the conglomerate label with pride, diversity was in itself a merit and asset disposals were unlikely to become a burning issue. Once, however, a more refined version of a conglomerate was adopted, under the chairmanship of Michael Blakenham, sector comparisons took on an altogether sharper edge. For Pearson, this process can be dated from 1986 with the disposal of the engineering division, a mere six years after its acquisition of Fairey Holdings.

Pre-interest operating margins of nine major sectors are available for the period 1985 to 1989 (see table 12). Merchant banking, for which this performance measure is irrelevant, is omitted.

During the period covered, Penguin's operating margins were consistently below those of the other book publishing interests and typically below those of the other divisions. While comparative information is not available for the period 1990 to 1996, Penguin's own pre-interest margins averaged 7.8% in those years. It would have been highly surprising if such ratios had not prompted some discussion of the longer-term future of Penguin within the Pearson Group.

James Joll, Pearson's finance director from 1980 to 1996 and main board director with a watching brief over the book companies from 1985 to 1996, does not recall that at any time there was a serious possibility of Penguin being sold. While accepting that 'there was a school of thought within the board that this was not the sort of business we should be in, I, and others, took the view that we should be able to do better and that this was not yet reflected in the numbers'. The critics, most vocal among whom was Elsevier's Pierre Vincken (who was on the Pearson board from October 1988 to May 1991), were influenced by the limited growth prospects of trade publishing, coupled with its obstinately cash-absorbent characteristics. Such hesitations did not, however, lead to Penguin being denied funds for acquisitions. Furthermore, the board members' decision in 1993 to concentrate Pearson's resources in media and entertainment, thereby renouncing their conglomerate past, went far to confirm Penguin's security of tenure within the Group. There is also one other important consideration: Peter Mayer maintained very good relations with Michael Blakenham, and this gave Penguin much added protection.

How did Penguin, operating in an area of publishing which has become a by-word for change and impermanence, maintain its presence in the masthead of a major publishing corporation?

The first point that an historical survey of this kind brings out is Penguin's own record of change.

From its origins as a quality fiction paperback reprint house, it broadened into paperback originals, into hardback non-fiction, into hardback fiction, into publishing for the mass market. Helen Fraser, now group managing director of Penguin UK, is hard put to name examples of books published today for which Penguin has acquired merely the paperback reprint rights.

From being an exporter to Commonwealth and former colonial countries, Penguin has been at the heart of the development of local publishing houses, notably in Australia, New Zealand, Canada, and, last in time, India.

The USA saw the most dramatic changes, with the quality hardback publisher Viking being first linked to Penguin's small paperback importing business; to this was added a mass-market paperback publisher, NAL, and ultimately, in a reverse takeover in management terms, these interests were absorbed into a major US trade house, giving Penguin Putnam total coverage from minority interest titles to bestsellers.

Arising out of such developments, Penguin has been alert to the opportunities of global publishing, involving the exploitation across world markets of titles within a single organization. While the number of suitable titles is fewer than some imagine, it will have done Penguin no harm to have taken from

HarperCollins the paperbacking in the UK of Tom Clancy in the wake of the Putnam Berkley acquisition. The importance of North America was recognized by Penguin at an early stage, with its sales in the US first exceeding those in the rest of the world in 1986 following the NAL purchase. The Putnam Berkley acquisition tilted the business yet further in the direction of the USA. This geographical emphasis was first and foremost a recognition of the attractions of the single largest English-language market. It was also reinforced, as Peter Carson expresses it, by the fact that 'in trade publishing, there has been in many respects a creative shift to New York from London over fifty years'.

In its battle to survive and develop, Penguin has demonstrated huge adaptability, but not to the point of becoming a protean creation. The Penguin name has taken care of that. This remains one of the most cited reasons for the company's continued prominence. At one stage a generic term for all paperbacks, it then received the marketing accolade of a 'consumer brand' in an area of the retail trade where the customer is notoriously insensitive to seductions of this kind. Penguin's ascendancy is periodically endorsed in surveys: one conducted in the UK in 1998 went so far as to maintain that 'Penguin is the only publishing brand that can actually act as a purchase influence on consumers'. The strength of such general responses is unsurprisingly linked to the duration and scale of Penguin's presence in different geographic markets, in descending order the UK, Australasia, Canada, the US.

While the book-buyer may be in a bit of a fog, for an author to have Penguin as publisher still brings on for many the same glow of satisfaction that membership of a distinguished club with a distinctive tie carries with it. This sentiment is echoed by Christopher Sinclair-Stevenson, speaking as a literary agent: 'People pay attention if it is a Penguin book.' Penguin has inspired powerful loyalties. These can take on a semi-proprietorial tone. The sense of betrayal at Penguin's publication of such examples of big-time commercial 'schlock' as Shirley Conran's *Lace* or Jane Fonda's gymnastic books emerges clearly in Richard Hoggart's book of reminiscences published in 1992. While recognizing that Penguin still produces some very good titles, he laments that it is 'also willing to produce quite awful bestsellers. The "Boule de Suif" argument, that the whores can protect the virtuous women, doesn't suit artistic matters.'

Outrage in artistic matters may be an endangered sentiment in today's climate, but the nurture of freedom of expression continues to command attention. By this measure, Penguin has no equal: *Lady Chatterley's Lover* in 1960, *Portnoy's Complaint* in Australia in 1971, *Spycatcher* in 1987, *The Satanic Verses* in 1989, and *Denying the Holocaust* in the year 2000.

If credit for such publishing is to be given, the publisher needs to share it with the proprietor – where the two are distinct. In this respect, Pearson deserves many more plaudits than it has ever received. The case of *Spycatcher*, which Viking Penguin published in the US, despite heavy-handed efforts by the British Government to bully Pearson into cancellation, makes illuminating reading. On a totally different order of magnitude, there is the Rushdie affair where the attempted censorship was foreign.

This illustrates the wider point that, among the reasons given for Penguin's continuing leading presence, one of the most important – perhaps indeed the most important – is the fact that when it lost its independence, it did so to Pearson rather than to another predator.

From 1970 to the present, Pearson has bankrolled Penguin's acquisitions, starting with Viking in 1975 and extending to Dorling Kindersley in 2000.

Pearson's respect for editorial integrity – and this applies as much to its newspaper interests through the *Financial Times* and *The Economist* – serves as a lesson from which other media owners could profit.

Notwithstanding critical scrutiny on some occasions, Pearson has remained committed to Penguin, a commitment that was strengthened when Pearson's conglomerate label was replaced by the 'focused' media group label.

The trading performance of the Penguin Group over the past five years is unlikely to have shaken this commitment, with operating profits rising from £31m in 1996 to £79m in 2000 (but before charging £27m of integration costs in 2000). Over the same period, operating margins have risen from 8.2% to 10.5% (12.5% if Dorling Kindersley, which broke even on eight months' turnover of £125m, is ignored).

With this as background, where, one might ask, is the danger to Penguin's continued pre-eminence within Pearson's trade publishing interests? The answer lies in the management structure.

At Penguin's head is David Wan, who took over from Michael Lynton in January 2000 on the latter's departure to be president of AOL International. David Wan is not an editorial man, having occupied the post of chief financial officer since joining Penguin in 1998 from Simon & Schuster, where much of his time was in strategic planning. Answering to him as president of the Penguin Group (Michael Lynton's title had been chairman and chief executive) are three heads of operating companies, in descending order of importance, Penguin Putnam, Penguin UK, and Penguin Australasia. Encouragingly, flexibility exists, as witness the way geographic tidiness can be made to play second fiddle to publishing requirements: the world-wide operations of Dorling Kindersley, notwithstanding the importance to it of the US market, remain the total responsibility of Penguin UK and have not been shared with Penguin Putnam.

What is conspicuously absent, however, is the presence at the centre of a youthful Peter Mayer look-alike, a publishing driving force whose constant goal is to push Penguins into even the remotest corners of the world. This gap is all the more significant considering that the Penguin headquarters is in the USA, where the Penguin traditions have comparatively shallow roots and the international character of trade publishing is at its weakest.

Today's verdict is that Penguin's present position within the Pearson mastheads still appears largely to reflect publishing realities. But, given the managerial and the commercial swing to the USA, the circumstances under which this could become more and more of an historical reminder are well in place. Allen Lane's statement that 'very few great enterprises like this survive their founder' could still come true.

- September 2001 – resignation of Phyllis Grann as CEO and president of Penguin Putnam. David Shanks becomes CEO, with Susan Petersen Kennedy, president of Penguin Putnam, reporting to him.

- June 2002 – resignation of David Wan, Penguin Group president. John Makinson, chairman of Penguin Group since May 2001, becomes chairman and CEO. David Wan's responsibilities taken up in part by the three regional CEOs: David Shanks, Penguin Putnam; Anthony Forbes Watson, Penguin UK; Peter Field, Penguin Australia.

- Penguin Group headquarters now divided between London and New York City. John Makinson maintains an office and a place to live in both cities.

- Penguin Putnam renamed Penguin Group (USA).

- October 2003 – publication of *A Royal Duty* by Paul Burrell.

Comment. In the light of these developments, the managerial swing to the United States referred to above now requires heavy qualification. At the same time, the Phyllis Grann editorial legacy survives in the shape of continued commitment – some might say heightened commitment – to the mass market, even where it inflicts significant damage on Penguin's reputation for enlightened, principled publishing (the Burrell book).

Chapter 4

FOUR PUBLISHING TAKEOVERS

'TO SAY THE AMOUNT OF financial expertise (in UK publishing) is nil is no overstatement.'

'Let shareholders make their own decisions about charity and let the businesses in which they have invested be businesslike.'

'Is it a business or a charity? There are those who think because they are publishing books with artistic worth they don't have to worry about balance sheets. I love books. I could never work in ball-bearings or Mars bars, but publishing is a business. You have to sell to survive.'

These statements were made by three British publishers – respectively Paul Hamlyn in 1972, Tim Hely Hutchinson in 1991, and Anthony Cheetham in 1992 – who have at least one thing in common: They have all created publishing houses from scratch and converted them into publishing empires through marriages with companies much older than their own. Paul Hamlyn's Octopus (founded in 1971) acquired Heinemann (founded in 1890); Tim Hely Hutchinson's Headline (1986) bought Hodder & Stoughton (1868); and Anthony Cheetham's Century Publishing (1981) merged with Hutchinson (1887). Cheetham did it again when he started Orion in 1991 and in the same year bought out the company that George Weidenfeld had started in 1949.

What is it that attracts these lusty blades to these brides of a certain age? Was W. S. Gilbert right in proclaiming 'there's a fascination frantic in a ruin that's romantic'? Or is there something more to these unions?

In three of the four cases there is a disparity not only of age, but of size. Century merged with a company whose turnover was four times their own; Headline with one three-and-a-half times larger than their own. Orion didn't even have any turnover when they purchased Weidenfeld. While Octopus was some 30% larger than Heinemann in terms of sales and profit, the relative scale of the two businesses as reflected in their numbers of employees and titles suggests that the predator was living up to its cephalopodic name by making a distinctly ambitious catch.

Table 13 highlights not only differences of scale, but also disparities in profitability between the acquisitors and the acquired. At one extreme, Orion,

Table 13: *Comparative company statistics*

Company (year end)	Average no. of employees	Turn-over £m	Operating profit £m	Pre-tax profit £m	Pre-tax margins %	Backlist sales as % of publishing sales	Overseas sales as % of total sales	Titles in print (approx.)
Century (31/12/84)	29	5.25	0.60	0.52	9.9	15/20	19	300
Hutchinson (6/7/84)	679*	20.73	0.94	0.18†	0.9	20	30	3500
Octopus (31/12/84)	334	53.41	8.07	9.12	17.1	60	47	600
Heinemann (31/12/84)	700	40.89	6.16	6.88	16.8	65	40	8000
Orion (31/12/91)	(Trading not commenced)			–	–	–	–	–
Weidenfeld (31/12/9 1)	62	8.17	(0.64)	(0.76)	–	20	37	700
Headline (31/12/92)	118	15.71	1.68	2.05	13.0	24	20	1000
Hodder & Stoughton (30/6/92)	638	55.60	2.10	1.05	1.9	45	38	7000

* Including 217 in printing and binding.
† After exceptional charges of £323,000.

a newly started company, purchased a company that had just made losses of nearly 10% of its turnover. Seven years previously, the same management, under the name of Century, had merged with Hutchinson when the latter was barely profitable. Headline, with pre-tax margins of 13%, wooed and won Hodder & Stoughton, a company that had achieved a profit margin of less than 2% in its last full reported year. Once again, Octopus and Heinemann were the exception, having comparable profit margins.

Let us defer, for the moment, consideration of the amounts paid by the successful bidders. There were attractions on both sides before price was discussed. Firstly, why were the companies on the market? Not by any means for similar reasons.

1. **Weidenfeld**: For Lord Weidenfeld, the timing in 1991 was sound. He had been considering the problem of succession since he was in his late 50s. Now that he was in his early 70s the matter was of more than intellectual interest. Anthony Cheetham was a Weidenfeld author. They had had business links in the mid-1970s through a joint paperback company. Furthermore, Cheetham's heart was in publishing and Lord Weidenfeld's company was to be 'the corner-stone of a new communications group'. Finally, Weidenfeld had the oppor-

tunity to retain an equity interest in his own publishing creation, of which he owned 80%, by becoming a shareholder (albeit small) in Orion.

2. **Heinemann** had been part of the BTR conglomerate empire since June 1983, when BTR had taken over Thomas Tilling; Tilling were themselves an industrial conglomerate which had acquired full control of Heinemann in April 1961. Within the BTR portfolio, the intangible intellectual property assets of a publisher had always sat uncomfortably alongside the fixed assets of engineering and construction subsidiaries. Through Heinemann's sale to Octopus in 1985, BTR became a 35% shareholder in a publishing group two-and-a-quarter times the size of Heinemann in both turnover and profit and consequently that much better able to exploit the advantages of scale. At the same time, BTR had in effect passed over the management of their investment in publishing to Paul Hamlyn.

3. **Hutchinson** had been bought by London Weekend Television (LWT) in 1978 for £3.9m. Hopes of trading benefits from the interaction of television and publishing had been largely disappointed. Furthermore, Hutchinson's trading performance, which had suffered severely in the 1980-2 recession, was responding too slowly to remedial action. Through their merger with Century, LWT recovered their original investment and also were left with a 25% stake in a larger group. Century's profit record had been strong and the management was explicit in its ambitions to secure a public quotation. This meant that LWT had before them the prospect of being able to sell their holding at a later stage after what they hoped might be a satisfactory performance. This judgement was triumphantly vindicated four years later (without the need for a flotation) when Random House paid £64m in June 1989 for Century Hutchinson. By that time, turnover had risen to £38.6m and pre-tax profits to £2.3m. LWT's interest, after a further investment of £1.3m at the time of a rights issue, came to 23.4%, for which they received the thoroughly satisfactory sum of £15m.

4. **Hodder & Stoughton**: The possibility of a sale had been the subject of speculation in the trade press for some time. Indeed, towards the end of 1989, the Hodder board had concluded that some sort of alliance would make economic sense. Initially, they had been thinking of a European partner, probably French or German, with ambitions to expand in the world of English-language publishing. Hodder would then have constituted the UK and Commonwealth limb of a European publishing tree and would also have provided a useful entry into the American market. In the event, nothing came of this. The recession – particularly as it affected trade publishing – was beginning to have an impact and the need for additional capital resources, which had been at the origin of the continental initiatives, became increasingly evident. The sale of Hodder's famous medical journal, the *Lancet*, to Elsevier in October 1991 was a palliative. The solution came through the merger with Headline.

Hodder & Stoughton were a family business, 80% owned by descendants of

the founder, Matthew Hodder, with the balance largely in the hands of employees. Of the 160 shareholders, some were seventh generation descendants. Few
had any direct involvement with the firm. At the same time, they were not
as a group independently wealthy and, in the words of the chairman, Philip
Attenborough, 'a rights issue among our own shareholders would have
been a real lead balloon'. With no existing institutional shareholders and no
possibility, thanks to the recent trading record, of obtaining access to outside
capital by way of a quotation (or for that matter a private placing except on
penal terms), a sale had become inevitable. For Hodder some of the advantages
of the Headline merger were similar to those influencing Weidenfeld's sale to
Orion: Hodder's importance within the merged group as a guarantor of their
editorial integrity; the absence of overlaps, except in UK distribution; the
goodwill that stemmed from existing trading links; and the fact that Headline's
ambitions extended to the whole of the group. Furthermore, Headline were a
demonstrably successful publisher with a quotation and something of a stock
market following.

For the acquisitors, the four target companies offered, in addition to whatever
their balance sheets represented, a common set of strategic advantages:

   1. *Improved standing.* In each case, the acquisition/merger gave the acquiring company a standing that it previously did not have, notably in dealings with
authors and literary agents. It served to enhance each company's chances of
being included in literary agents' short lists, whether in auctions of titles by
existing authors or as a possible home for new or relatively untried writers.
Another benefit came with recruitment: The association with long-established
imprints can be seen as confidence-inspiring and likely to influence potential
recruits favourably.

   Recognition of such advantages was no doubt behind the decision to call the
product of the Century and Hutchinson merger 'Century Hutchinson'. An
even more explicit acceptance came with the naming of Hodder Headline,
where the acquisitor chose second position. This also ensured that the idle
would not drop the second name – as had earlier occurred with Hodder &
Stoughton – and that the merged company would have alliterative appeal.

   2. *Enhanced scale.* In ascending order of importance, Octopus, Headline,
Century, and Orion greatly increased the scale of their businesses. For
Octopus, magnification was not such an important factor. It was already one of
the largest independent publishers in the country. For Orion, the resulting
expansion was almost unlimited.

   For Century, according to Anthony Cheetham, the merger with Hutchinson
'gave them a critical size and, while it brought margins down initially, it seemed
to make them safer'. Critical size was particularly evident in paperbacks.
Hutchinson's paperback imprint, Arrow, found themselves towards the bottom
end of the second division. They had also had a succession of disasters, some
of them self-inflicted, and many affecting their Australasian business. The

result was that the hardback editors at Hutchinson had limited confidence in their own company's paperback effectiveness and were reluctant to have their authors paperbacked under the Arrow imprint. The merger with Century brought additional paperback turnover which, when added to Arrow's, meant that total sales by 1988 had risen to some £12m. At that level, and after some sensible management decisions, notably in the handling of Australia, the paperback division was making a useful pre-tax profit margin of around 8%. Interestingly, this owed little if anything to the repatriation to Arrow of paperback rights that had been licensed to outside houses.

Increased scale will often change the relationship with suppliers. Opportunities for keener prices from printers are an obvious example. Warehousing and distribution present more complex issues. While in theory the option of sub-contracting these functions is beguiling, in practice, publishers of any size normally seek to undertake their own warehousing/distribution. This reflects concern over the lost control that sub-contracting involves and, in the event of some disaster, over the unlikelihood of being able to switch swiftly and painlessly to a suitable alternative. Consequently, in most mergers, the parties involved will already have their own warehousing and economies of scale will require consolidation. The occasion may also be taken to introduce a new improved computer system. The trading results can be variable.

On the positive side, the closure in 1987 of Heinemann's warehouse in Kingswood, Surrey and concentration at Rushden, Northants of warehousing and distribution proved a considerable success in terms both of increased efficiency and of cost savings. Headline's purchase in July 1992 of Bookpoint, at Abingdon, Oxfordshire, where Headline were already being distributed, was in part to prevent it passing into the hands of another publisher. Headline management rejects the view that there is no money to be made in warehousing and distribution. Bookpoint is a profit centre – and a profitable one at that – and consolidation of Hodder's operations at Bookpoint, with the closure in early 1994 of the Sevenoaks, Kent centre, is expected to reinforce this profitability. Much the same thinking was behind Orion's purchase in 1993 of Gollancz Services. Weidenfeld had been warehoused at the Littlehampton centre for some years and Orion from their inception had also been with Gollancz Services. Within Orion it is treated as a profit centre and there are ambitious plans for expansion to accommodate Orion's own expected growth and also to look after additional outside clients. In the Century Hutchinson merger, Century were already being warehoused at Hutchinson's Tiptree, Essex centre.

The collapse of Tiptree's systems in 1993 is a reminder of the hazards to which even a long-established, well-regarded business is exposed. The unhappy experience of Edward Arnold, acquired in 1987 by Hodder & Stoughton, who were required to close their Woodlands Park centre in Berkshire and transfer to Sevenoaks, also serves as a cautionary tale.

It is clear that reorganization and redundancy costs are an essential ingredient in any merger of warehousing capacity. The financial solution is to have the sale proceeds of the centre that has been made redundant pay for the move and expansion of the centre that is being retained. A neat trick if you can do it – and quite often this has been achieved.

Another obvious consequence of enhanced scale in the supplier and client relationships lies in the strengthening of the publisher's hand in his discussions with retail booksellers, particularly the chains. This is also where the publisher who has made a point of staying close to his market and cultivating his customers stands to gain maximum advantage.

3. *Geographical diversification.* For Headline, Hodder's extensive overseas exposure was a major attraction. This included companies in Australia and New Zealand which had been set up in 1971 (having previously been branches) and in South Africa, where the company was formed in 1986. Hodder's non-UK sales were 38% of their total, as compared with Headline's 20%, and were supported by an overseas staff of 165, 26% of their total at year end.

Hutchinson also provided Century with a valuable overseas infrastructure – a major benefit cited at the time by Anthony Cheetham. As with Hodder, Hutchinson's overseas companies were in Australia, South Africa, and New Zealand. The first two had been set up in the 1960s and the third in 1977. The numbers employed came to a little over sixty, some 10% of the group total, while overseas sales represented 30% of group sales. While these were lower percentages than Hodder's, they represented a useful base on which Century might build. In the Australian companies of both Hodder and Hutchinson a limited amount of local publishing was undertaken.

Heinemann had easily the most extensive overseas interests. Their eight subsidiary companies in Australia, New Zealand, USA, Hong Kong, Singapore, Malaysia, Kenya, and South Africa, and their associate companies in Nigeria, Jamaica, and Zimbabwe were primarily linked to Heinemann's educational business, total sales of which in 1986 were running at around £25m, 35% overseas and 65% in the UK. In Australia, where the investment in local publishing had been greatest, sales were made up of 55% imports, 45% indigenous. The subject mix was 70% educational, 30% trade. For Octopus, whose sales were already 47% overseas, the foreign content of Heinemann's business was not in itself novel. What was novel was the network of foreign companies and the geographical spread extending to Asia and Africa.

Finally, Orion's purchase of Weidenfeld gave them ownership of a company with a high export content (37% of 1991 group turnover of £8.2m), half of it in the USA and nearly 30% in continental Europe. There were no overseas subsidiaries. This pattern mirrored Lord Weidenfeld's own cultural and business links and brings to mind Emerson's saying, 'an institution is the lengthened shadow of one man'. Some shadow! Missing from all four transactions was a US publishing base. Weidenfeld's American business consisted entirely of exports.

4. *Product diversification.* Small publishing companies taking over larger ones

always add some new dimensions to their lists. Century Publishing's strengths lay in middlebrow fiction, illustrated coffee table books and strong computer and health/fitness lists. Through Hutchinson, this was expanded to encompass sport and leisure (Stanley Paul); art books (Barrie & Jenkins); the occult (Rider Books); illustrated reference, maps, and guides (Geographia and Nicholson); education (school and university); academic lists; sponsored books (Benham); and above all a mass-market paperback imprint (Arrow).

For Headline, who had set themselves up in low to middlebrow fiction and had only recently been extending their scope to non-fiction, the merger with Hodder had an explosive impact on their subject lists. Popular fiction, Hodder's stock-in-trade, was given a new dimension. New areas for Headline included religious books, school textbooks, academic titles (Edward Arnold), home education (Teach Yourself series), tertiary textbooks, and juveniles.

Octopus's original publishing emphasis had been on heavily illustrated hardbacks related to leisure for a popular audience. It had been broadened by the purchase of children's publisher Brimax in 1983 and of children's picture book licences, and the aggressive marketing of such titles. On the eve of Octopus's takeover of Heinemann, between one-fifth and one-quarter of their publishing turnover was sales of children's books. Diversification on this scale said much for the attractiveness of the juvenile book market. It also no doubt reflected management's recognition that the growth potential for heavily illustrated popular non-fiction hardbacks was finite. The Heinemann acquisition brought to Octopus:

(a) ownership of one of the leading UK educational publishers, with a major overseas exposure, a market where rapid changes were favouring the larger groups;

(b) cross-over opportunities whereby Octopus's marketing skills would be employed to exploit educational titles in high street outlets;

(c) a considerable boost to children's publishing through Heinemann Young Books plus the Kaye & Ward and World's Work imprints, with a combined UK market share rising to some 20%; and

(d) entrée into fiction and belles lettres through William Heinemann Ltd and Secker & Warburg. Heretofore, Octopus had not been a serious entry in the Booker Prize stakes.

For Orion, the purchase of Weidenfeld gave the company a substantial exposure to hardback non-fiction together with the literary and reference lists of J. M. Dent's Everyman's Library and Dent Children's Books. Weidenfeld had bought J. M. Dent in December 1987, but in the course of 1990/91 had sold (to David Campbell Publishers) the Everyman list, the paperback rights to which were then licenced back to Weidenfeld.

Not all diversification hopes were fulfilled. Century found the capital-hunger of educational publishing more than they wished to face. Feeling that the economics were increasingly favouring the larger units, they sold the Hutchinson educational business (sales of £3.5m) to a subsidiary of Wolters

Kluwer in May 1989. Less than a year later, they sold Hutchinson Academic (turnover of some £600,000) to Unwin Hyman. They had already sold the map and guide division (Geographia and Nicholson) because it needed substantial investment in map-making equipment and fell outside the group's mainstream publishing interests.

At Orion, somewhat the same pattern emerged. Weidenfeld's academic, law, and economic lists were sold within twelve months of being acquired.

The strengths of a publishing house – even a large one – often reflect the publishing enthusiasms of the man at the top. Anybody running the educational division at William Collins during the era of Sir William (Billy) Collins was well advised to recognize that it was an 'also ran' job so long as the chairman's consuming enthusiasms were for Hammond Innes, Boris Pasternak, and Joy Adamson's lioness Elsa. Similarly, Anthony Cheetham turned his face against educational and professional publishing – notwithstanding their highly profitable characteristics – and concentrated, both at Century Hutchinson and at Orion, in the areas that he knew and liked. Thereby he gave both houses a clear-cut publishing profile and renounced any claims to being a publishing 'mini-conglomerate'. By contrast, Paul Hamlyn at Octopus and Tim Hely Hutchinson at Hodder Headline had objectives well beyond their personal publishing interests and wore the conglomerate badge with pride.

5. *Backlist strengths.* In the vocabulary of merger justification, 'strengthening the backlist' comes second only to 'broadening the base'. It is the publishing equivalent of expressing support for motherhood. But whereas the consequences of motherhood are pretty evident, no such clarity surrounds the backlist. For Octopus life-style books, a backlist is achieved when a title reaches a second printing. In the context of a vertically integrated trade publishing house, Orion defines backlist sales as paperback sales. At Hodder a title selling for more than a year used to enter the backlist. To other trade publishers, however, the backlist consists of titles that do not appear in their current catalogues. Some publishers of academic titles start recognizing backlist sales only after two years. And then there are the definitional complexities of straight reprints and new editions.

What is abundantly clear is that different types of publishing have different backlist patterns. In the Hodder Headline merger document, where backlist sales are defined as sales of books published in previous financial years, Hodder's gross backlist sales are shown at £20m, 45% of total gross sales from publishing. Within that total, the backlist ratios were 71% for religious books, 67% for Edward Arnold academic titles, and 57% for educational titles. Headline's own ratio was put at 24%. (In this instance, gross backlist sales are shown as a percentage of net sales.) The merger has therefore resulted in a significant shift from front list publishing towards backlist publishing. Other things being the same, this increases the predictability (and quality) of publishing turnover.

The estimates in Table 13 show the backlist proportions for Octopus and Heinemann at 60% and 65% respectively. In this instance, the merger served to maintain an already high percentage. For Octopus, this reflected the long shelf-life of many of their life-style books, as well as the importance of children's books, where successive generations of children allied to the nostalgia of parents create for some publishers not a mere gold mine, but a diamond drift. At Heinemann the high ratio of backlist sales was a direct reflection of their heavy involvement in children's books and educational titles, more than offsetting their front list fiction publishing.

Hutchinson's low backlist ratio of around 20% is in part a consequence of their modest presence in educational books and juveniles. In part it reflects the leakage of titles to outside paperback imprints. Hutchinson also suffered from the cumulative effect of tight financial restrictions over several years. The backlist was not properly replenished.

Copyright licences rather than sales percentages may well offer the best indication of the potential that exists for a Century Publishing or a Headline that gains control of a Hutchinson or a Hodder. The permutations available to a publisher intent on exploiting a store of copyright licences are immense: reprinting of titles; their repackaging and repricing; licensing others to reprint; recovering from others the reprint rights; issuing new editions.

The extension under European Community law of copyright protection to life plus seventy years from life plus fifty years from 1 July 1995 has added to the value of such inventories of intellectual property. The intensity and effectiveness with which they are exploited is very much a function of the verve and imagination of their new owners.

6. *Nuturing trading links.* While the nurture of existing trading links between the two parties is unlikely to be a determining consideration in a publishing merger/acquisition, it can be influential. Of the four instances under review, Octopus and Heinemann had the closest trading connections. These were concentrated on the series of hardback omnibus editions developed under the code name 'Operation Pickles', named after Charles Pick, managing director of Heinemann. They consisted of inexpensive compilations of the bestselling titles of major Heinemann authors, which were marketed by Octopus. They were launched in the UK in 1976 and in the USA three years later, and by 1985 had sold more than five million copies. This happy commercial experience must have given Octopus management a taste for the backlist benefits of a quality trade fiction list. It no doubt also guaranteed the inclusion of the Heinemann name in any compilation of suitable candidates for purchase.

As far as the other mergers were concerned, the connections between the parties were more modest, being almost entirely in warehousing and distribution. Headline were warehoused and distributed by Hodder in Australia and New Zealand: 10% of Headline's turnover as a result went through Hodder. Century Publishing already used Hutchinson's Tiptree centre, while Orion joined Weidenfeld from the start at Gollancz Services.

Reasons for mutual attraction being established, comes the key issue: What did the predators pay? Second after a set of balance sheets, a potential acquisitor studies a target company's trading record. At Weidenfeld, the three years preceding their sale to Orion had clearly been difficult, with the company reporting cumulative losses that came to nearly 6% of turnover. That period also saw the sale for £250,000 of the rights to the Everyman editions. Losses persisted in the early months of 1992 leading up to the 8 May 1992 date of sale to Orion, albeit at a reduced rate compared to 1991 (see table 14).

In the case of Hutchinson, the year to 6 July 1984 saw pre-tax profits of £183,000 on turnover of £20.73m. Profits were struck after exceptional write-offs and reorganization charges of £323,000 (see table 15). The nadir of Hutchinson's fortunes came in 1979/80. Over the ensuing four years, there was a strong turn-around of over £2.5m, which lifted the group out of deficit into profit. However, whether one adjusts for exceptional charges or not, the profitability achieved was still marginal.

The trading record of Hodder & Stoughton in the period up to the merger is complicated by a change of year-end, as well as by the incidence of redundancy and reorganization charges in early 1991. There were signs of recovery after a setback in the middle of the period. The results for the six months to 31 December 1992 reflect the seasonally strong Christmas period, the first six months of the calendar year normally coming close to break-even (see table 16).

In October 1991, the *Lancet* was sold to Elsevier for £11m net of costs. The money was used to reduce UK borrowings. The element of *Lancet* turnover, included in the results to 30 June 1992, came to £1.195m.

The four years preceding the 1985 acquisition of Heinemann were characterized by a strong advance in both sales and profits. The improvement in margins was also marked (see table 17).

These snapshots of the trading records of the four target companies just prior to their acquisitions/mergers reveal that three of them presented turn-around opportunities. The acquisitors were coming on the scene at times of significant trading losses (Weidenfeld); of marginal profitability (Hutchinson); or when the recovery shoots were still young and tender (Hodder). Heinemann were once again the exception, displaying as they did rosy health, with a radiance exceeded only by that of their acquisitor (see table 18).

In the event, Octopus paid £100m for Heinemann; Headline's purchase of Hodder cost them £48.9m; Orion acquired Weidenfeld for £3.6m. The merger of Century and Hutchinson attributed a value of £16m to the combined companies. These figures have little meaning until stated as multiples of the turnover and profits of the target companies (see table 19).

At the top end of the scale is the purchase by Octopus, a highly successful quoted company, of Heinemann, an extremely profitable division of BTR, which over many years under the direction of Sir Owen Green had become a byword for the maximizing of shareholder value. The price paid to BTR in

Table 14: *Weidenfeld*

Year to 31 December	1988	1989	1990	1991
Turnover (£000)	10,486	9993	10,876	8166
Pre-tax profits (£000)	282	(593)	(359)	(758)

Table 15: *Hutchinson*

Year to July	1980	1981	1982	1983	1984
Turnover (£000)	15,617	15,491	16,748	17,199	20,730
Exceptional charges (£000)	(538)	(424)	(246)	–	(323)
Pre-tax profits (£000)	(2323)	(1791)	(318)	181	183
Pre-tax margins	–	–	–	1.1%	0.9%

Table 16: *Hodder*

	12m to 31/3/90	15m to 30/6/91	Annualized	12m to 30/6/92	6m to 31/12/92
Turnover (£000)	60,074	74,229	59,383	55,603	31,360
Pre-tax pre-exceptional profits (£000)	663	(4909)	(3927)	1049	2220
Exceptionals (£000)	+187	−2442	−2442	–	–
Pre-tax profits (£000)	850	(7351)	(6369)	1049	2220
Profit margins	1.4%	–	–	1.9%	7.1%

Table 17: *Heinemann*

Year to 31 December	1981	1982	1983	1984
Turnover (£000)	28,278	30,692	37,831	40,888
Pre-tax profits (£000)	3662	4292	5202	6883
Pre-tax margins	12.9%	14.0%	13.8%	16.8%

Table 18: *Octopus*

Year to 31 December	1981	1982	1983	1984
Turnover (£000)	24,476	30,751	37,157	53,407
Pre-tax profits (£000)	3833	4824	6334	9123
Pre-tax margins	15.7%	15.7%	17.0%	17.1%

FOUR PUBLISHING TAKEOVERS

Table 19: *Takeover statistics*

Transaction	Predator company	Company	Consideration	Historic turnover	Multiple of turnover	Historic pre-tax	Multiple of pre-tax	Net debt[1]
					Target company			
March 1985		Century	£8.0m	£5.3m	1.5×[5]	£0.52m	15.4×[5]	£0.6m
		Hutchinson	£8.0m	£20.7m	0.4×[5]	£0.18m[3]	44.4×[3,5]	£6.3m
		Century Hutchinson	£16.0m	£25.9m	0.6×	£0.70m	22.9×[3]	£6.9m
August 1985	Octopus	Heinemann	£100.0m	£40.9m	2.4×	£6.88m	14.5×	Nil
May 1992	Orion	Weidenfeld	£3.6m[2]	£8.2m	0.4×	(£0.76m)	–	£1.3m[2]
June 1993	Headline	Hodder & Stoughton	£48.9m	£55.6m	0.9×	£1.05m[4]	46.6×	£5.5

1 As at the balance sheet date prior to the transaction.
2 Bank borrowings at the time of acquisition of £1.3m are included in the consideration.
3 After adding back to Hutchinson profits exceptional charges of £323,000, Hutchinson's historic pre-tax is £0.50m and Century Hutchinson's £1.02m; corresponding multiples are 16.0× and 15.7×.
4 Results for the full year to 30 June 1992. In the six months to 31 December 1992, pre-tax profits were £2.2m.
5 See text.

Octopus shares was adjusted to compensate BTR for relinquishing certain voting rights. Under these, so long as Paul Hamlyn and his family owned 20% of Octopus's voting shares, Hamlyn would be entitled to vote such of BTR's holding of 35% as afforded him at least 50.1% of the votes of Octopus. The granting of this sweetener naturally had the effect of raising the price paid by Octopus for Heinemann. Nonetheless, the 2.4× multiple of turnover paid was not hugely dissimilar to other transactions involving educational and professional publishing assets, where similar adjustments were not required. Examples include Pearson's March 1988 purchase of Addison-Wesley on a 1.7× multiple of turnover; Time Inc's purchase of Scott Foresman in October 1986 (2.6×); and International Thomson's December 1986 acquisition of South Western Publishing (2.9×).

At the time, however, a widely held view was that a full price had been paid by Octopus for Heinemann. That it was not an excessive price was demonstrated two years later when Reed International bought Octopus (as enlarged by Heinemann) for £535m on a multiple of turnover of 3.4× and on a multiple of pre-tax profits of 20.6×. This gave BTR a profit on their holding of £78m.

The Orion-Weidenfeld transaction differs from that of Octopus-Heinemann in that neither of the participants had a quotation. This in itself may have had some dampening effect on valuations and contributed to the low purchase multiple of less than half one year's turnover. The consideration of £3.6m included the £1.3m of bank borrowings in the Weidenfeld balance sheet. Undoubtedly, however, one of the most important determinants of the amount paid by Orion was the fact that Weidenfeld was in deficit and had just experienced three consecutive years of significant losses. Another factor was the absence of a current fiction list and the related lack of a paperback arm. In a publishing environment where the merits of vertical hardback–paperback publishing are now taken for granted, such gaps in a trade publishing portfolio constitute a major weakness. For Orion, however, where paperback skills were strongly entrenched, this was no real drawback. Rather the reverse, since it had the effect no doubt of cooling the enthusiasm of some other potential bidders.

The mix of skills and assets within Orion started to work in the 1992 results, which consolidated Weidenfeld for seven-and-a-half months and showed pre-tax profits of £56,000 on turnover of £8.8m. In 1993, pre-tax profits rose to £202,000 on a turnover of £19.9m. Anthony Cheetham is quoted as having a turnover target of £50m in about five years. On margins of, say, 10%, a ratio that he sees as sustainable in trade publishing and one that he achieved at Century Publishing just ahead of the Hutchinson merger, pre-tax profits of £5m would be indicated. This would provide ample justification for a stock market quotation – a case of third time lucky, since Century were heading for a quote before the Hutchinson opportunity presented itself and Century Hutchinson were on their way to the Stock Exchange when they were intercepted by Random House.

The Century Hutchinson deal was a merger. Under its terms, ownership of the new company was first of all divided equally between Century Publishing and LWT. LWT then sold half of their interest, by way of a placing to institutions at a price of £5 a share, receiving net of expenses £3.9m. This established a value for Century Hutchinson as a whole of £16m, in which LWT retained at the outset a holding of 25.12%.

The disparity in size between the two companies, with Hutchinson's turnover at £20.7m and Century's at £5.3m, and the equality in share ownership in the merged company need explaining. In part they reflected contrasting profit records, albeit a short one for Century. In part they reflected balance-sheet differences, with Hutchinson contributing to the merged company their debt of £6.3m (as at the balance-sheet date of 6 July 1984 and including £3m owing to LWT), while Century Publishing contributed net debt of £567,000 (as at 31 December 1984). Equality between the two participants was an elegant way of sidestepping what might have developed into a destructive accounting debate in a situation where the important merger decisions had already been taken. LWT, having recovered their original investment in Hutchinson through the placing, wanted their remaining interest in publishing to be managed by Anthony Cheetham and his team, while Century were happy to defer getting a quotation for Century Publishing in order to have an even more splendid stock market launch as Century Hutchinson.

The Century and Hutchinson ratios given in table 19 are hard to interpret because this was a merger between unequals. There was no possibility of the kind of adjustments based on stock market capitalizations that were to be used in the January 1993 Reed Elsevier merger. Attention should be focussed on the combined totals, which show the £16m valuation as being equivalent to 60%

of combined turnover and 22.9× combined pre-tax profits (15.7× after adding back exceptional charges).

The Headline purchase of Hodder has many interesting features. The valuation on a multiple of revenues of 0.9× was richer than in the Century Hutchinson and Weidenfeld cases, but well below the Heinemann statistic. If one makes some adjustment for the fact that around £10m of Hodder's turnover was made up of agency business, this comment still stands. The price was also below the valuations achieved in other transactions involving broadly based publishing groups. For example, News Corporation purchased William Collins in January 1989 on a 1.8× multiple of revenues and Random House purchased Century Hutchinson in June 1989 on a multiple of 1.6×.

Considerations influencing the Headline Hodder terms included Hodder's unspectacular record in recent years, which entailed a sharp dividend cut in 1990/91, as well as the fact that the vendors were getting the benefit of exchanging an illiquid investment in an unquoted company for a liquid one in a quoted company. Most important of all to the success of the bid, Hodder shares, which were traded infrequently on a matched bargain basis, were hugely undervalued. Prior to the bid, the price at which they had last traded was £9.50 a share, well down from a high some years previously of around £15. The Headline offer valued them at £108.75. For many Hodder shareholders, it must have looked as if Christmas had come in June.

While the bid looked generous in the eyes of the Hodder shareholders, it appeared undemanding when viewed by Headline shareholders. There was widespread confidence that Headline management would be up to the task of delivering many of the benefits of scale and diversification. In short, it looked like an earnings-enhancing acquisition.

The most intriguing aspect of the transaction was that by setting the terms on the basis chosen, Headline looked like doing themselves a considerable favour and thereby heightened the prospects of a positive reaction in the stock market to the announcement of the merger. In the event, Headline's price, which ahead of the announcement was 290p, rose swiftly to 400p. Hodder shareholders thus saw a 38% increase in the paper value of the bid they had just received for their company.

Under the terms of the bid and after giving effect to the accompanying rights issue (which raised £12.5m), the Hodder shareholders became entitled to 49.7% of the enlarged equity capital of Headline. This had the paradoxical result of giving to the Hodder interests apparent control of the new group. The expectation, however, was that many Hodder shareholders would sell part of their Headline holdings. This they duly did. By early 1994, their combined stake probably stood at less than 30%.

For the Headline management, the share price performance also had its satisfactions of a personal nature, bearing in mind their own shareholdings in the merged group amounting to some 6%. More generally, however, it under-lined for them the advantages of a stock market quotation. In Tim Hely

Hutchinson's words, 'the quoted market is much more efficient than the venture capital market, being both quicker and less expensive'. Furthermore, if a takeover can be structured as a merger, this enables the predator to avoid paying the premium price that a straight takeover often requires in order to gain the acceptance of the target company's shareholders. In this particular case, the premium duly emerged, but it came after the merger terms were set and was enjoyed by all shareholders on both sides.

There are six main conclusions from this study:

– One – the most significant – is that all four of the deals came about because of the firmly held views and personal ambitions of the three entrepreneurs.

– Second, they were all agreed. There were no hostile bids making marvellous newspaper copy and leaving the victor with a balance sheet in tatters, e.g. Time Inc + Warner or Viacom + Paramount, and, absurdity of absurdities, endowing the expansion-driven group with a pressing need to retrench.

– Third, agreement was not just a matter of finance, but took account as well of past commercial links between the participants and a general familiarity with each other's business.

– Fourth, in all cases the mature attractions of the acquired companies exerted a fascination on the purchasers. To revert to W. S. Gilbert, in three instances, these attractions might be said to have been partly ruinous, if by that is meant overgrown, but not to the point of decay.

– A fifth point is that in two cases the stock market had an immediate and central role to play and in two others has been promised a deferred role.

– Finally, the timing of the four transactions cannot be faulted.

Chapter 5

ASSOCIATED BOOK PUBLISHERS

Question: How might one treble one's money in the space of three months?
Answer: Buy Associated Book Publishers shares in May and sell them in July.

The twist is that this opportunity came only once and that was in 1987, when ABP changed ownership.

Going over these events nine years later evokes feelings of nostalgia. But it also provides an opportunity to probe the motives of the various participants and to draw conclusions from some aspects of company takeovers.

To set the scene, one needs to remember what constituted Associated Book Publishers. The antiseptic name, and the even more unmemorable acronym, ABP, indicate the multi-faceted nature of the group. The name was assumed in June 1958 after Eyre & Spottiswoode (Publishers) had joined forces with Methuen & Co. Four and a half years later, in January 1963, the group took on its distinctive shape through the merger with Sweet & Maxwell.

By the mid-1960s, therefore, ABP was a holding company with 15 sub-sidiaries, in which trade publishing accounted for somewhat less than 25% of turnover and legal, scientific, and academic publishing over 75%. Included in these percentages were two important overseas interests: Associated Book Publishers of Australia and New Zealand (57% owned) and Methuen of Canada, with its 51% voting interest in the Carswell Co.

The company's major imprints by category in 1963 were:

General trade and children's publishing: Methuen, Eyre & Spottiswoode

Social sciences, academic, religious: Tavistock, Methuen, Eyre & Spottis-woode

Scientific, technical: Chapman & Hall; E.&F.N. Spon

Legal: Sweet & Maxwell, W. Green & Son, Stevens & Sons, Carswell (Canada), Law Book Company (Australia)

During the next twenty-odd years, management dedicated itself to rein-forcing these publishing strengths. Admittedly, there were some diversions, the most sustained being the backing given to Charles Hammick, the engagingly inspirational, but decidedly erratic, founder of Hammicks Bookshops. There were also some initiatives which came to nothing, notably the launch of a mass-market paperback imprint, Magnum, in 1976 (it survived five years), and a more short-lived trade publishing presence in the USA at the end of the 1970s.

But the overwhelming impression is one of steady resolve on the part of management leading to a considerable degree of success in the pursuit of the chosen objectives.

Specific measures taken included the purchase of the minority interests in the Australian company, with ABP's stake being lifted from 57% in 1965 to 64% in 1973 and to 100% in 1980. In Canada, ABP's voting interest in Carswell, 51% in 1963, was progressively raised to 72%.

By contrast, the acquisition of outside businesses fell almost entirely into the last few years of ABP's independent existence:

1983 A.H.&A.W. Reed Ltd, New Zealand's principal general publisher, for £540,000 (cash)

1985 Routledge & Kegan Paul for £4.41m (of which £1.14m cash and £3.27m shares)

1986 Croom Helm for £3.5m (of which £2.48m cash and £1.02m shares)

1986 Pitkin Pictorials for £1.05m (cash)

Given this burst of predatory activity, it was perhaps not entirely surprising that Associated Book Publishers should have announced in April 1987 its first ever rights issue, to raise £11m net of expenses. By way of explanation, chairman Peter Allsop pointed to the cash element in the last three acquisitions, the cost of the development of the UK distribution centre at Andover, completed in 1986, and the accelerated investment being made in academic, scientific, technical, medical, and legal publishing. At 31 March 1987 the group's net indebtedness (total debt of £11.5m less cash holdings of £1.8m) already stood at £9.7m, approaching 60% of shareholders' funds.

On 3 June 1987, only six days before the closing date for subscription to the rights issue, Peter Allsop advised shareholders, in the desiccated prose appropriate to such occasions: 'It has come to the attention of the board of Associated Book Publishers plc that an approach has been made to a major shareholder which may lead to an offer for the company at a price in cash substantially higher than the current market price.'

The question immediately presents itself: was it coincidence that the rights issue and the bid approach should have materialized simultaneously? To find an answer, one needs to explore what spurred both the sellers and the buyers into action.

In the history of ABP, the analysis can be usefully extended to the Routledge & Kegan Paul and Croom Helm takeovers, which are key elements in the development of ABP and also serve to illustrate the rich variety of considerations that lead to the same result – the change of ownership of a business.

ROUTLEDGE & KEGAN PAUL

Routledge can trace its history back to 1834. The links with the Franklin family date from 1902, when Norman Franklin's grandfather, together with associates, bought Routledge from the receiver. The chairmanship fell to his son in 1946 (after 15 years as managing director) and to his grandson 20 years later in 1966. The merger with Kegan Paul had taken place shortly after the war, following an extended period of collaborative publishing.

In 1967 the company secured a quotation on the London Stock Exchange. In contrast to some other UK publishers that went public in the 1960s, primarily to simplify valuations for estate duty purposes, Routledge did so to raise the finance for the construction of an important warehouse and distribution centre at Henley. This also had the unfortunate side-effect of acting as an untoward stimulus to trading, so much so that a cash crisis struck in 1969.

The US publisher Crowell Collier Macmillan emerged in the role of saviour when it subscribed to a convertible loan stock, maturing in 1974, which gave it 25% of the enlarged equity. Soon thereafter, however, disenchantment with the UK publishing scene set in – influenced perhaps by the unsettling sight of the Pergamon-Leasco debacle. CCM became sellers.

Enter Camellia, a holding company controlled by a Canadian, Gordon Fox, whose investments were primarily in tea plantations. One of its board members, later to become managing director, was David Bacon. For the purposes of this article, he was notable for his bookish credentials through his interest in the well-known bookshop, G. Heywood Hill, in London's Curzon Street.

Camellia had already acquired a small holding of 2% or thereabouts in Routledge & Kegan Paul, and this was quickly raised by the purchase of the bulk of CCM'S stock, as well as the 10% stake owned by Norman Franklin's cousin Colin when he left the firm to become an antiquarian bookseller.

By early 1977, Camellia had built up its holding to the 30% level. Subsequently, with the blessing of the Routledge board, Camellia took advantage of the Stock Exchange provision allowing a holding of that size to be increased by up to two percentage points a year without the investor being required to make an offer for the whole of the capital. David Bacon had joined the Routledge board and in 1979 was appointed vice-chairman.

The precise moment at which the botanical charms of the camellia were replaced by the ornithological threats of the cuckoo is impossible to pinpoint. What is clear is that this major investor became more assertive as its investment rose – the last purchases, made in 1984/85, lifted the holding to 39% – and as the trading experience of the company deteriorated. From a profits peak in the year to 31 March 1979, the company slid into loss in the year to 31 March 1983 and stayed in the red throughout 1983/84.

One response of the board to the profits collapse had been to commission Spicer & Pegler to prepare a consultants' report. Implementation of some of the recommendations led to the appointment in October 1983 of Philip

Sturrock, previously with Pitman Books, as group managing director. As reported to shareholders, this also had the merit of enabling the chairman 'to devote more time to longer-range planning and studying new developments in the rapidly changing fields of publishing'.

More immediate action followed Philip Sturrock's appointment: the sale and lease back of the Henley property; withdrawal from retailing; the move to new offices in Leicester Square (combining in one building activities previously spread across six); the departure of four directors and the introduction of such operational initiatives as profitability hurdles for new books.

Operating profits in the year to 31 March 1984 improved significantly over the previous year's, but heavy exceptional charges from the restructuring and reorganization resulted in a substantial loss. In the six months to 30 September 1984 the trading improvement was carried a step further and pre-tax profits of £105,000 were reported against losses of £49,000 a year earlier, neither result being affected by exceptionals.

Other action taken by the board involved the discontinuance of dividend payments on the ordinary capital for the whole of the period 1 April 1982 to 30 September 1984. In family-controlled firms, dividends often arouse strong emotions. Routledge & Kegan Paul was no exception: the monolithic 52% figure for family ownership (representing the holdings of family members who were subsequently those to accept irrevocably ABP's offer) breaks down into eleven specific holdings, with Norman Franklin accounting for 28.6% (over half non-beneficial) and the others ranging in size from 4.9% down to 1%.

Little imagination is required to picture the underlying strain at family gatherings as dividendless shareholding relations (plus their nearest and dearest) sipped sherry with the chairman of the family company. One should also pause for a moment to consider the likely speculation as to the priorities of an established investment company such as Camellia, by then markedly the largest single shareholder in Routledge, and getting larger. As Norman Franklin conceded: 'I'm not sure what drives Camellia.'

With this as background, the outcome of the chairman's deliberations on longer-term planning was to point him in the direction of a sale.

A large number of shareholders, and beneficiaries at one remove, whose common characteristics may extend no further than their family ties, is inherently a source of potential instability. Add to this the presence of a big corporate shareholder with unknown targets. The pressures may well have appeared acute at the time, generating a sense of urgency that superseded the rule of thumb whereby to get a good price for a business that has experienced hard times, you aim to sell when it is well into a recovery, rather than at the recovery's birth.

Advised by Barings, Norman Franklin set about finding a home for the 52% stake he felt able to speak for. This was done with considerable circumspection. Over the years, friendly lunches had taken place, with many a publisher looking to 'help' Routledge to greater riches – if only it were prepared to part with its independence. Doubtless a number of them were now approached, though their names remain discreetly hidden.

The company that came forward as the keenest and most appropriate buyer was ABP. Its existing, relatively modest academic side stood to be transformed by the inclusion of Routledge & Kegan Paul. Geographically, the £1m of north American sales being achieved by Routledge from its Boston base represented a considerable boost to ABP's still embryonic academic sales in the USA. More generally, Routledge constituted a mine of copyrights and licences, the profitability of which offered considerable scope for improvement.

The confidential discussions with ABP lasted some six weeks, at the end of which Norman Franklin secured the unconditional agreement of the holders of 52% of the equity to the terms ABP offered. The day on which the last of the signatures were received by Norman Franklin coincided with a Poetry Society meeting to which he had cycled from the ABP offices. Final confirmation only came late that evening, and it was from a coin-operated public payphone that he contacted a shocked Philip Sturrock at 10 p.m. to tell him that the business was well on its way to being sold.

ABP's terms valued Routledge & Kegan Paul shares at 386p, 36% up from the closing price of 283p on 14 March 1985, the day preceding the announcement. The offer was two ABP shares plus £3 in cash for every three RKP shares; with ABP then standing at 430p, this implied a total value of £4.41m, made up of £1.14m cash (26%) and £3.27m shares (74%).

The immediate response of the RKP board, minus the chairman, was to try to find a way of preserving the company's independence. Its merchant bankers, Morgan Grenfell, did in fact obtain indications of support from institutional investors prepared to put up some £2m to buy out the family stake, subject to thorough investigations by professional advisers. The indicated value of the counter offer came to some 350p per Routledge share, falling short of the ABP offer. It was not a firm offer at that stage and time precluded any other discussions.

Reluctantly the board bowed to superior planning and recommended acceptance of the ABP offer while lamenting that 'RKP should lose its independence at this stage of its recovery'.

For those who might have felt that the exit valuation owed more to recent misfortunes than to future potential – and indeed £4.4m for a business with sales of £5.5m meant that for each £1 of sales ABP was paying a mere 80p – the directors drew attention to the fact that shareholders who chose to hold on to the ABP shares would continue to have an indirect interest in the future success of the company; it was indeed no accident that the equity content of the bid was as high as it was.

Those who pursued this course subsequently had ample reason to be reconciled (on financial grounds) to Routledge & Kegan Paul's loss of independence. One who didn't was Camellia, an early seller of the ABP shares it had received in exchange for its Routledge stock.

CROOM HELM

The purchase of Croom Helm was an altogether simpler affair. Founded a mere 13 years earlier, in 1972 by David Croom and Christopher Helm, it published overwhelmingly for the academic market, specializing in the social sciences, humanities, and health fields. In addition, about 15% of its business was in general titles, notably natural history.

Croom Helm grew rapidly, with sales reaching £1.1m in the year to 31 March 1980, £2.6m in 1983/84 and £3.1m in 1984/85. Pre-tax profits advanced from £52,000 in 1979/80 to a peak of £219,000 in 1983/84. The following year, however, profits fell back sharply to £120,000.

In 1985 Croom Helm experienced two items of bad news. One was a bolt from the blue when the company's Australian distributor went into receivership, leaving Croom Helm with a sizeable bad debt. The resulting write-off went some way towards explaining the halved profits in 1984/85. The other was more subtle in its effects and stemmed from management action rather than divine intervention.

Following a decision to set up an operation in the USA, in March 1985, the company purchased 85% of Auburn House Publishing Co., a Boston-based social science and professional publisher started five years previously, for $150,000. Within six months, it became clear that the two Auburn House founders – who had retained the 15% minority holding – and Croom Helm management were operating on different wavelengths. As David Croom describes it, this was a clash between a Boston Irish Jesuit in his mid-50s and Kent-based Scottish Presbyterians in their late 30s.

However, extricating the company from an awkward diversification proved much simpler than might have been expected. The *Boston Globe* had developed publishing ambitions outside newspapers and approached Croom Helm that autumn in the hope that Auburn House might be for sale. After an appropriate display of profound reluctance, Croom Helm sold the business in early December for rather more than it had paid in March.

These two events coincided with, and contributed to, a growing divergence in the business objectives of David Croom and Christopher Helm, who was devoting an increasing amount of time to the non-academic side, notably through his work in building up ornithological and gardening lists.

David Croom, meanwhile, had had the seed of a possible sale planted in his mind when Peter Preston of the *Guardian*, who was at that time casting around for diversification opportunities, invited him to lunch. As a precautionary move ahead of this meal, he sought professional advice. This consisted of a half-hour conversation with Munroe Pofcher. Just before Pofcher boarded Concorde, he threw out the guideline: 'If the business is profitable and doing £3.5m, it's worth about £4m.'

The idea of a sale picked up momentum that autumn, and Munroe Pofcher was invited to enter into discussions with potential buyers. In contrast to the

Routledge cloak-and-dagger drama, this was a pretty open auction, albeit one controlled by the vendor, who selected those who were to be invited to participate. Six sets of papers went out. The recipients included groups such as Thomson and Kluwer, but ABP quickly established itself as the front runner.

The potential advantages of such an acquisition to ABP were abundantly clear: Croom Helm greatly enhanced the scale of its academic business, the areas of specialization fitted well with the subject areas of Methuen, Tavistock and Routledge & Kegan Paul, while the geographic breakdown of sales strengthened the group's presence in the Australian and north American markets. Most important of all, Croom Helm's underlying record was evidence of dynamic and skilful management.

The ownership of Croom Helm was fairly widely spread. The founders each held 17% and Investors in Industry, the specialist venture capital investment group now known as 3i, had 15%; the remaining 51% was dispersed among family members and friends. The key to shareholders' endorsement of the decision in principle to sell the company lay in their recognition that the two founders, the company's joint managing directors, had drifted apart.

ABP confirmed its intention to buy Croom Helm on 10 December 1985 and the terms were announced on 14 April 1986. The sale excluded the loss-making general books division, which was acquired by Christopher Helm (Publishers) Ltd.

The business that ABP purchased had sales of £2.6m for the year to 31 March 1985 (and related pre-tax profits of £277,000). The consideration was £3.5m, indicating that for every £1 of sales ABP was paying 135p, a considerably higher rating than that accorded Routledge & Kegan Paul. Of the £3.5m payment, cash accounted for £2.48m (70% of the whole) and ABP shares for £1.02m (30%).

This was the mirror image of the Routledge terms and reflects in part the natural desire of many entrepreneurs, when they sell the businesses they have created to realize some of the equity they have built up, especially if their continued involvement ceases or is greatly weakened. In the event, Christopher Helm went off to found his own company while David Croom joined ABP in June 1986 as managing director of the academic division.

Any serious student of the British publishing scene who took the time to study the record of Associated Book Publishers up to the end of 1986 would have been struck by the accelerating rate of change in the company. The earlier pattern of growth had been organic, allied to a policy of mopping up minority holdings in subsidiaries.

Since 1983, and most particularly in 1985 and 1986, this had been supplemented by a series of acquisitions which not only brought in publishing assets (Routledge & Kegan Paul, Pitkin Pictorials) but also management (Croom Helm). A further indication that ABP was more and more in tune with the times came in 1985 with the introduction of a share option scheme. Conclusive evidence of change came, however, in April 1987, with the announcement of the first rights issue in the company's history.

Rights issues mean different things to different people. For managers of pension funds, one of whose greatest challenges is to find a home for the pension contributions that build up throughout the year, much rejoicing usually accompanies the announcement of a cash call: in their position as existing shareholders, the critical decision to buy into a company has already been made and, provided the use to which the new money is to be put is not too outlandish, the decision to take up the rights will often fall into the easy 'no brainer' category beloved of hard-pressed fund managers.

For other investors, however, rights issues often give rise to headaches: if there are no cash reserves, subscribing means selling something else, while not subscribing means suffering a decline in one's stake in the company (the number of shares held as a percentage of the capital as enlarged by the rights).

A holding will also become diluted when a company makes an acquisition, issuing shares to the vendor in whole or part payment. While dilution is not a material consideration for most individual investors, it is highly relevant where a holding is of a size that gives it 'strategic' importance. This was the case at Associated Book Publishers.

At its formation in 1958, ABP had as its chairman and dominant shareholder Sir Oliver Crosthwaite-Eyre. Following the Sweet & Maxwell merger his holding in the enlarged company amounted to 40%, and in 1966 these shares were transferred to a Bahamian trust. The beneficiaries under the trust were his grandchildren, including the three infant children of his son Antony Crosthwaite-Eyre.

Sir Oliver retired at the end of 1973. Antony Crosthwaite-Eyre, who had joined the board in a non-executive capacity in 1973, became non-executive vice-chairman in 1974. Starting in the early 1970s, the Bahamian trust's 40% holding was shown in the ABP accounts as forming part of Antony Crosthwaite-Eyre's share interests. While this was a Stock Exchange requirement, it nonetheless readily lent itself to misinterpretation.

The diluting effect of the Routledge & Kegan Paul and Croom Helm acquisitions is reflected in the fall in the Bahamian holding as a percentage of the issued ordinary capital, from 39% at the end of 1984 to 36.7% twelve months later and to 35.9% by the end of 1986. One judgement on this shrinking percentage, presented in *The Bookseller* of 23 March 1985, was that it made the company itself 'less invulnerable' to a bid than was the case when the '*rock solid Crosthwaite-Eyre family holding*' (my italics) stood at more than 39%.

The rights issue announcement of 24 April 1987 put to the test the density of this particular rock. While the Bahamian trust found the £4.1m needed to take up its share entitlement, thereby maintaining its percentage stake, Alan Turnbull, then president of Carswell, has it clearly fixed in his mind that 'as soon as the rights issue was announced, the auction started; it showed that

84

ABP was raising money mostly to pay off debt, not just to expand further'.

The man who started the bidding was Richard Snyder, chairman of Simon & Schuster, the book publishing arm of Gulf & Western. But he may not have been the first. His recollection was that 'what triggered our bid were rumours that somebody else was interested and we decided to jump in'.

Richard Snyder, with Munroe Pofcher at his elbow, correctly judged that the attitude of the Bahamian trust was of critical importance. The conduit was Antony Crosthwaite-Eyre. On any dispassionate analysis, his ability to influence events was negligible. He had not set up the trust in the first instance; this had been done by his father, who had furthermore made his grandchildren, rather than his children, the beneficiaries. He was not a trustee; all the trustees were Bahamian lawyers. He could speak for a personal holding of a mere 7740 shares. He was a firmly non-executive director of the company.

In practical terms, however, he was a man of much greater substance. This stemmed from the Kafkaesque invisibility of the Bahamian trustees. They had never been sighted in Britain, and such contact as the top management had with them was via Antony Crosthwaite-Eyre, notwithstanding repeated efforts to establish a more direct form of communication. The one exception was a visit to Nassau by David Evans, group deputy managing director, to prepare the ground for the rights issue.

Antony Crosthwaite-Eyre had effectively embraced the internal role of go-between. From an outsider's point of view, he also had about him the aura of influence enjoyed by a family member representing the family shareholding. He was the ideal person to carry Simon & Schuster's bid to the trustees; he was also promised a role in the restructured company.

Simon & Schuster's sighting shot was £5 a share. Important contrasts emerge at this point with the Routledge & Kegan Paul and Croom Helm takeovers. In the case of Routledge, a 52% fait accompli was presented to the world after weeks of negotiations behind closed doors. Croom Helm changed hands following discussions with a selection of potential purchasers, the choice being made by the vendors.

With ABP, however, any hopes that Simon & Schuster might have had of stealing a march on rivals fell foul of the fiduciary obligations of the trustees: by entertaining a bid of x, they were bound to test the water for x plus something. Hence the statement by Peter Allsop on 3 June 1987 advising shareholders that a bid approach had been made to a major shareholder. This had the intended effect of declaring open the public auction of the company.

With directors' holdings a mere 2.4%, it did not take the board long to realize that the business was going to be sold over their heads, an outcome they became swiftly resigned to. Nor can this have come as a total surprise to them, although the timing might have been hard to predict. ABP had been intermittently subject to bid rumours; in early 1979, for example, these were particularly intense and the financial commentators of the day persuaded themselves that they could see flames beyond the smoke.

Management resignation to a loss of independence did not, however, translate into management inactivity. With the interests of shareholders in mind, the board recognized that its chief role lay in influencing the price that would ultimately be paid.

Tim Rix, then chief executive of Longman, remembers a call from Peter Allsop with the terse message: 'It looks as if we could be for sale.' For Tim Rix and his colleagues at Pearson the news itself was not astonishing, 'but we did not think it would come loose as soon as it did'.

Sir Gordon Brunton recalls that International Thomson senior management stayed in touch with ABP 'for many years. They knew very clearly of our interest, without it, however, having ever led to direct financial talks.' Under the code name 'Zulu', they kept their file on ABP up to date – a telling lesson in forward planning!

Richard Snyder, for his part, acknowledges that, while S&S had followed ABP for some time, this did not begin to compare with Thomson's period of courting.

Expressions of interest came from other groups, Reed International, Collins, and Elsevier being three that were cited at the time. In the case of Reed, monopoly considerations, given its ownership of Butterworths, made any serious approach highly implausible. The contest for ABP quickly settled down to a three-cornered fight: Simon & Schuster vs Pearson vs International Thomson.

One view from within ABP was that Simon & Schuster was primarily interested in the trade book side. This is vigorously disputed by Richard Snyder: 'Trade publishing was not the driver.' Instead he cites ABP's geographic strengths – 'We wanted very much to establish a presence in the UK, and ABP dovetailed nicely' – and the legal attractions. 'We had little legal publishing at the time and we would have used ABP as a cornerstone for an international legal publishing business. We didn't get ABP and we didn't develop into the legal market. Nor did we go after any trade publisher afterwards.'

Pearson looked at Associated Book Publishers and liked all it saw – or almost all. Longman had acquired Oyez Publishing in 1980; the subsequent expansion had been rewarding, and as a result it had big ambitions for legal publishing. The addition of Sweet & Maxwell, Carswell, and the Law Book Company would have crowned these. Longman Academic and Scientific Publishing stood ready to take in Chapman & Hall (whose scientific list was particularly appreciated) and Routledge/Croom Helm, while Methuen's general and children's publishing in the UK, Australia, and Canada would have fitted nicely into Penguin.

International Thomson had its sights trained on ABP's legal riches. Scientific and technical publishing found some favour in its eyes, and the academic business was tolerated. Alan Miles, managing director of ABP's UK publishing, was struck by the fact that Thomson made no attempt to disguise its distaste for general trade publishing, influenced perhaps by some earlier unsettling experiences.

All three bidders had in common the belief that, in the area of profitability, they could do better than the existing management. The Pearson view centred on underpricing of legal products and insufficient pressures on overheads. Simon & Schuster also focused on margin improvements, incorporating redundancies. International Thomson's attitude is epitomized in the criticism recalled by ABP main board director Richard Stileman, that ABP top management spent too much time trying to fix the bit that was broken rather than encourage the bit that worked.

Whatever the individual merits of these judgements, in its last five years of independent existence ABP's margins had 'done a Duke of York': group pre-tax profits as a percentage of sales rose from 10.9% in 1982 to a high of 12.1% in 1984, whence they had slipped to 10.2% in 1985 and 9.5% in 1986.

The mechanics of the bidding process required the presence of the protagonists in London, where their financial advisers were to be found, as well as the company they were seeking to acquire.

The International Thomson team, led by Michael Brown and including Bob Jaquino, set up camp in the Westbury Hotel; they were advised by Warburgs. Richard Snyder brought with him Jeremiah Kaplan; ironically, Bill Mackarell, main board director of ABP in charge of the Australian side, found himself staying in the same hotel as Jeremiah Kaplan. Simon & Schuster had Charterhouse as its merchant bank. Pearson, for its part, fielded a team of three, Lord Blakenham, James Joll, and Tim Rix. They had no hotel requirements. Their advisers were Lazards.

Kleinwort Benson acted for the board of Associated Book Publishers. The burden of negotiations naturally fell on chairman Peter Allsop and deputy chairman and group managing director Michael Turner. The Bahamian trust employed the services of County Bank.

All three bidders attended individual presentations organized by ABP in its New Fetter Lane offices. In addition, they had further meetings that varied in scope. Simon & Schuster concentrated its contacts at the chairman/managing director levels. The same was true of Pearson, though the point has to be made that most of the ABP executives were already well known to many in Pearson. Thomson, by contrast, conducted extensive interviews with all the ABP executive directors and a number of the other senior executives, a professional approach that impressed many. This had some bearing on the popularity stakes of the bidders within ABP's ranks.

Pearson emerged top, largely by reason of the fact that its interest in ABP encompassed virtually the whole group. Other factors were its past acquisition record in the UK and the simple matters of familiarity and nationality. However, Pearson's lead over International Thomson was to be measured by reference to nose rather than length. Thomson's assiduous courting over many years and the businesslike way in which it conducted its bid stood it in good stead.

Simon & Schuster came a bad third, on the score of the poor perceived 'fit' between the two businesses, and for more personal reasons. Richard Snyder cheerfully acknowledges the latter: 'We have always told people up front what they had to expect. Others hold back and then make the redundancies.'

As noted earlier, Simon & Schuster's initial bid for the Bahamian trust's stake had been £5 a share. It was an all-cash bid, the only type that the trustees had made clear they might entertain. The price of ABP shares immediately prior to Peter Allsop's announcement that an approach had been made to the trust was 273p. A 500p bid represented therefore an advance of 83%; at that level, the shares were selling at a multiple of 30 times 1986 earning per share of 16.7p and yielded 1.7%.

Under 'normal' circumstances, this would be a pretty full rating. Perhaps this was the reasoning behind the opinion delivered by the Kleinwort Benson representative to the board that £5 was probably about as good a price as they could reasonably expect. Alan Miles remembers demurring and suggesting – to everybody's amusement at the time – that £7 was a more likely figure.

Kleinwort Benson's limp view on price is consistent with James Joll's recollection that Kleinwort Benson failed to impose itself on the bidding process and that it was instead County Bank, acting for the trustees, that made the running. In this, County Bank benefited from ABP management's work in making certain that the company's assets and strengths were well understood.

The deadline for the final bids was set at 17 June. All interested parties met at the offices of Kleinwort Benson, where the sealed envelopes were opened one by one. The Thomson bid was for 730p cash. The Pearson bid was a mixture of cash and equity worth 745p a share, with a cash alternative of 715p. The Simon & Schuster bid was 650p cash per share. It was the last to be opened.

The Thomson bid was accepted by County Bank on behalf of the trustees, and recommended by ABP over the objections of Lazards. Despite the Pearson bid being the highest of the three, Thomson's was the highest in cash terms, and cash was what the major holder wanted. As Pearson chairman Michael Blakenham had occasion to point out a few days later, 'The full body of shareholders didn't have the opportunity to consider Pearson paper.'

At 730p, the company was being valued at a multiple of 1986 earnings per share of 44 times and on a yield of 1.1%. The total sum paid for ABP was £210m; this represented a multiple of 2.5 times 1986 turnover of £85.1m and 25.9 times 1986 pre-tax profits of £8.1m. Looked at another way, for every £1 of turnover, Thomson paid 247 pence; if the retail turnover of the barely profitable Hammicks (£12.2m) is excluded from the calculations, for every £1 of publishing turnover Thomson paid 288 pence. This made ABP one of the most 'expensive' publishing company purchases in post-war history.

Mark Knight, vice-president of the International Thomson Organization, justified the price paid with the comment, 'You only get one crack at this sort of opportunity. We have taken a long-term view.' James Joll concedes that 'some Pearson colleagues felt that we were quite bold to offer the price we did and that it was stretching it, but then Sweet & Maxwell was a great prize'. Richard Snyder's camp was 'astonished at the price it fetched'. Michael Turner for his part was quite taken aback by the inadequacy of Simon & Schuster's final offer.

In bid situations, the losers normally question the financial judgement of the winner. In this instance, one of the losers, Pearson, had actually bid more than the winner. But then, so it could: in contrast to its rivals, the dovetailing of activities – the one plus one equals three argument – applied across the whole range of ABP's publishing activities.

In losing to Thomson, Pearson fell foul, however, of a group whose commitment to professional publishing was a lot greater than its own, thereby raising the possibility that Thomson would be able to profit most from what were ABP's dominant business interests. As for the parts Thomson did not want, these could always be sold. Thomson also had a reputation for paying up for businesses that fitted with its strategy. The emphasis on long-term rewards was greatly helped, furthermore, by a share structure which featured the Thomson family as 73.5% controlling shareholders. Financial cares were not a family concern, while International Thomson itself generated cash.

In the case of Simon & Schuster, it was seeking to acquire through ABP businesses that were in the main going to have to stand on their own feet. Only in trade publishing in the UK would a significant element of dovetailing of interests have existed, with the attendant opportunities that that creates. In addition, Richard Snyder reported to Martin Davis, chairman and chief executive of Gulf & Western. While the creation of long-term values was a cardinal Gulf & Western objective, the demands of the US quarterly reporting treadmill on a high-profile corporation such as Gulf & Western and on a high-profile chairman such as Martin Davis should not be overlooked: Richard Snyder would not have been thanked for endowing the group with an acquisition that knocked holes in near-term profits.

The comparative disadvantages from which Simon & Schuster suffered were thrown into increasing relief as the bidding rose. By setting out to influence the price, ABP management was also in effect influencing the outcome. Whether or not this was an explicit objective is uncertain. The end result, however, was that the bidder who was a close second in the popularity stakes within ABP won the prize, and the bidder about whom there were the greatest reservations, and who aroused most apprehension, was sidelined.

We have come a long way from the formation of ABP in 1963. What comments can one make and what conclusions can one draw from this account?

Family control, especially second and later generation control, is an inherent source of instability as the family ownership becomes more diffused and the objectives of family shareholders and those of management diverge. The rock-solid Crosthwaite-Eyre holding that *The Bookseller* identified proved friable. Or as Michael Turner expresses it, 'If you have a ruling family interest, you can never sit comfortably in your seat.' To the question, does this also apply to ABP's own purchaser, the Thomson Corporation? the answer must be yes, but it would be advisable not to hold one's breath.

A financial performance that falls short of perfection invites change. It can be grounds for action by existing investors. The build-up of the Camellia stake in Routledge was stimulated in part by concerns of this nature. The parting of the ways of Christopher Helm and David Croom owed something to a profits hiccup. It can also arouse predatory thinking among outsiders: all three bidders for ABP were struck by the group's lacklustre profitability and were confident that, under their ownership, the situation could be transformed.

Threats or perceived threats to a dominant position in the share register may goad an investor or a group of investors into action. The Franklin family's collective holding in Routledge & Kegan Paul was being challenged by the apparently inexorable build-up of Camellia's stake.

The Bahamian trust holding had already suffered dilution as a result of ABP's acquisitions. The rights issue – even though the trust took up its entitlement – served notice on the trustees that dilutive pressures in the future might well come from ABP's future capital needs, as well as from any further acquisitions paid for through the issue of shares. Were the trust to try to protect its percentage stake, it would find itself having to add to its investment. Even assuming that funds were available, the matter of a prudent balance in the trust portfolio would certainly arise – i.e., the inadvisability of having too many eggs in one basket.

Controlling stakes in companies can command a premium in terms of price and also in terms of the punch they carry. As in the case of a leasehold in the property market, however, once they fall below a certain level, this premium can run off quite quickly.

The experience at ABP points up some of these privileges of scale. The desire of the Franklin family to sell overrode the wish of the rest of the board to maintain the company's independence. More tellingly the preference that the Bahamian trustees had for cash led to the acceptance of an all-cash offer. This was actually below Pearson's part cash, part equity offer. Furthermore, since the acceptance of the Thomson offer clearly crystallized a capital gain, little account was taken of the tax position of the other shareholders, who were merely given the option of deferring their liability to capital gains tax for up to five years by taking a loan note instead of cash.

Finally, I come to what is one of the great mysteries in this account of the takeover of Associated Book Publishers. When the Nassau lawyers demanded cash in June 1987, was it because they just wanted the security of being able to count it? Or did they anticipate the collapse of stock markets around the world on 17 October 1987? For timing, they come second only to Paul Hamlyn, who held out until July that year before selling Octopus to Reed – but then he went and took payment mostly in paper!

Chapter 6

OCTOPUS

THE OCTOPUS IS A CREATURE 'hideous in form and obnoxious in character'. Not so, said Paul Hamlyn: 'it's a loving, cuddly beast'. To investors, Octopus has been a marvel, wonderful to behold and hugely rewarding to own. To the publishing community, it was a great creation that ultimately came to grief in a conglomerate maze.

Octopus Books was formed early in 1971 as a subsidiary of News International. At the time, Paul Hamlyn was the company's joint managing director with Rupert Murdoch, a doubly bizarre linking of two supreme individualists. As Paul readily conceded, it was a daft arrangement and one that could not last. After a year, and having purchased the Octopus business, he left News International, though he stayed on for a further fourteen years as a non-executive director.

In September 1972 the first 33 Octopus titles were published to a challenging fanfare from Paul Hamlyn – 'to say that the amount of financial expertise (in UK publishing) is nil is no overstatement', being a fair sample. But even without the teasing remarks, the launch of Octopus was thoroughly newsworthy. Paul Hamlyn had already earned his entrepreneurial spurs with the creation in 1949 of Paul Hamlyn Books. This developed, from its start as a remainder merchant, into a leading mass-market and promotional publisher. In 1964 the company was bought by the International Publishing Corporation for £2,275,000, thereby making Paul Hamlyn a book publishing millionaire at the age of 39.

Following IPC's purchase, Paul Hamlyn occupied a commanding position in the industry; he became chairman of IPC's massive books division, heavily unionized, highly centralized, and based in Feltham.

In his years at IPC, which he did not enjoy, one of Paul Hamlyn's initiatives that deserves special mention was Music for Pleasure, the joint venture he established with EMI in August 1965. It was set up to market a budget range of long-playing records (one-third classical, two-thirds show music, jazz, pop, and the like); they were for the most part reissues, priced at 12/6 (62½p) and sold through a variety of retail outlets. It was a radical innovation for the time. By the end of three years, Music for Pleasure had sold twelve million records, making it the biggest selling long-playing record label in the country; turnover had reached £1.4m and pre-tax profits were at £237,000. He had opened up a new market.

Reed's purchase of IPC in 1970 – about which Paul Hamlyn had had quite a few misgivings – left him a free man.

When he set out on his second publishing venture, he came to it not only trailing clouds of glory, but with the practical advantages that his past achievements gave him in recruiting staff and establishing commercial ties with both suppliers and customers.

A fundamental tenet of Paul Hamlyn's was that the market is very much larger than most people think. To reach those consumers, he sought to supply attractively produced books that offered exceptional value. As to the subject matter, one can do a lot worse than turn to an interview he had with Judi Bevan in the *Sunday Telegraph* in February 1984: 'I only understand one kind of publishing and that is books of wide appeal that improve the quality of life from the stomach to the mind.'

One of the earliest measures taken by Paul Hamlyn in the establishment of Octopus was the formation in 1971 of Mandarin Publishers, later renamed Mandarin Offset. This was a Hong Kong based print broker, responsible for overseeing Octopus's book manufacturing needs. He appointed as managing director Geoffrey Cloke, who had previously worked for him at Feltham. The ability to offer 'exceptional value' to customers depended on Octopus gaining access to sound, reliable colour printing and despatch facilities at competitive prices. Little wonder that this should have been one of the top priorities at Octopus's birth.

The hiring of senior staff in London also had strong Hamlyn/IPC overtones. Sue Thompson, managing director, who joined in 1971, Ronald Setter, publishing director (1971), and Peggy Singleton, UK marketing director and general manager (1973), had all worked previously at Hamlyn. And there were other Hamlyn alumni. Altogether, quite a commentary on the personal loyalty on which Paul Hamlyn was able to draw.

Derek Freeman joined in January 1974 as Octopus production manager. While also from the IPC stable, he had not been in any way connected with books, an omission that Paul Hamlyn and Sue Thompson were happy to overlook in the face of the applicant's overweening self-confidence, as Derek recalls. The appointment in 1973 of Tim Clode involved a genuine outsider, coming as he did from the *Financial Times*, where he was advertising and marketing development manager. He joined as Octopus group marketing director and from an early stage was involved with Paul Hamlyn in overseas sales.

The IPC roll-call can be said to end with the arrival in 1977 of Gordon Cartwright as finance director; he had previously been finance director of IPC and briefly director of strategy at Reed. Recruitment of a man of his experience was impressive evidence of the seriousness of Octopus's ambitions.

The first commercial development that caught the attention of the book world was the exclusive distribution agreement reached in 1972 with W. H.

Smith. Under this agreement, Octopus took responsibility for editorial, production and pricing as well as general publicity and advertising. W. H. Smith for its part handled trade advertising, warehousing, accounting, sales representation, and the selling and distribution to wholesalers and retailers. Its purchases from Octopus were firm; the discount on the cover price – a mere £1 on the initial titles – was 60%. The formula in the UK was applied overseas with the appointment of sole distributorships in Australia (initially Angus & Robertson), Canada (Doubleday), and continental Europe (Doubleday's subsidiary Feffer & Simons). In the USA Crown Outlet was chosen, but in 1979 W. H. Smith Inc. took on the role. As Tim Clode points out, W. H. Smith, in conjunction with the overseas distributors, was effectively bankrolling Octopus, providing a start-up publisher with a remarkably risk-averse beginning.

With the distribution arrangements falling happily into place, the next challenge was the publishing programme. Initially, this was fed in part through the purchase of rights from other publishers, Weidenfeld & Nicolson, for instance, contributing to those first offerings with their attention-catching £1 prices, and increasingly from within Octopus as the publishing design teams got into their stride. Nonetheless, there was a growing hunger for more books.

In 1975 agreement was reached with the British Printing Corporation whereby Octopus gained access to BPC's extensive part-works material for republication in book form. This was a rich seam that Octopus mined successfully; particularly rewarding titles covered witchcraft and mythology and the two world wars.

The second and more important development, in terms of both scale and significance, came the following year with the joint venture with Heinemann code-named 'Operation Pickle'. September 1976 saw the publication of ten omnibus volumes of such twentieth-century authors as George Orwell, D. H. Lawrence, Somerset Maugham, Wilbur Smith, and John Steinbeck. They appeared under the joint Heinemann/Octopus imprint, and the division of labour was such that Heinemann dealt with the contracts and supplied the authors, while Octopus took responsibility for production and marketing, using its existing exclusive distributors.

Charles Pick and Tom Rosenthal, the two managing directors of the literary imprints William Heinemann and Secker & Warburg respectively, conceived the idea in summer 1975 of squeezing additional profit out of their backlists by combining several titles of a given author in an omnibus edition that offered outstanding value for money. But try as they might, they could not find a way of producing the volumes for less than £5, implying a retail price of some £12.50. At this point, Charles Pick decided to call on Paul Hamlyn, whose publishing was synonymous with value. The retail price point worked out by Paul, based on print runs of 50,000, was £3.95, at which level they stood out as hardbacks at paperback prices. Little surprise that sales exceeded expectations by a wide margin, with print runs of 100,000 becoming 'normal'.

In 1979, the series was introduced into the USA. By 1983 the omnibus titles

93

covered fifty authors and cumulative worldwide volume sales exceeded four million copies. For Octopus, the Pickle experience had not only generated a valuable stream of profits but had also given the company status within trade publishing.

Another significant publishing innovation involved the launch of ranges of own-label books for leading store and supermarket chains in the UK, the USA, and Australia. The titles themselves were the creation of Octopus's design department, working in collaboration with the client. For many of them, book-selling was a novelty, so the creative and hand-holding role played by Octopus was hugely important. Programmes were developed for groups such as Sains-bury, K Mart, Waldenbooks, G. J. Coles, and Myer. Dwarfing these, however, was the association formed with Marks & Spencer, the commercial importance of which to Octopus is difficult to exaggerate.

David Frost (with whom Octopus had close links through the jointly-owned Sundial Publications set up in 1973) introduced Octopus to Marks & Spencer during the course of 1975. Tim Clode recalls that Octopus's initial pitch con-cerned records (an echo of Paul Hamlyn's initiative with Music for Pleasure in his IPC days). This idea was turned down but, in a throw-away line, Marks & Spencer's chairman Marcus Sieff said, 'Why not do some books for us?' In 1975, Octopus duly launched, through Sundial Publications, a test range of finely produced own-label books under the St Michael imprint. Priced at £1.99, they were referred to by one wag as coffee-table volumes for the council estates.

This was the start of what was to become a highly successful commercial partnership. It was underpinned by the establishment within Octopus of a design team dedicated to the Marks & Spencer account; in its heyday the team originated up to fifty books a year for the St Michael imprint. Furthermore, many of these titles proved suitable for sale in overseas markets. The *Microwave Cookery Book*, which sold close to one million copies in the UK at £1.99 for M&S, also achieved sales (after some re-editing) of a further 100,000 in Australia at a retail price of A$25 under the Octopus imprint.

In 1980 Octopus set the seal on its individualistic approach to publishing with the creation of Tigerprint, a company formed to specialize in the design and sale of stationery products, notably an own-label range for Marks & Spencer; this was seen as a natural extension of its gift ranges. Octopus had identified a gap in the market between expensive imported stationery and the domestic Basildon Bond products. The creative side, under Loretta Dives, was confident of its ability to come up with well-designed stationery at high-street prices and at the same time secure for Octopus an acceptable profit margin. From stationery, Tigerprint expanded into giftwraps, cards, diaries, toiletries, and even food products. By 1984 turnover had grown to £6.4m; on pre-tax profits of £428,000, margins were 6.7%.

At this point, it is worth dwelling on the distinctiveness of Octopus within book publishing. As Derek Freeman puts it: 'The success of early Octopus was that it was a marketing machine. It was never a traditional publisher. It did things differently. It did things quickly.' It was also disciplined: an essential feature of the Marks & Spencer account, for which Tim Clode retained responsibility notwithstanding his appointment as group managing director in 1977, was the closeness of the links built up and maintained at all working levels with the opposite numbers at Marks & Spencer.

The ebullient, entrepreneurial Octopus spirit is as evident in the response to challenges as in the seizing of opportunities. In 1981, W. H. Smith withdrew from the USA. This meant the loss of Octopus's dedicated distributor in a significant market where sales were running at over £4m. A replacement had to be found. The decision taken was to go direct to the retail chains, B. Dalton, Waldenbooks, and K Mart. Remarkably, Octopus was successful in introducing the three chains to the discipline of firm sales by using the attractive Heinemann/Octopus omnibus titles as a lever. Given the American retail community's attachment to sale or return, this was a considerable achievement.

The development of imprimatur publishing in the early 1980s came in response to a switch in consumer tastes, from the pictorial leisure-oriented book to titles with greater information content. The *Laura Ashley Book of Home Decorating*, published in 1982, was an early example. Such titles appeared under the Octopus imprint, but carried the authority in the title (and in the text, which had to be approved) of the partner involved. *Vogue Complete Beauty*, which sold nearly one million copies, was also remarkable for the fact that *Vogue* had never before entered into a co-operative agreement of this kind.

Bounty Books, the budget-label imprint launched in 1981, is an example of Octopus identifying and exploiting a silver lining in an economic cloud. The recession had made consumers increasingly cost-conscious and responsive to bargains. The recession had also hit publishers hard, and this presented Octopus with the opportunity of buying from them, on attractive terms, the rights for publication under the Bounty imprint of selected titles and series; at the same time, it provided an additional outlet for many of Octopus's own titles. Octopus took the publishing risk and Websters, through its subsidiary, Bookwise, had the exclusive UK distributorship, buying firm from Octopus.

Bounty Books represented for Paul Hamlyn a return to the promotional book market of his Paul Hamlyn Books days. It also fitted in with his operating practices as established at Octopus – no stocks, no warehouses, high volumes, alluring prices, and the use of somebody else's sales force. Growth was rapid: in 1981 turnover came to £1m, in 1982 to £2.2m, and in 1983 to £4m – the year that saw the end of Octopus's existence as a private limited company and its transformation into a publicly quoted company.

OBTAINING A QUOTATION

Paul Hamlyn's familiarity with the worlds of business and finance was crucially important to Octopus's development. For him business held no terrors. Quite the reverse: throughout his life he found it endlessly stimulating, and from the ranks of businessmen came many of his oldest friends.

The close friendship with Robert Gavron goes back to 1963, one year before Bob Gavron founded St Ives, the highly successful printing group which went public in 1985 and of which he remained chairman until 1993. The friendship with Rupert Murdoch also dates from the early 1960s. When News International began fighting Robert Maxwell for control of *News of the World*, Paul lent Rupert his flat on the Chelsea Embankment while he himself was away in Australia. One national newspaper that had blown Murdoch's cover was almost persuaded to publish Paul's impish explanation that Rupert was there to look after two precious Siamese cats. The story was spiked when the sub-editor, on checking with an Australian colleague of Murdoch's, was told 'Rupert hates f*****g cats'.

The links that go back further than most are those with Claus Moser – he claims to have a clear recollection of Paul aged three – who became vice-chairman of the merchant bank N. M. Rothschild. Philip Jarvis is a chum from the IPC days, when he was chief executive of the non-professional side of the book division.

No account of postwar publishing can fail to mention that rising star, Robert Maxwell. The only recorded business dealing Paul Hamlyn had with Robert Maxwell was in December 1965 when, as head of the book division within IPC, he sold Maxwell for £1m the Newnes subscription book side, whose main asset was *Chambers Enclyclopedia*. As Paul Hamlyn explained at the time, encyclopedias gave IPC a bad name due to aggressive door to door sales practices. Furthermore, sales and profits had been on a declining trend for the previous four years, leading to a loss in 1964/65.

Some will remember the prominent role played by Maxwell's encyclopedia interests in the damning investigation into the affairs of Pergamon Press, published in 1971 by the Department of Trade and Industry – a report, incidentally, that certain professional advisers, hungry for fee income, subsequently deliberately chose to ignore, to their eternal discredit.

One development that caught the attention of the examiners, R. O. C. Stable and Sir Ronald Leach, was the 'turnround' in the fortunes of the Newnes subscription book division. In the seven months immediately following its purchase by Pergamon, from being loss-making the previous year, it had apparently achieved profits of £205,000, while in the six months to 31 December 1966 it apparently made profits of £246,000. These results were supported by a remarkable plunge in the 'cost of sales': for the seven-month period this was given as a mere 13% of sales, while for the second half it was miraculously trimmed to 0.3% of sales. One million pounds was a good price for the vendor and IPC was well served.

Throughout his life, Paul Hamlyn was a spirited investor. While he had access to a raft of investment advisers and counsellors over the years, a more or less continuous presence from a very early date was Toby de Lotbiniere.

This connection was firmly grounded in pure fluke. One morning in 1968, Toby de Lotbiniere was at his desk in the stockbroking firm Grenfell when the telephone rang. 'This is Paul Hamlyn. How long would it take you to execute an order?' 'About five minutes.' 'Well then, buy me x number of shares in company y at such and such a price. I've been talking to NatWest and every 20 minutes I get a call to say that they haven't dealt. They tell me that Grenfell is one of the brokers they use.'

The transaction was executed in four minutes, and reported. The satisfied client then indicated that he was likely to make further use of this swift service. A little later, he expressed a readiness to listen to any bright investment suggestions. The first proved to be a recommendation to buy a few Martins Bank shares on takeover talk. Barclays' bid for Martins several weeks later cemented the link. This typically involved at a minimum one daily telephone call, wherever Paul Hamlyn might be, and the transmission of a stream of information on market trends, company developments – by no means confined to the publishing sector – and the general flow of Stock Exchange stories.

As other suppliers found, the connection was not free from turbulence: there were at least two occasions when Toby de Lotbiniere was sacked (only to be reinstated some months later); but the gradual build up of trust, based on successfully meeting Paul Hamlyn's demanding requirements, generated business and led to friendship. It also made for excitement.

Paul Hamlyn's personal attitude to wealth was explored in an interview he gave to the *Guardian* in September 1972. By that stage – with many possessions to his name – he had as it were graduated to the 'tenth two-piece suit' level, whose utility is clearly less than that of the ninth is less than the eighth and so on downwards to the essential first suit. As he explained, what his money could then do for him was provide an index to his having been successful. A stock market quotation had the incidental merit of giving him a continuously updated measure of achievement. But this was not so compelling a consideration as to make him unblinkingly committed to flotation.

He had indeed scotched such a move in 1982. Factors influencing the decision will have been a profits record that took in only the first year of recovery following the recession and a stock market that was itself still at an early stage in its recovery. Both considerations would have borne down on the valuation that Octopus might have achieved. In addition, Paul Hamlyn had a natural reluctance to go public as a small company, a disability that promised to be mitigated, if not eliminated, by postponement.

The question has still to be asked: Why seek a quotation in the first place? After all, neither the company nor the controlling shareholder had any need to raise money. Perhaps the best answer is, to reward the executives and staff in the business.

Paul Hamlyn held out to those he recruited the possibility of making money, and this was a prospect that his past record rendered distinctly credible. From the start he had also made clear that Octopus was not to be a family company.

Table 20: *Octopus factsheet at flotation*

	1972	1978	1979	1980	1981	1982
Profit and loss						
Turnover (£m)	1.85	18.26	21.78	22.37	24.48	30.75
Operating profits (£m)	0.27	2.67	1.45	1.50	3.34	4.04
Operating margins (%)	14.6	14.6	6.7	6.7	13.6	13.1

Notes:

Balance sheet (31 December 1982)   *Operating statistics*
Debt: Nil   Turnover 60% UK, 40% overseas
Cash: £8.15m   Backlist: 60% of sales
                                                            Staff: 250

He encouraged staff to buy shares, and in two instances enabled them to do so by loaning them the funds. In short, he derived considerable satisfaction from having the employees participate in the company's performance. It also happened to make good business sense. This may also go some way towards explaining the tensions that arose over resignations where the individuals concerned were viewed as acting in a disloyal and ungrateful fashion.

May 1983 was indeed a good time to choose for a stock-market flotation. The British economy was recovering strongly from the 1979-80 recession, helped by a currency that had already fallen some 35% from its 1980 highs against the dollar. Investors were feeling their oats in happy anticipation of a period of rising profitability. Corporate activity had started to pick up, but the flow of new issues was still relatively subdued. A company coming to the market with a good story was consequently almost assured a good reception. And Octopus had a good story, as table 20 demonstrates.

The salient characteristics of the company were those of a well-balanced business; the one contentious statistic, book and stationery sales to Marks & Spencer accounting in 1982 for nearly one quarter of group turnover. The optimists saw this percentage as a great accolade, the pessimists as worrying dependence. In the event, the optimists were in the ascendant. They were also stimulated by encouraging comments in the prospectus on current trading.

Pricing is a matter that occupies the forefront of the minds of all concerned the moment that an issue gets under way. In view of Octopus's unique position in publishing, which ruled out any helpful comparisons with companies already quoted, the decision was taken by the financial advisers (N. M. Rothschild as issuing house and Rowe & Pitman as brokers) to offer the shares for sale on the basis of a tender. A conservative minimum tender price was set (at 275p), but it was open to would-be investors to pay more.

In total, 3.1 million shares were offered on 18 April 1983 to the public (of which 2.4 million were supplied by Paul Hamlyn and his family and the balance by the other directors and staff who were typically taking profits on a small percentage of their shareholdings). The issue generated considerable interest: it was over-subscribed five times and the actual striking price that investors paid was 350p, 27% above the minimum level. Furthermore, at that price investors received a mere quarter of the number of shares they stood ready to purchase. The size of the premium – reflecting what the *Financial Times* described as the wide-eyed enthusiasm of the new issue market that was then prevailing – fully justified the tender offer. The scale of investor interest provided management with an exhilarating debut to Octopus's new existence as a public limited company.

Following the issue, Paul Hamlyn retained 67% of the capital of the company. At the price of 350p a share, Octopus was valued in the market at £55m. This represented a multiple of 1.8 times the 1982 turnover of £31m and 11.5 times pre-tax profits of £4.8m.

Paul Hamlyn described the prospectus as the most difficult and costly book they had ever produced. It was also the most rewarding.

Whenever a company such as Octopus obtains a quotation for its shares, top management must learn a set of skills for which their previous status will not have equipped them, namely, establishing and nurturing links with the City, whether it be security analysts, stockbrokers' sales teams, institutional investors, or merchant banking advisers.

Many company chairmen and chief executives have difficulty adjusting to this novel role. Paul Hamlyn took to it effortlessly. He knew exactly how a big investor feels – he was already one of them. He also appreciated the merits of keeping the argument simple: not for him the over-elaborate explanation that revels in product complexities.

Furthermore, he was an enthusiast, who cared more to look at the opportunities to be seized than to agonize over the state of the economy and the fickleness of governments. In this he was helped by his delight in playing the role of the 'enfant terrible'. No, he did not believe in the Net Book Agreement; Frankfurt – or at least 80% of it – was a waste of time; he saw no merit in joining the Publishers Association. He also understood that optimism, a sense of fun, and, when judged appropriate, the ability to charm the birds out of the trees were not alone sufficient to satisfy investors: he had to deliver.

After the excitement of the quotation, preparations for which had inevitably taken up a lot of senior executive time, there was a return to the familiar emphasis on publishing and marketing.

One important new venture announced in October 1983 was the setting up of a company to be known as Conran Octopus, 50% owned by Habitat Mothercare – of which Terence Conran was chairman – and 50% by Octopus, but with provision for the later issue of shares to executives. Its publishing emphasis was to be lifestyle books, distributed through Octopus's existing sales network. It made a promising start, achieving in 1985 – little more than two years after its launch – turnover of £3.4m and pre-tax profits of £240,000.

In November 1983, Octopus made its first acquisition: Brimax Books, publisher of colour illustrated books for children, chiefly in the three- to five-year age range. Turnover was running at £2.3m, with pre-tax profits of £775,000; the balance sheet was debt-free and held cash at the latest year-end of over £2m. The company employed 21 people in its Newmarket offices and warehouse. The consideration was £4m, entirely cash, £1m of which was subject to achieving certain operating targets.

The terms of purchase were extremely favourable from Octopus's point of view; consolidation of Brimax's results promised to enhance Octopus's earnings per share from the very start. Paradoxically, the newly quoted acquisitor did not take advantage of its shares to make the purchase, since the vendors insisted on cash. Operationally, while Brimax's children's titles were said to complement Octopus's existing lists – 10% of Octopus's 1982 publishing programme had been accounted for by children's books – no attempt was made to 'consolidate' children's publishing following the purchase. Brimax was a successful business which continued to be managed quite separately by George Rogers, his wife, and his daughter. Octopus viewed the resulting 'untidiness' of having two centres of children's publishing as totally inconsequential.

The next event in Octopus's life as a public limited company relied heavily on its possession of a quotation for its shares. On 7 March 1984, Octopus announced that it had acquired options on 13.45% of the shares of W. N. Sharpe, the Bradford-based greetings card group, and that it wished to discuss a bid worth 390p a share; this would have valued the whole company at £28m.

On this occasion Octopus used Morgan Grenfell, rather than N. M. Rothschild, as its merchant banker; Roger Seelig, who remained a close friend and adviser of Paul Hamlyn, was the corporate executive involved and the man said to have originated the idea. Even after Octopus was able to claim to have received the support of investors holding a further 16.53% of the capital (bringing the total to just under 30%), W. N. Sharpe felt little immediate pressure to enter into discussions with Octopus, its share price having risen to 495p, well above Octopus's sighting shot. Ten days later, all was over; the W. N. Sharpe board recommended an offer of 500p a share by Hallmark of Kansas City, which valued the company at £36m.

Octopus's unsuccessful foray into the greetings card market showed it to be happy developing its interests outside books. It also demonstrated the company's readiness to use its highly valued shares in acquisitions. The share price had risen to 605p from 350p ten months earlier, and the rating, as measured by the price:earnings multiple, had achieved levels that stockbrokers were pushed into justifying through reference to Octopus as a 'concept stock'.

Octopus emerged with a useful profit on its W. N. Sharpe shares of £1m. It was also that much the wiser after its direct experience of some of the pitfalls to which hostile bidders are vulnerable. Perhaps this was what Paul Hamlyn had in mind when he said that he had learned more in two weeks than he might have gleaned from two years at the Harvard Business School.

The bid that marked Octopus's first successful use of its quotation came eight months later when it announced on 14 November 1984 an agreed offer for the Websters Group, parent company of Bookwise and exclusive distributor of Bounty Books. The terms of the basic offer were one Octopus share plus 545p in cash for every ten Websters shares, valuing the bid on the announcement at £21m.

For Octopus, Websters was at that time a big buy: 1983 turnover of £52m (compared to Octopus's £37m); employees 1168 (261); tangible assets £6.4m (£1.1m). It was at the profit level that the disparity reversed, with Websters' 1983 pre-tax profits of £2m trailing far behind Octopus's pre-tax profits that year of £6.3m. At the halfway stage the inequality had been further magnified, with Websters reporting a loss to 30 June 1984 of £181,000 against Octopus's first half pre-tax profits of £3.42m.

The acquisition of Websters represented a significant diversification into the retail market, as well as the decisive abandonment of Octopus's long-cherished policy of subcontracting wherever feasible. Websters' core business was book distribution, with turnover of £37m. Half of this – Bookwise – was accounted for by the merchandising of paperbacks for sale in non-traditional outlets. The other half of book-distribution revenues was divided fairly equally between: a paperback wholesaling operation serving traditional retail book outlets; a hardback distribution service aimed at its paperback merchandizing customers; the Bounty Books business; and Books for Students, a unit supplying paperbacks to schools and public libraries.

In addition, Websters was developing a book retailing presence of its own through Websters Bookshops, which had eight outlets in south-east England. Websters' activities were rounded off by a heavily loss-making audiovisual training venture, an increasingly problematical merchandizer of personal computers and computer games, and minor weekly newspaper and printing interests.

Backing up all these varying activities was a significant infrastructure: seven warehouses and depots spread across the country; sales forces for all its divisions, the most numerous being the 140-strong army of merchandizers/sales representatives at Bookwise; and a central head office complex at Godalming.

The main attraction of Websters lay in its core business; its customer list included Woolworths, Boots, Asda, Safeway, House of Fraser, as well as Martins and the other confectionery, tobacco, and news chains. As Paul Hamlyn explained at the time, 'we can feed Octopus books into an efficient marketing machine'. The prospect of obtaining 100% of the profits from Bounty Books, where Websters was demonstrating its marketing effectiveness, also had its appeal.

On analysis, however, so long as the exclusive distribution arrangement with W. H. Smith lasted, encompassing all titles under the Octopus imprint, the scope for feeding titles into Websters' distribution machine was relatively limited. The thought also existed, however, that Bookwise would become a vehicle for the sale of stationery and other products of Octopus's subsidiary Tigerprint that fell outside the own-label ranges.

Financially, Octopus management had from the very start the intention of disposing of non-core parts of the Websters portfolio. There was also a 'turn-round' appeal to Websters that had been absent from the Brimax acquisition: the 1983 results had been struck after losses of £655,000 on the audiovisual side and these had persisted into the first half of 1984. Loss elimination by a new owner was a real option.

One other point: Websters' indifferent first-half results had raised fears in some quarters about the long-term future of the company. With its subsidiary Bookwise accounting for 25% of the paperback market, the larger trade publishers were bound to treat any fears of this kind seriously; this would have been the case at William Collins, whose recent acquisition of Granada had given it a much enhanced paperback presence. Takeover talk and rumours no doubt reached Octopus, providing it with a further stimulus to forestall any real or imagined predatorial initiatives and thereby to protect the valuable Bounty operation. The final word may go to Richard Charkin, whose retrospective judgement is that the acquisition of Websters had the merit of making Octopus itself that much larger (and potentially attractive to an eventual predator), i.e. adding bulk to the business.

The stock market reacted positively to the Websters acquisition, Octopus shares rising 25p to 800p on announcement of the bid and further to 855p in mid-December. The Octopus 1984 results, released the following April, did nothing to dampen enthusiasm in the light of a 44% advance in pre-tax profits. The company also announced the sale to W. H. Smith for £9m of two divisions, Websters Bookshops and Books for Students, thereby cutting its Websters acquisition cost to £12m. By this time, the shares had risen to 1025p and the market valuation, taking the capital as enlarged by the Websters purchase, came to £176m.

THE HEINEMANN PURCHASE

Those impatient spirits looking for further transformation in Octopus's business and financial position had a mere three-and-a-half months to wait. On 29 July 1985 it was announced that Octopus was to merge with Heinemann, the publishing subsidiary of BTR, the major conglomerate (a term of admiration rather than derision in those days).

Heinemann had developed a habit of being under conglomerate ownership. In 1961 it became a wholly-owned subsidiary of the conglomerate Thomas Tilling, and in June 1983, when BTR bought Tilling (a case of one piranha gobbling up another), Heinemann found itself occupying a fairly minor position in a much larger portfolio dominated by engineering, transportation, and construction companies. In short, it did not fit, but at the same time

Owen Green, chairman of BTR, felt no urgency to achieve an immediate disposal.

Heinemann was known to Paul Hamlyn from his earliest publishing days, when he would travel down to Kingswood to buy their remainders. In the life of Octopus, a strong trading partnership had been in place since 1976 through the immensely successful 'Operation Pickle'. A further link was forged when Charles Pick, having retired as managing director of the Heinemann Group in February 1985, accepted Paul Hamlyn's invitation to become associated with Octopus. He was duly appointed a consultant – not a 'medical consultant', to the chagrin of an employee suffering from severe chest pains, who applied for immediate relief on Charles's first day at work.

The spark that may have started the fire – or perhaps it was the nudge that set the toboggan down the Cresta Run – was the comment of a BTR executive to Charles Pick to the effect that 'there's no future for Heinemann in this set-up'. Charles remembered duly relaying this to Paul Hamlyn who was, at the time, staying in his house in the south of France. He experienced one of those protracted silences that those unfamiliar with Paul's telephone manner found so unnerving. Some weeks later, the silence was broken when Charles answered the telephone to hear an exultant Paul – 'I've just shaken hands with Owen Green on a merger. I'm in control.'

The term merger as signifying the union of two companies having broad statistical equality was appropriate: in the calendar year 1984, Octopus's sales were £53m (Heinemann £41m); pre-tax profits £9.1m (£6.9m); pre-tax margins 17.1% (16.8%); backlist sales 60% (65%); and overseas sales 47% (40%). One sharp contrast, however, lay in the number of titles in print, which came to 600 for Octopus and 8000 for Heinemann.

Under the terms of the merger, Octopus was issuing to BTR 18.75 million new shares, giving BTR a 35% stake in the enlarged group. BTR was thereby acquiring an important interest in a business that, from Heinemann's perspective, had more than doubled in size. It was doing so at a time when the benefits of scale in publishing were being proclaimed with increasing stridency. At the same time BTR was subcontracting a slice of its portfolio, which fitted awkwardly, to a publisher with an outstanding record. It was converting an illiquid asset into a liquid asset. The sacrifice was its loss of control.

For Octopus, the considerations surrounding the merger were more far reaching: no question of disengagement, very much the reverse.

By acquiring Heinemann, the innovative, iconoclastic fourteen-year-old Octopus was transforming itself overnight into:
– a long-established UK educational publisher through Heinemann Educational Books and Ginn & Company, which gave it a market share at the primary level of some 20% and at the secondary level of 10%;
– an international publisher with a network of eight subsidiaries, operating almost entirely in the educational market, spread across Asia, Africa, and Australasia;

– one of the leading UK trade publishers, through William Heinemann Ltd, which traces its origins to 1890, and Secker & Warburg Ltd, plus a one-third interest in Pan;
– a company with a dominant position in the UK children's book market through Heinemann Young Books, Kaye & Ward, and World's Work, which, when combined with Brimax and Octopus's own children's titles, gave it a UK market share approaching 20%; and
– the possessor of all the warehousing and other infrastructure that go with such interests.

At Octopus board level, the arguments were a mixture of the defensive and the expansionary:
– some directors felt that the market for Octopus-type books was showing signs of being finite and that, taking into account the growing activities of competitors – for instance in own-label publishing that originally Octopus, having effectively invented the formula, had had to itself – it would be extremely unwise to assume a continuation of past rates of growth;
– the opportunity of securing in one move a commanding position in educational publishing had distinct appeal; to Paul Hamlyn, this was the most financially interesting part of Heinemann;
– in the way that Octopus's standing had benefited from the Heinemann/ Octopus omnibus programme, actual ownership of two prominent literary publishers was seen as carrying the process very much further;
– in Heinemann, Octopus was acquiring a highly profitable business, one that could trade blows with them on equal terms in any margin contest. This meant that any immediate pressures on Octopus's management in the aftermath of a merger stood to be contained;
– the two groups' publishing activities were genuinely complementary, hence no calls for rationalization; Octopus was diversifying, not taking out a competitor. The one area where they shared common ground was in children's books, where they were supplying a nicely growing market; and
– the advantages of scale were increasingly recognized as a springboard for establishing a publishing presence in the United States.

There were also advantages that were more personal to Paul Hamlyn. One of the most remarkable aspects of the merger was the concession made by Owen Green to Paul Hamlyn whereby, so long as Paul and his family and other interests owned at least 20% of Octopus's voting capital, Paul would be entitled to direct the voting of such of BTR's holding as afforded him at least 50.1% of the votes of Octopus. Hence Paul's triumphant call to Charles Pick.

The merger terms took these factors into account. The issue of 18.75 million shares to BTR valued Heinemann at £100m. This was 2.4 times turnover and 14.5 times pre-tax profits. While this price included an element to compensate BTR for voluntarily ceding its voting tights, it was by no means dilutive, given Octopus's then current rating of 3.5 times turnover and 20.2 times historic pre-tax profits. The price, however, was higher than in the case of some other publishing transactions, and the view that Octopus had paid a pretty full price for Heinemann gained currency.

Nor was this view confined to outside observers. Tim Clode, Octopus's managing director, recalls having felt the price to have been a bit steep. More fundamentally, he was critical of a move that converted Octopus into a mainstream publisher and was so much at odds with the entrepreneurial trading spirit of the group. 'We were much more like Saatchi & Saatchi than Heinemann. We were not traditional publishers.' In this he can be seen as the defender of Octopus in the purity of its early days, and this led him to conclude, 'I just had a gut feeling that it wasn't right for our type of culture.' Furthermore, he was not convinced that Octopus's size ahead of the Heinemann purchase – a market capitalization of £185m – was the bar to expansion in the USA that others were suggesting. He had, after all, been advocating a merger with Octopus's first US distributor Crown Outlet, whose sales were running at $200m.

Sharp-eyed readers of the offer document for Heineinann will have seen the outcome of this dissenting opinion in Appendix VII Note 8 (a) (i), whereby Tim Clode's seven-year service contract, dated 30 March 1983, was being amended to permit more rapid termination by either side.

On the announcement of the merger, Octopus's shares rose 50p to 585p (1170p if one takes account of the one-for-one split of June 1985), valuing the new group at £311m. This was more than five-and-a-half times the £55m at which the stock market had capitalized Octopus on its flotation little more than two years previously.

This positive response perhaps owed something to vague thoughts of benefits that might flow from Octopus' entrepreneurial management skills being put to work on the 'staid' Heinemann businesses. A stronger but even less reasoned explanation was that the market was simply responding to the way the pot was being kept boiling. To change the metaphor, deals were being piled on to yet more deals in Pelion fashion. The bulking process associated with the Websters purchase was being pursued with even greater vigour than before.

One important consequence of the Octopus–Heinemann merger to which sufficient attention has not yet been drawn is the alliance formed between Paul Hamlyn and Owen Green. An unlikely alliance, many might have thought: on one side, an ebullient, irreverent Paul Hamlyn, full of panache and prepared to spend money on the good things in life, and on the other, a shy, frugal figure, who half believed that working for BTR was reward enough for its employees and in whose own life balance sheets and management accounts seemed to occupy pride of place. And yet the two men got on well. 'He used to give me hell,' Paul Hamlyn recalled, 'but I'm still very pally with him. He was just so unbelievably professional.'

The Octopus board became Cadbury-compliant in respect of non-executive directors well before the publication of the Cadbury report on corporate governance. After the Heinemann purchase, Octopus had four non-executives: Owen Green and Michael Smith, representing the BTR interests, joined Robert Gavron, Octopus director since 1975, and Claus Moser. Iain Burns, who had succeeded Gordon Cartwright as finance director in the summer of 1985, remembers the board meetings, chaired by Paul Hamlyn, as 'essentially an Owen Green show. Paul didn't think board meetings all that important; Owen Green did. At every one, in good non-executive fashion, he took us to pieces.' And ever present was Bob Gavron, 'who always asked the right questions'.

On the executive side, there had been some changes as well. In the wake of the Websters acquisition, Stuart Wallis had been recruited to be in overall charge of the non-publishing interests (Websters and Tigerprint), becoming a board member in June 1985. Nicolas Thompson, who had taken over from Charles Pick as managing director of Heinemann, joined the board following the merger.

It was not long, however, before the board, under the spur of the four non-executive directors, came to the conclusion that a group chief executive was needed to push the strategy along. Tim Clode, the managing director, was not realistically a candidate being out of sympathy with the strategy (he was to resign in June 1986). An outside appointment was called for.

The man chosen was Ian Irvine. He was between jobs following the acquisition by United Newspapers of Fleet Holdings. As managing director of Fleet, Ian Irvine had presided over a powerful turnround in trading; he had also been heavily involved in breaking the Reuters trust which led to the distribution to newspaper groups of Reuters shares, to their great financial advantage.

His wish to move away from newspapers made him welcome the approach from Octopus. It would take him into another aspect of publishing, and one of which he had had no previous experience, but in terms of personalities, Octopus was not a totally unknown quantity to him: in the accounting firm of Touche Ross (where he later became one of the senior partners), he had been assistant to the partner who acted for Bob Gavron in 1964 when St Ives was set up. And before that, he had been a student of Claus Moser at the London School of Economics.

Ian Irvine's appointment as group chief executive of Octopus was announced in mid-December. He was given 'overall responsibility for the development of the group', taking up his position on 1 January 1986.

His assessment of Octopus was that 'they were a public company without a real structure'. And while the system of financial reporting was well developed – how could it be otherwise with BTR having given it its blessing – there was a lack of corporate direction.

Over the ensuing eighteen months, this complex portfolio of publishing interests was given a clear divisional structure, comprising eight main profit centres plus the group services division. A group executive committee was established, chaired by the chief executive, whose membership included the divisional heads, the finance director, and the head of publishing development, a post created when Paul Richardson was recruited in January 1986.

From an early date, the divisions were required to prepare three-year strategic plans, and a review was swiftly made of the real estate holdings and fixed assets of the group. The purchase in March 1986 from Reed International of the Hamlyn Publishing Group – Paul Hamlyn's original company – included a warehouse and distribution centre at Rushden, Northamptonshire. This presented the opportunity to close Heinemann's distribution centre and warehouse at Kingswood, Surrey, and transfer the activity to Rushden; realization of the Surrey property for over £6m neatly covered the costs of closure in Surrey plus expansion in Northamptonshire. The longer-term plan was that it should become an integrated book distribution centre for the whole of the group.

Concentration of office accommodation was a medium-term objective. It did not escape people's notice when Paul Hamlyn and Terence Conran joined forces in July 1985 to buy the well-known South Kensington Michelin building, owning 66.5% and 33.5% respectively. In the event, it was not until the spring of 1987 that Octopus Publishing committed itself to 52,000 sq ft of office space in Michelin House; the actual move took place in April 1988 and gathered under one roof trade imprints previously occupying space in seven different London locations ranging from Twickenham to Poland Street.

The task of pushing the strategy along resulted in several in-fill acquisitions. As mentioned, March 1986 had seen the acquisition of Hamlyn Publishing; payment was a nominal £1000 plus the assumption of about £10m of debt. Hamlyn Publishing, which had a turnover of about £16m, had become an isolated and unprofitable unit in Reed International.

A year later, in May 1987, Octopus added Mitchell Beazley to its portfolio of lifestyle publishing interests; this included 75% of Millers Publications. Mitchell Beazley had moved into the black in 1985-6, reporting pre-tax profits of £321,000 on turnover of £7m. The consideration was £4.85m, mainly taken in shares.

The wider objective of securing a publishing base in north America continued on the agenda and led to a number of conversations with potential candidates; none of the talks, however, got further than the exploratory stage. In Paul Richardson's view, the urgency to succeed in this quest was somewhat blunted by the continuing success of the three main streams of publishing activity: Octopus, selling as before considerable quantities of books into the US promotional market; the trade houses, William Heinemann and Secker & Warburg, selling and buying rights as actively as ever; and the educational publishers Heinemann Educational Books and Ginn, performing strongly without any US presence.

This was duly reflected in group results. After a restrained performance in the first half of 1986, the figures for the full year were reported at the top end of brokers' estimates, with pre-tax profits (excluding an exceptional gain on a trade investment and the benefits of a pension holiday) of £23.8m, a 17% advance on a year earlier. In his chairman's statement of 21 April 1987, Paul Hamlyn was pleased to tell shareholders that he found the prospects encouraging. This might be interpreted as pointing them in the direction of an increase in 1987 profits of some 15% to 20%. It did not – nor could it – prepare them for the sale of the business to Reed International three months later.

In circuses the high-wire artist starts with the splits fifty feet above ground. Then he goes one better with a somersault. And finally comes the climax – a double somersault. These feats are heralded with drum rolls of ever-increasing volume, followed by absolute silence. The analogy with Octopus is close: first the flotation, next Heinemann, and finally Reed. The main difference lies in the sound effects: silence precedes the achievements (except in a flotation, when it is broken by the rustle of underwriters earning their fees) and the drum-roll comes after. The echoes of the Reed drum-roll reverberate still.

On 2 July 1987 Reed International announced an agreed takeover of Octopus on the basis of nine Reed shares for every ten Octopus shares. At Reed's closing price on the day, this valued Octopus at £535m, or 491p per share. At the same time, there was a cash alternative for those who did not want to accept Reed shares, of 475p per share.

The share offer was equivalent to 3.4 times Octopus's 1986 turnover of £159m and 20.6 times pre-tax profits of £26m (22.5 times if the exceptional gain and pension holiday worth £2.25m are excluded). The £535m value placed on Octopus was 9.7 times its capitalization at the flotation in May 1983. This was a reflection not only of the expansion of the business, both by acquisition and organically, but also of the high stock-market ratings that publishing had come to attract.

At the level of the individual investor, the performance can be assessed as follows: had he managed to subscribe to, say, 1000 shares at the flotation price of 350p, paying £3500, he would have ended up holding 4000 shares as of July 1987 (reflecting the two one-for-one stock splits of June 1985 and May 1987). These would then have been worth £19,000 taking the 475p cash alternative, or slightly more, £19,600, on the basis of a price of 491p per share. This represented five-and-a-half times what he had invested. This advance had occurred during the space of little more than four years.

Such stark sums tell one nothing, however, about the circumstances surrounding Reed's agreed bid for Octopus. They are as it were the drum-roll.

The first point to recall is that the whole atmosphere in 1987 was feverish, as much within the publishing industry as on all main stock markets. Takeovers in the first seven months included Random House's purchase of Chatto, Virago, Bodley Head, and Jonathan Cape; News Corporation's purchase of Harper & Row; Wolters Samson's heavily contested acquisition of Kluwer; and, most dramatically, International Thomson's emergence as the successful bidder in the auction for Associated Book Publishers.

Swirling around such events were rumours of all hues, such as those sparked by the revelation of Rupert Murdoch's minority positions in Reed International and Pearson. Gulf & Western, owner of Simon & Schuster, was a failed bidder for Associated Book Publishers, and any sightings of Dick Snyder, then in charge at S&S, were imbued with immediate significance.

Octopus itself was not immune: one national newspaper told its readers in all seriousness that BTR was on the point of bidding for the 65% it did not already own; the argument was weakened somewhat by the description of Octopus as 'the Pan book publishers' and was further undermined by a dateline of 1 April.

Beneath all the feverishness was the spreading conviction that the path to prosperity in virtually all types of book publishing was an international one. Still high on the list of Octopus's desiderata was a worthwhile north American presence. Ian Irvine had inherited this strategic objective, but efforts to implement it had not so far borne fruit. The argument now ran that greatly increased scale was a prerequisite. The term 'critical mass' was invoked.

In the wake of the purchase by Reed, Paul Hamlyn indeed rejoiced, saying, 'I believe I can now make Octopus bigger and better and do all the things I have dreamed about.' Additional considerations that gave the Reed link particular appeal for Octopus were the shared history that stretched back to IPC days, the totally credible expectations of operational independence – Reed was adding a new division to its publishing portfolio – and the fact that the Union Jack flew from the masthead.

A further telling argument was that, in approaching Reed, Paul Hamlyn was still exercising control: it was he who was managing the selection process. An auction of the kind ABP had experienced filled him with distaste. He also drew journalists' attention to the fact that people do suffer thromboses and that to ignore this was an act of irresponsibility; the onset of Parkinson's can actually be dated from about then. Factors such as these may well be behind his statement that by selling to Reed he was securing the future of Octopus. At the time, the argument seemed at best paradoxical, as pointed out by Tim Clode in one of his critical letters to *The Bookseller*.

The mechanics of the transaction were greatly helped by the fact that Paul Hamlyn could speak, to all intents and purposes, for close to 70% of the votes, his own block plus the BTR holding. The story has it that the invitation 'to have a look at Octopus' was extended by Paul to Les Carpenter, his mate of long standing and the Reed chairman, over a cup of coffee on the latter's birthday.

Like all good stories, this has become oversimplified in the telling. Before the congratulatory cup of coffee with Les had come a discussion with Peter Davis, the group chief executive. What is unchallenged is that the negotiations lasted only seven days, conducted by Paul Hamlyn having Owen Green as a wholly supportive adviser on the end of a telephone.

From this process, Paul Hamlyn emerged with a fortune of £200m (including family interests and shares held in a trustee capacity). From this he donated to his foundation the considerable sum of £50m. He retained a personal holding of 24 million Reed shares (4.4% of the Reed capital as enlarged by the acquisition), while the Paul Hamlyn Foundation retained seven million shares (1.3%). Owen Green for his part received £178m in cash for shares that had been valued at £100m some two years previously.

A life and times of Octopus divides neatly into two volumes. The sale to Reed marks the end of volume one. It also offers an opportunity for a few moments of reflection.

When Octopus was set up in the early 1970s it appeared to start life as something of a recreation for Paul Hamlyn, certainly with limited publishing objectives. When Octopus gained a quotation in 1983, the goals again seemed restrained. Those who took such appearances at face value were overlooking the character of the founder. His competitive spirit allied to his professionalism in business – qualities that made him a highly demanding employer as well as a formidable rival – were such that Octopus would never be allowed to develop into a mere also-ran in the publishing stakes; nor was it possible that Octopus would ever be allowed to treat its possession of a quotation as a marginal attribute.

As Bob Gavron points out, Paul Hamlyn had the distinction of being talented at both the micro level – the creation of highly desirable books in his chosen fields – and at the macro level – overall strategy and conjuring up big corporate deals. What lay between needed to be somebody else's responsibility.

To these characteristics can be added a quality admired above all others in the City, namely a sense of timing that has occasionally suggested possession of a sixth sense. This was first evident when he ignored the early calls to obtain a quotation and later came to the market on the crest of a wave of investor enthusiasm. The broadening of the base with the purchase of Heinemann anticipated any falling off in the traditional businesses and preceded the acceleration in publishing valuations. The sale to Reed came at the peak of the acquisitive euphoria sweeping over publishing. It also came just three months before the great stock market crash of 17 October 1987.

Chapter 7

REED AS A TRADE PUBLISHER

REED'S ACQUISITION OF Octopus came at the halfway stage in its repositioning from a widely diversified conglomerate into a publishing and communications group: 1985 had already seen the disposal of the building products and decorative products divisions and in the spring of 1987 came those of the paint and DIY division. Still in the wings were the sales of the European packaging and paper divisions in July 1988, and of the north American paper business in August the same year.

The opportunity to acquire a major position in publishing, a sector that had at the time a growth label attached to it, offered considerable attractions. Octopus had been building itself up – a bulking exercise – and this enabled Reed to achieve prominence in books at one stroke. The price being asked might look high – 3.4 times Octopus's 1986 turnover and 20.6 times reported pre-tax profits – but this could be a once in a lifetime opportunity, given the presence of rapacious international rivals that were circling anything that looked like possible prey.

Justification of this nature for such an acquisition was plausible in the climate of the day. Reed threw in two additional arguments: first that its lengthy involvement in north America would be a material help to Octopus in its quest for a US publishing business; and second that investors could 'expect considerable synergy to develop between book publishing and magazine publishing'. This carried little conviction, and indeed had the whiff of strategic thinking formulated on the hoof after an evaluation process that had lasted all of one week.

Paul Hamlyn and Ian Irvine duly remained chairman and chief executive respectively of the Octopus Group. Both joined the main board. This terse statement makes it sound a formality. In fact, it was agreed to in a concluding one-to-one meeting on 2 July 1987 of the two chairmen, Leslie Carpenter (Reed) and Paul Hamlyn (Octopus), ahead of the acquisition announcement.

Reed chief executive Peter Davis's own view had been that one directorship was appropriate and that two gave Octopus greater main board representation than was justified by its economic size. In addition, he feared that this might inhibit Reed in the management of its new acquisition, leading to a 'don't send your scooter onto our lawn' attitude within Octopus. The definitive acquisition terms were also established at this concluding meeting of the two chairmen.

The first announcement Octopus management was called upon to make from its new corporate home was distinctly unhelpful. In September 1987 the publishing community was startled to read that Octopus was selling its half interest in Pan to Macmillan, which was the holder of the other 50%, leaving Octopus shorn of any paperback involvement. The explanation given was that the transaction had been triggered by a clause which provided that, in the event of a change of ownership of one of the partners, the other had a pre-emption right on the former's stake. No hint of the existence of this clause had previously emerged, but it was a risk of which Reed had been made aware ahead of its purchase of Octopus.

Following Pan's launch in 1946, the shares had been fairly widely held until 1961 when a consolidation took place, leaving Heinemann, Collins, and Macmillan each holding a third. As is common in companies whose shares are unlisted, a shareholder wishing to sell or reduce his stake is obliged to offer such shares in the first instance to the other shareholder(s). This is indeed what happened in October 1986 when Collins decided to dispose of its one-third interest. With Fontana and Granada paperbacks in its possession, the desirability of retaining a minority interest in what was becoming more and more of a competitor was questionable to all concerned. Collins's Pan shares were gleefully taken up by Octopus (Heinemann's new parent) and Macmillan, whose holdings each rose from one-third to one-half. It was at this point that the 'change of ownership' clause was inserted. The clause was put forward by Octopus and agreed to by Macmillan. The thinking behind its introduction was in both cases a precautionary, rather than an adrenalin-stirring, move in a game of poker. With Robert Maxwell an ever-acquisitive presence on the publishing horizon, the danger that he might somehow obtain a stake in Macmillan could not be entirely ruled out. After all, it is a truth universally acknowledged that in family-controlled companies the priorities of individuals vary and this can lead to instability in the share register. Octopus had no appetite for finding itself saddled with Maxwell as a fellow Pan shareholder, hence the appeal of the clause. For Macmillan, it made sense in as much as it removed an attraction to a would-be predator and consequently served as a built-in deterrent, a kind of poison pill.

Whatever the precautionary origins of the clause, Nicholas Byam Shaw, managing director of Macmillan, had no hesitation in invoking it: indeed, he did so when the ink was barely dry on the completion documents for Reed's purchase of Octopus. As Paul Hamlyn was to tell *Publishing News* some fifteen months later, 'Of course we were very reluctant sellers. We actually offered Macmillan more for their share than they paid us, but Byam Shaw wasn't to be moved. A very static gentleman.' It has not been given to many to out-negotiate Paul Hamlyn.

As a palliative, however, the price received looked healthy: £22m for a 50% interest, valuing the whole business at £44m. This compared with the £30m valuation for Pan established only a year earlier, when Octopus and Macmillan between them bought Collins's one-third shareholding for £10m.

A more encouraging piece of news for investors came in December 1987, with the acquisition of Methuen, the general publishing division of Associated Book Publishers, from the International Thomson Organization. The main attractions were Methuen's children's, humour, and drama lists; also included was Pitkin Pictorials. The consideration was believed to be in line with turn-over, which was running at £13m. Another in-fill acquisition was that of George Philip and its associated companies in April 1988. In addition to the map production side, the business included Osprey's aerospace, automotive, and military lists. Turnover was around £8.5m, generating profits of some £750,000, and the consideration was estimated at £10m. A purchase on a larger scale was made in September 1988, when Octopus paid W. H. Smith £52m for its 50% share of Book Club Associates (Bertelsmann owning the other 50%).

But the momentous event that month was an approach by Reed to Pearson about a possible merger. In what Peter Davis recalls as 'a polite but distant conversation', he had suggested to Pearson's chairman, Michael Blakenham, that they combine their international publishing interests. Reed was by then at the end of its disposal programme of all of its non-publishing assets. The proposal was that Pearson for its part would hive off its non-publishing interests into a separately quoted company.

This plan would then permit the creation of a single publishing/communi-cations group of international standing. In book publishing – not by any means the sole driving force behind the proposal – Reed's presence in educational publishing stood to be transformed through the addition of Longman and Addison-Wesley and in trade publishing through the addition of Viking and Penguin. The forced sale of Pan would have then taken on the proportions of a mere pinprick. The benefits of critical mass would have been demonstrated beyond dispute. Paul Hamlyn's wildest ambitions would have been satisfied.

One characteristic the two companies had in common was Rupert Murdoch on their share registers, but his 2.5% stake in Reed was a mere bagatelle compared to the 20.3% stake he had in Pearson. The assumption can safely be made that conversations would have taken place aimed at putting Rupert Murdoch 'on side' before Peter Davis paid his call on Michael Blakenham. That nothing came of this can be attributed in part to the fact that the Pearson family and friends could muster a collective stake in excess of News Corpor-ation's. Furthermore, for 'merger', Pearson read 'takeover', and it had every intention of remaining independent.

Pearson's response was two-pronged. First of all, a share swap which gave Pearson a 19% stake in Elsevier and Elsevier an 8.7% stake in Pearson. This complicated life for a would-be predator; it was also intended to be a first step towards marriage. Accompanying this action was the outright rejection of

Reed's offer, leaving Reed's chief executive, Peter Davis, expressing at the time considerable surprise that his 'friendly approach was apparently not considered by the Pearson board before doing the deal with Elsevier'.

Ploddingly and painfully Octopus had after all to achieve the vertical hardback/paperback integration that had become a necessary feature of large-scale trade publishing. The announcement that it was to create its own paperback imprint was made in June 1988, together with the appointment, to take effect two months later, of Richard Charkin as director responsible. In some respects, this was a surprising appointment, given Charkin's academic press background at Oxford University Press; but his irreverent spirit appealed to Paul Hamlyn, who saw him as a first-class marketeer with a first-class brain.

The new imprint, Mandarin (originally Octopus Paperbacks but re-christened because of the distribution arrangement giving W. H. Smith exclusivity on all Octopus titles), was presented with the challenging launch date of early April 1989. This was not the only challenge facing Richard Charkin. Paul Hamlyn had let it be known: 'I will be surprised if we are not profitable by the end of year three. We hope to be among the top three paperback houses in the country by then.' That implied sales of more than £20m by 1992.

The publishing programme called for some four hundred titles in the first year. In addition to Mandarin, there was the B-format list published under the Minerva imprint and the children's lists under the Magnet and Teens (later Mammoth) imprints. The great majority of titles was to be originated internally, with all Octopus's new books acquired jointly by the hardback and paperback imprints.

For the April lead titles, Octopus had bought volume rights to Michael Jackson's *Moonwalk* and Thomas Harris' *Silence of the Lambs*, paying for the latter an advance of £250,000. In addition, there were the reversions of titles currently licensed to other publishers, and this promised to develop from a trickle into a stream. Names included John Steinbeck, Somerset Maugham, Neville Shute, Olivia Manning, and Wilbur Smith. The actual launch was supported by a £1m promotional budget. The initial overall investment was put at £10m.

Inevitably, a number of the measures taken swiftly became controversial. None more so than the repatriation of rights: not every author who had been happily paperbacked by a Pan or a Penguin took kindly to being shifted to an untried Mandarin, however large the financial backing the new imprint was receiving.

The compulsory reversion of backlists in favour of Mandarin was capable of generating ill-will, most notably in the case of Wilbur Smith; the additional piquancy, if one may express it this way, was provided by the fact that Charles Pick had become Wilbur Smith's agent on his retirement from Heinemann, and he therefore presided over the author's switch, which took formal effect in 1991, from Heinemann to Macmillan as his primary publisher. Pan, which had previously sold 21 million copies of Smith's books in paperback, was at the same time confirmed as the author's paperback imprint for future titles.

Nor was it only a question of facing disaffected authors. There were margin implications, since terms often had to be renegotiated and frequently contained a financial sweetener to compensate authors for the unknown quantity implicit in an untested imprint. At the retail end, incentives needed to be given to secure adequate shelf space. To help with finances, an innovative initiative was to keep a tight control on selling costs while channelling funds into marketing: the domestic sales team was nine strong, rather than say twenty, which would equate with the sales objectives they had given themselves. Management also had very much in mind Bookwise Extra, its own retail merchandizing subsidiary, to give it material support.

In short, large sums of money were being committed and the group's internal resources were being deployed to maximum effect. This was a combination that, it was hoped, would turn out to be winning. After all, the base from which this attack on the paperback market was being made could hardly have appeared stronger.

Reference to Bookwise Extra may have seemed to readers familiar with Websters' Bookwise paperback merchandizing operation to have been a copy editor's lapse. This is not the case. It refers to a business that started trading in January 1988 when Octopus's Bookwise Services and its direct competitor, W. H. Smith's Book Extra, merged to form Bookwise Extra, a massive book wholesaling and merchandizing group supplying non-trade outlets, with sales approaching £50m. Octopus owned 75% and W. H. Smith 25%.

Within three months of Bookwise Extra's formation, it lost its single largest contract, worth over £5m in turnover, when Woolworths decided to buy direct from publishers. This followed hard on the heels of another blow when the Martins Retail Group sold 60 of its larger shops, with the loss to Bookwise Extra of £4m of book turnover.

The consequent reorganization of Bookwise Extra involved the progressive closure of its regional depots and concentration of offices and warehousing in a new £4m dedicated centre at Rushden. Implementation was halted, however, with the decision, announced on 26 May 1989, to sell the whole business to the Dublin-based book merchandizer and wholesaler, Overseas Publications. This in turn fell through when the prospective purchaser pulled out, declaring that 'in our opinion we were becoming more involved in a rescue operation than a turnround'. The trading figures gave support to that view: in the three months to 31 March 1988, the company had made losses of £1.15m on turnover of £8.2m; in the 12 months to 31 March 1989, losses amounted to £4.2m on turnover of £29.2m (no longer 'approaching £50m' please note).

W. H. Smith had by then sold its share of Bookwise Extra to Octopus; the closure decision taken in mid-June was made by Octopus as sole owner. Over the preceding two to three years, Bookwise and Bookwise Extra had illustrated how it was possible to expand and yet become smaller. And its demise was painful. As the then head of children's books at Octopus, Paul Richardson, recalls, not only was it a blow to the marketing expectations of Mandarin, but it also generated huge ill-will for Octopus in the retail trade, especially with the big multiples such as Boots and the supermarket chains – not to mention among other paperback houses.

The closure also marked the end of Octopus's strategic move into book retailing through the 1984 acquisition of Websters. For this diversification, Paul Hamlyn took responsibility: 'without any doubt a mistake of mine'.

Important as individual developments may be, the single most significant statistic in the wake of a purchase such as that of Octopus by Reed is its over-all contribution. It can usually be traced for a relatively short time before the figures become hopelessly muddled by subsequent acquisitions, disposals, and rationalizations. This was indeed the case with Octopus.

For the eight months from 1 August 1987, deemed to have been the date of purchase, to 31 March 1988, being the Reed year-end, the Octopus Group turnover was given as £133m and trading profit as £11m. In the full year to 31 March 1989, the Octopus results were incorporated into those of the Reed book division, whose turnover was £324m and operating profits £48m. Within this total, the Octopus contribution to operating profits was said to have been in excess of £24m.

This was to be the last time that the outside world was given any quantification of Octopus's performance within Reed. While there were no comparisons with earlier periods, outsiders did take note of the fact that £24m of operating profits was little changed from the £23.8m reported in 1986, being Octopus's last full set of accounts as an independent company.

Even though the dangers of comparing oranges with lemons were recognized (different year-ends, intervening acquisitions and disposals), the general implication was that Octopus's performance was distinctly subdued. The narrative evidence in the Reed results statements, brief as it was, tended to confirm this overall impression. Looking beyond the period immediately following the acquisition, there was a change in tone from the initial, somewhat defiant, optimism to more objective assessment. References to the educational side were for the most part positive or absent – a case of no reference being interpreted as a relatively encouraging sign. On the other hand, the declining profitability of the consumer book interests – albeit interrupted by the occasional profit rebound attributable to cost reductions – attracted regular comment.

For Reed to have paid a very full price for a set of businesses that from the outset provided the proud new owner with disappointments, as reflected in overall performance figures and such specific events as the loss of Pan and the later closure of Websters/Bookwise, was deeply embarrassing. Ian Irvine, as chief executive of Reed's book interests but until recently in the camp of the vendors, had the challenging task of justifying to the purchasers the substantial investment they had chosen to make. His personal quandary was somewhat analogous to that of Rabelais' Gargantua, who alternated between rejoicing at the birth of his son Pantagruel (sale price of Octopus) and lamenting the death in childbirth of his wife Badebec (declining fortunes of the business). The reality of his position was such that he could not spend much time openly rejoicing.

Ian Irvine's responses to pressure from the Reed board automatically turned the spotlight on his style of management. A Fleet Street newspaper background naturally breeds a certain toughness where the stick is used to great effect. It does not, however, automatically produce the right results when exported to the more tender environment of book publishing. Even less so when the wielder of the stick appears to view the industry with a certain degree of impatience. Indeed, the suspicion that Ian Irvine did not find book publishing totally absorbing gradually gained ground.

Such crucial issues in trade publishing as relations with authors require a light touch, otherwise damage can ensue. Sloppy, let alone inaccurate, royalty statements can be hugely unsettling. And there is the prickly business of advances to big-name writers. Catherine Cookson's move from William Heinemann to Transworld (already her paperback publisher) occurred in October 1986 on an important multi-volume contract. From one angle, this shows Octopus management in a robust mood, determined not to get sucked into a spiral of competitive bids. From another, it may be regarded as a serious misjudgement of the publishing realities of the day and of the vital interests of William Heinemann.

In the history of Octopus, the Michelin building occupies a position that is infinitely greater than one might expect of a piece of real estate, however distinguished. In addition to its role as a workplace for the 380 people who moved there in April 1988, the Michelin building was where the strategies for the business were evolved, fought over, and implemented. For the critics of Reed's management of the Octopus publishing assets, it occupies top slot in their demonologies.

At a practical level, however, it has had its admirers as well as critics. The administrative and operational advantages of having businesses that share a degree of common ground, whether it be in products or markets, is widely accepted. But, undoubtedly, many of the seven imprints that moved into Michelin House found the change deeply shocking for a number of reasons:
– going into an open-plan office is often resented, notwithstanding the resulting improvement in communications;
– adjusting to the bureaucracy of a large office building with executive gradings covering such matters as the size of desks and the height of partitions excites either mirth or outrage;
– conforming to rules of behaviour is irksome – no pets on the premises being one that presented particular difficulties for a few dog-owning trade editors;
– most of all there was the shock of being one of several hundreds in a regimented head office.

The view of Richard Charkin, now chief executive of Macmillan, that 'it was bound to happen in a centralized structure', is difficult to find fault with. IPC had it in its blood, whether at Feltham in the 1960s for books or in the King's Reach Tower on the South Bank for magazines. It takes a rare publishing company such as magazine publisher EMAP to resist the centralizing arguments. Reed was never going to be another EMAP.

The most intriguing aspect to Reed's policy of centralization lies in the breadth of its ambitions. In the first instance there was the pursuit of overhead economies, most dramatically achieved in Michelin House itself. In the case of the educational imprints, this objective led to their being rehoused under one roof in Oxford in June 1988. The children's imprints, which outgrew their Michelin quarters following the acquisition of Methuen, were moved in 1989 into a separate building not far distant in Hans Crescent.

The pursuit of overhead economies extended beyond office space and was at its most determined in the area of warehousing and distribution. In the 1990s Rushden became the successor to IPC's Sunbury centre in the 1960s as the book division's warehousing/distribution capital.

The other objective that Reed had – and this may have evolved gradually and not been explicit from the start – was the fusion of businesses sharing very different cultures, for which Michelin House came to be seen as the symbol.

Paul Richardson illustrates the diversity of Reed's interests in publishing by asking the question of three executives in a hypothetical budget meeting: 'What are the star items on your list for the autumn?' The Secker/William Heinemann executive would reply in terms of authors, 'a new Tom Sharpe'; the Octopus/Hamlyn executive in terms of format, '20 K 48s' (48-page crown quartos) and '10 P 160s' (160-page de luxe coffee-table books); and the Heinemann Education/Ginn executive in terms of subjects, 'a revised secondary maths course'. He recalls how, in the Michelin environment, the clever young deal-makers on the mass-market illustrated books side were suddenly given managerial roles. 'Their skills were buccaneering. Instead they were producing monthly reports.'

Nicolas Thompson, managing director of the Heinemann Group at the time of Reed's purchase of Octopus, saw very little merit in linking the two trade imprints with the traditional Octopus business. 'I thought plans to merge marketing, sales management, and production were wrong.' It is the firm belief of David Blunt, who was with Octopus from January 1987 to February 1989, much of it as chief executive of the imprints in the Michelin building, that the fundamental mistake made by Reed in its diversification into books was to imagine that all companies were operating in the same business. Reflecting on these issues, Sir Peter Davis, now group chief executive of J. Sainsbury, felt that 'what replaced the Paul style was not the right one for the business'.

True or not, one of the features of management within the book division was frequency of change. This did little for continuity and could be taken as evidence of internal disharmony or at the very least bumpy progress towards the achievement of strategic goals.

The careers within Reed of Ian Irvine and Richard Charkin deserve to be charted.

The Octopus companies had been divided into nine divisions reporting to Ian Irvine as chief executive. On the consumer side, there were among others the two literary imprints, the Octopus and Hamlyn adult illustrated books, and children's books.

– As mentioned, Richard Charkin joined Reed in August 1988 with the precise brief to create a leading paperback imprint.

– In January 1989 Charkin's role was expanded, with perfect logic, to include responsibility for trade publishing as a whole.

– In March 1990 Reed International Books was established, bringing together all the Reed Group's book publishing and associated activities. This gave Ian Irvine, already chief executive of the Octopus companies, additional responsibility for Butterworths. Three months earlier his role within Reed had been expanded on his appointment as one of two group deputy chief executives.

– With the formation, in March 1990, of Reed International Books, Richard Charkin's own administrative responsibilities were greatly increased following his appointment as chief executive of Reed Consumer Books, largely made up of the literary imprints, the illustrated adult division, children's books, Tigerprint, and Mandarin Offset.

– In January 1993 Reed International merged with Elsevier to form Reed Elsevier. The latter's flirtation with Pearson, which dated back to 1988, had ended some time previously with the unwinding of the share exchange. Once again, Ian Irvine's responsibilities grew as he joined the executive committee of Reed Elsevier.

– In July 1994 Richard Charkin took over from Ian Irvine as chief executive of Reed International Books. Ian Irvine, for his part, had just been appointed co-chairman with Pierre Vinken of the Reed Elsevier executive committee and chairman of Reed International following the surprise resignation of Peter Davis.

– In July 1995 Richard Charkin moved to head office with a role in corporate strategy. In January 1996 he resigned from Reed International.

– In July 1996 Ian Irvine retired as co-chairman of the Reed Elsevier executive committee and in April 1997 as chairman of Reed International.

Both careers reveal an impressive degree of upward mobility, leading ultimately to their spinning out of the Reed orbit. Richard Charkin's assumption of ever-increasing administrative responsibilities resulted in the rapid dilution of his contribution at the operating level.

The divisional heads within the book division also displayed at times a bewildering degree of mobility, as illustrated in table 21. The snakes-and-ladders career of Derek Freeman is especially remarkable.

Underlying these management changes were difficult trading conditions. These prompted a number of integration measures, including:

(a) the move of George Philip to Michelin House soon after its acquisition in April 1988;

(b) centralization under one person of direct hardback promotion for Methuen, William Heinemann, Secker & Warburg (July 1989);

(c) reduction in October 1990 of sales forces, from six to four, with the merging of adult and children's sales and the merger of George Philip and Hamlyn sales; separate sales forces for Mandarin and Bounty were retained; the export sales force was reorganized into a single integrated unit serving all imprints;

(d) reduction in the output of new titles and pruning of the 15,000-strong backlist (October 1990);

(e) creation of a single vertical publishing structure for William Heinemann and Mandarin (September 1991), featuring also a single publicity department and a single marketing department;

(f) move into Michelin House of Mitchell Beazley from its Soho premises in August 1991. This had been preceded by mass resignations, notably those of the managing director and the publishing director, in protest at the loss of autonomy and of independent location, both of which had been undertakings made when Mitchell Beazley was bought by Octopus in May 1987, ahead of the Reed purchase.

Rationalization went hand-in-hand with integration. In November 1990 the illustrated books division had its staff reduced from 75 to 55 as part of a corporate plan to cut the numbers employed across publishing as a whole from 600 to 500. The professional division (chiefly Butterworths) also faced significant redundancies that year. The consolidation of Mitchell Beazley into Michelin House in 1991 led to yet more job losses, notably those of six senior executives, but in this instance occasioned by resignations rather than dismissals. In October 1992 the illustrated books division suffered a further reduction in staff of 19.

Measures of this kind were being taken by other publishers faced with a difficult trading environment. The spur to action within the Reed book division may have been somewhat sharper. For one thing, the climate for developing an important new paperback imprint was proving thoroughly unfavourable.

In the first full year paperback turnover had reached £5m, and there had been in Thomas Harris' *Silence of the Lambs* a critical success which two years later, when the film was released, became the commercial envy of other paperback publishers. But Mandarin Paperbacks was proving unequal to the task of getting within striking distance of the leaders. In June 1989 closure of Bookwise Extra was a serious setback. The backlist, weakened by such defections as Catherine Cookson and Wilbur Smith, was too thin; so the onus

Table 21: *Divisional responsibilities*

Date	Illustrated books	Children's books	Trade books	Tigerprint	Mandarin Offset	Total consumer books[5]
End 1987	Derek Freeman	Bill Mitchell	Helen Fraser, Heinemann David Godwin, Secker Geoffrey Strachan, Methuen	Derek Freeman	Derek Freeman	David Blunt[5]
January 1989	Derek Freeman	Paul Richardson[4]	Richard Charkin	Derek Freeman	Derek Freeman	Ian Irvine[1]
January 1990	Tony Bovill	Ingrid Selberg	John Potter	Derek Freeman	Derek Freeman	Richard Charkin
Spring 1994	Robert Snuggs	Ingrid Selberg	John Potter	Peter Murphy	Derek Freeman	Richard Charkin
January 1995	Chief executives[2] Hamlyn Bounty Mitchell Beazley George Philip Pitkin Osprey	Jane Winterbotham[3]	John Potter	Peter Murphy	Derek Freeman	Sandy Grant
April 1996			Helen Fraser			

1 Chief executive of Octopus Publishing Group, including the educational imprints.
2 Sandy Grant and Derek Freeman were the board members through whom the chief executives of the illustrated books imprints reported.
3 Peter Murphy was the board member to whom Jane Winterbotham reported on children's books.
4 It was through Paul Richardson that the Heinemann, Secker, and Methuen managing directors reported into the board.
5 Chief executive of publishing imprints in Michelin House.

was placed to an unhealthy extent on an inevitably unpredictable front list. At its peak, turnover managed to push through £10m. That the £20m to £30m level eluded it was not for want of investment – but then throwing money at a publishing venture has never guaranteed its success.

One action being taken that was special to Reed might be described as the homogenization of illustrated books. This came as part of the 1992 reorganization which brought six imprints – Bounty, Hamlyn, Millers, Mitchell Beazley, Osprey, and George Philip – into an integrated structure. Of the 19 staff then made redundant, there were several on the editorial side; others were in rights, design, and production, for which the individual imprints had previously been responsible.

At the time, Tony Bovill, in overall charge of illustrated books since 1990, explained that his intention was to form a less rigidly demarcated publishing force. 'It makes more sense for us to decide whether a cookery book, for example, goes to Hamlyn, or maybe to Mitchell Beazley. Bringing imprints together gives us a much more coherent structure.' An alternative view, colourfully expressed by Derek Freeman, is that all he could observe was 'a treacle of people making books, not knowing the market for which they were making them'. Such products then went through a central design department to central production, to be promoted by the central marketing department, to be sold by centralized sales forces from the group's distribution centre. Once again the IPC mentality would have applauded the resulting tidiness.

The trading consequences – not forgetting of course the difficult market conditions – were generally unhappy, as the Reed Elsevier interim and full-year reports laconically record:

– Year to 31 December 1993: 'Although Illustrated's results were disappointing, both children's and trade had very successful years.'
– Six months to 30 June 1994: 'Operating profit of Reed Consumer Books was below that of last year, reflecting weak UK sales.'
– Year to 31 December 1994: 'In the UK 1994 was a difficult year, with the lack of consumer confidence leading to subdued sales and book retailers reducing their stocks. Overseas, the US and Australian markets were more buoyant.'
– Six months to 30 June 1995: 'The UK and Australian retail book market showed little sign of improvement and the results of Reed Consumer Books were down on the first half of 1994.'
– Year to 31 December 1995: 'Weak overall consumer demand in 1995 resulted in a slowdown in book sales in both the UK and Australia. In addition the collapse of the Net Book Agreement during the year particularly impacted Book Club Associates.'

Help was close to hand, however. The appointment in July 1994 of Sandy Grant, long-serving head of Australian operations, as chief executive of Reed Consumer Books heralded a significant change of direction in management strategy. True, it involved yet another restructuring, but this time one that harked back to an earlier period when imprints were the profit centres rather than divisions with such generic titles as 'Illustrated Books' and 'Children's Books'. To Helen Fraser, at the time publishing director of the trade division, the appointment of somebody with Sandy Grant's extensive publishing experience was like a breath of fresh air. 'We were very happy to work with him.'

His brief was broad in the extreme: to restore morale, which was low, and publishing, which had been falling away. He had found, for instance, major product gaps on the children's side and in the adult illustrated publishing programmes. His return to earlier patterns of publishing meant that decentralization took pride of place, leading to the elimination of such positions as group marketing director and group sales manager. The individual imprints were progressively endowed with their own dedicated design teams and sales forces.

Even the centralized distribution/warehouse complex, what might be regarded as the touchstone for publishers in quest of critical mass, was first called into question and then repudiated. The closure of Rushden and the outsourcing to Exel Logistics, which took place in April 1997, had been mooted from the start of 1995. Its implementation had taken longer than expected, however, due to Reed's formal announcement in July 1995 that it would be disposing of its consumer publishing interests. This had been preceded by Reed's merger with Elsevier in January 1993, the two developments being intimately linked.

In merging with Elsevier (January 1993), Reed had chosen a partner of roughly equal size in terms of market capitalization and profits. Furthermore, this was a company whose profits had grown during the previous ten years without interruption. This record was more consistent than Reed's and was accompanied by a steady rise in pre-tax profit margins from 6% in 1982 to 23% in 1991. The key to this remarkable achievement was a shift out of low margin businesses, such as printing and trade publishing, into high margin businesses, such as scientific journals and professional publishing. At the same time, Elsevier was moving away from businesses that were consumers of cash and expanding into those that were generators of cash.

It did not take long for observers from both inside and outside the company to realize that the merger with Elsevier spelled an end to the further development of the consumer book interests. As Ian Irvine recalls, 'the more you looked at the strategic direction of Reed, the more you had to look at scientific, high-margin cash generation'.

The formal announcement that Reed Elsevier wished to dispose of its consumer book interests was made in July 1995. It was part of a strategic decision to withdraw from consumer publishing that also called for the sale of the provincial newspapers in the UK, national newspapers in Holland and consumer magazines in the US and Holland. IPC Magazines in the UK was given a reprieve.

Four months later, the results of this programme were announced: £740m had been raised (£685m net after taxes and fees) from the sales of (a) Reed Regional Newspapers – £205m; (b) Dagbladunie – £346m; (c) Cahners Consumer Magazines and various Dutch properties – £189m. At the same time, Reed Elsevier said that the remaining asset sale, that of consumer books, would probably be completed the following February.

Any account of Reed's exit from consumer book publishing is complicated: the process was, contrary to Reed's expectations, long and drawn out; the assets being offered changed over time; the dividing line between exploratory conversations and serious expressions of interest is hard to draw; the confidential character of any sale leads to reliance on rumours, the quality of which is inevitably variable. The account that follows needs to be read with these caveats in mind.

The sale exercise started before the formal announcement in 1995. Thorn EMI was the interested party in the autumn of 1994. Included in its ambitions were Butterworths and the half interest in Book Club Associates. This all-encompassing approach did not find favour in Reed's eyes.

In July 1995 the talk was that Richard Charkin, then chief executive of Reed International Books, had offered £400m plus for the whole of the book division, excluding Butterworths but including the 50% interest in BCA. This offer related to businesses with turnover of £350m and pre-interest profits of some £45m.

Reed turned Charkin down, having every intention of retaining the educational imprints. Instead, it invited him to declare an interest in Reed Consumer Books on its own, the turnover of which was £166m and operating profits £18m to £20m. Charkin's appetite not being whetted, Reed turned to Goldman Sachs to conduct an official auction. From the start, John Mellon, the Reed board director overseeing the disposal, declared that the only bids to be considered would be those for the whole of the consumer books portfolio.

During the autumn of 1995 expressions of interest abounded, leading to at least seven presentations, ahead of an auction deadline of January 1996. The list was eventually refined to three names: Richard Branson's Virgin; the venture capital arm of Electra House; and a management buyout led by consumer books chief executive Sandy Grant.

In the meantime, trading conditions, as noted earlier, had been deteriorating, and the 1995 operating profits, on which the bids to be submitted in January would be based, were coming out 60% below those of a year earlier. About half of this had an exceptional character to it – write-offs against profits on cautious evaluations of stocks for instance. The immediate consequence was a drop in Reed's indicated asking price from £150m to at least £100m by the end of the year, both figures excluding the half interest in BCA.

At this point, Virgin was given an exclusive period of seven weeks to do its due diligence and make a firm offer. Instead of £100m, it came in with £85m. Electra, with advice from former Octopus financial director Iain Burns, got into the final stage and, after a tour of the businesses, indicated an interest at a much lower level than £100m – more in the region of £70m. The management buyout team was in a curious position in the sense that the financial buyers were using existing management as part of their purchase strategy. They were therefore almost pushed into becoming bidders in their own right.

On price, Sandy Grant's view was that they would be in the lists at £80m, ahead of a due diligence exercise that could well point to a firm bid at a significantly lower level: 'I didn't want to be involved in a stretched management buyout. If there were to be a bargain we would be happy. If not, happy to be employees.' In the event, they were not taken seriously and the two other candidates were turned away. In March 1996 Reed withdrew the consumer books division from auction.

The removal of the uncertainty regarding ownership – albeit temporary since Reed indicated that this was likely to be a reprieve – gave renewed heart to the division. Helen Fraser, who had replaced John Potter in April 1996 as head of the trade imprints, recalls a surge of activity, with morale high among executives who, having been 'bonded by adversity', were intent on proving their worth (and proving Reed management wrong). The six-month figures to 30 June 1996, which showed increased losses in the consumer books division, were, it was felt, more an echo of the past than a guide to the future.

It is against this background that the reaction to Sandy Grant's abrupt dismissal in November 1996 needs to be understood. Remembering the event two months later, Tom Weldon, publisher of William Heinemann, commented: 'My loyalty broke down the day John Mellon fired Sandy Grant. It was an act of incredible stupidity.' January 1997 was to see Tom Weldon's departure to Penguin, together with Louise Moore, editorial director of William Heinemann. This took place within hours of Helen Fraser's own arrival as managing director of Penguin's general publishing division – Penguin having initiated discussions with her immediately after Sandy Grant's dismissal.

Grant's departure marked in fact the next stage in the dismantling of the old Octopus group after the failed public auction, namely its piecemeal liquidation. The ultimate indignity.

John Holloran, Sandy Grant's successor as chief executive of Reed Consumer Books (whose appointment was announced in November 1996), came to the task with a background in printing, through the British Printing Corporation and McCorquodale, whence he had a clear view of publishers as customers – not necessarily the most endearing prospect. His brief was such, however, that he could have joined the ranks of publishers himself by mounting a bid for all or part of the portfolio. But this put him in an invidious position, and 'it didn't feel right to be buyer and seller'.

His task of finding homes for the various companies that made up the consumer books division was helped by the financial support that Reed continued to give. 'Reed never said no to investment, and right through my tenure

Table 22: *Realizations and closures of book interests*

	Turnover ($£$m)		Price realized ($£$m)
Realizations			
February 1997	20.0	Trade division sold to Random House	17.5
August 1997	9.0	Tigerprint sold to management	12.5
March 1988	–	Osprey sold to management	Combined est. of
April 1988	1.0e	Pitkin Guides sold to JNG	3.0e
May 1998	25.0	Children's Books sold to Egmont	13.5
May 1998		Rights to Thomas the Tank Engine sold to Britt Allcroft	13.5*
August 1988	45.0	Illustrated Books Div. sold to management	33.0
1997–98		Australian adult and children's assets sold to several buyers	3.5e
		Total realizations	96.5e
Closures			*Closure costs*
April 1997		Rushden	(2.0e)
April 1997	50.0e	Mandarin Offset	(1.0e)
		Closure costs	(3.0e)†

e = estimate. * Based on profits of $£$1.2m. † See text.

investment was available and given.' This, undoubtedly, was heartening to executives in the various companies, some of whom would have been giving thought from an early stage to management buyouts.

From November 1996 to the final asset disposal some 22 months later, seven main and a number of minor businesses were sold, and there were two closures. The considerations shown in table 22 have been taken uncritically from press reports. Where no figures are given, estimates have been made.

First of all, the closures and the costs. The closure of Rushden, announced in October 1996, confirmed a decision that operating management had been promoting for some two years previously but had been unable to implement because of Reed's declaration in mid-1995 that it would be selling the whole division. Now that the publishing assets were being sold off piecemeal, Rushden had become even less desirable – nobody wanted to be left holding that particular baby once the music stopped.

The reasons behind the April 1997 closure of Mandarin Offset, the Hong Kong print broker, are altogether more subtle: it was judged to be worth more dead than alive. This was notwithstanding the fact that as recently as March 1996 it had been singled out for special praise in the Reed Elsevier annual report for its good results in a year when the consumer books division as a whole had announced a 60% decline in profits.

The argument ran as follows. Had an attempt been made to sell Mandarin

Offset as a going concern, the profits of a Hong Kong print broker would have been lowly rated; furthermore, it was argued, Mandarin had enjoyed high margins at the expense of Reed's UK imprints and its closure would lead to the repatriation of some of these healthy profits to the UK imprints. (Better terms would be secured by going direct to Far Eastern printers, notably Toppan, with which a 'strategic alliance' was being formed.) In turn such profits would be seen as publishing profits and rated as such by prospective purchasers. However, the 40% of Mandarin Offset's turnover that came from third-party business (some £20m at the point of closure) would have to be sacrificed.

How much of an influence this ratiocination had on the purchasers of Reed publishing imprints is hard to tell. In the event, closure costs were limited since David Martin, the managing director, resigned in protest, thereby saving Reed a sizeable severance payment.

Reed's disengagement from consumer book publishing had other important cost implications, over and above direct redundancy costs and such matters as receivables that proved irrecoverable. For the disposals to have any chance of success, it was necessary to secure the services of senior executives. This took the form of substantial bonuses to be earned by key personnel, provided they saw the sale processes through to their conclusion.

An idea of the gold content to these handcuffs is to be had from their rejection by Tom Weldon and Louise Moore: as reported in *The Bookseller* (7 February 1997), they were offered respectively £150,000 and £120,000 if they would stay. Assuming that twenty people were designated as key to the sales – not an implausible assumption given the number of businesses to be disposed of – bonuses on this scale would have totalled more than £2.5m. All of this suggests that one needs to multiply the estimated direct closure costs in table 22 of £3m by two to three times to arrive at the overall liquidation costs.

Excluded from the table is the sale in June 1998 of the 50% holding in BCA to Bertelsmann. This is believed to have realized well under £40m and compares with a purchase price 10 years earlier of £52m. The changed circumstances of book clubs following the abandonment of the Net Book Agreement no doubt had much to do with this loss on disposal.

Next, the realizations. These started with the sale in January 1997 of the adult trade division to Random House. Turnover was £20m. If one goes back to 1985, hardback turnover of William Heinemann and Secker & Warburg (excluding children's) had stood at around £10m. This included nothing for paperback sales, since these were accounted for by the share of royalties received from Pan and other paperback imprints. Over the ensuing twelve years, additions to the division had included: (a) Mandarin Paperbacks, whose sales by 1997 were running at around £10m; (b) Methuen's adult lists, bought in 1987; and (c) Sinclair-Stevenson, the acquisition of which was completed in 1992. Trade publishing, far from growing, had experienced a contraction in its operations.

The price said to have been paid by Random House was £17.5m. Whether in fact this figure was reduced to reflect the staff defections that coincided with the sale is unclear. There is no way of knowing what value Octopus attached to the Heinemann trade side when it bought the whole group in 1986. It is a sobering thought, however, that the 50% interest in Pan sold to Macmillan in 1987 fetched £22m, more than the entire adult trade division ten years later.

This is perhaps the closest that an outsider can come to appreciate the extent of Reed's failed attempt to create its own paperback arm. It will therefore come as no surprise to learn that Random House attached no specific value to Mandarin Paperbacks when it made its acquisition, nor that the Mandarin and Minerva imprints should have since been very largely folded into Arrow and Vintage.

The sale in 1998 of the illustrated books division lies at the heart of this tale. This was by way of a management buy-out, with the company reviving the Octopus Publishing Group name as soon as it regained its independence. Turnover was £45m. Going back to the Octopus flotation prospectus, about 70% of the 1982 turnover of £31m comprised adult illustrated books, whose sales consequently amounted to £21.5m. In the next 16 years, some £37m of turnover was added through purchases of Hamlyn, Mitchell Beazley, George Philip, and the Conran-Octopus minority interest, giving a grand total of around £58m. When set against the 1998 turnover of £45m, once again this suggests significant underlying contraction.

As to valuation, 70% (as representing adult illustrated books) of Octopus's market capitalization on its flotation in May 1983 gives a figure of £38.5m. The £33m paid in the management buyout indicates that – notwithstanding subsequent acquisitions costing £15m to £20m for the equity alone – the overall value of the business suffered a marked decline. Affecting this, no doubt, were the changing economics of illustrated book publishing: in 1982, on Octopus Group turnover of £30.8m, operating profits of £4m gave an operating margin of 13.1%. By 1998, on turnover for the illustrated division of £44.9m, operating profits of £3.12m gave operating margins of 7%. Admittedly, the comparison is somewhat clouded by the inclusion in the 1982 group figures of children's sales and, more importantly, of the (lower margin) Tigerprint and print-broking turnover. Nevertheless, the evidence points pretty clearly to a halving in the profitability of adult illustrated book publishing.

Children's books provide perhaps the most startling instance of the downward adjustment to Reed's disposal ambitions. In mid-1995, when consumer book publishing was put up for sale as a unit, the children's books contribution to the asking figure of at least £150m was not far off £60m. By the end of the year, when Reed was hoping for a minimum of £100m, this had been trimmed down to £40m. Following the failure to attract a single buyer at an acceptable price, the consumer book interests were taken off the market until John Holloran's appointment in November 1996.

By July 1997, the Danish Egmont group was in negotiation for the whole of the children's division; talks broke down in November, but by then Penguin

Table 23: *Reed's investments in non-professional book publishing*

		(£m)
Purchase of Octopus	August 1987	535.0
Sale of 50% of Pan	September 1987	−22.0
Purchase of Methuen general books	December 1987	13.5e
Purchase of George Philip	April 1988	10.0e
Purchase of 60% of Budget Books Pty	September 1988	3.5
Purchase of minority Conran-Octopus	October 1990	Combined
Purchase of Sinclair-Stevenson	1991–92	est. of 4.0e
Total estimated investment		544.0

Note: Excluding purchase and sale of 50% of BCA.

was at the negotiating table. In March 1998, Egmont re-entered the auction but with lowered ambitions as to what it wished to acquire. At the end of April it was announced that the children's assets had been divided into two – the publishing business and the underlying rights to Thomas the Tank Engine – and that the buyers were Egmont and Britt Allcroft respectively.

The news was greeted with considerable relief, but at Reed Children's Books there was also utter astonishment that the winner should not have been Penguin, where practical arrangements, down to who would be given desks and where, had been concluded only days before. The price Reed secured for the two elements combined, £27m, was about half its initial aspirations.

The cumulative amount realized from the various sales was some £96.5m (see table 22). This was well down on management's earlier expectations of a good £150m and, in relation to 1994 divisional turnover of £166m, represented a restrained valuation of 58p per 100p of sales. If the estimated disengagement costs of, say, £8m are taken into account, the net total realized comes to £88.5m, equivalent to 53p per 100p of sales.

Given the damage inflicted by a very public failure at auction, the outcome must, however, have seemed reasonably satisfactory from the vendor's point of view. The high incidence of management buyouts, thereby limiting job losses, can also be viewed as something of an achievement, while the conversion of salaried executives into shareholders had the laudable effect of swelling the ranks of publishing entrepreneurs – Mandarin Offset excepted, of course.

Turning now to the broader picture, the main asset purchases and disposals made by Reed in non-professional book publishing amounted to £544m in the period from July 1987 to the end of 1998 (see table 23). Setting aside Octopus, there were several purchases, but these were minor and did little more than compensate for the enforced sale of Pan. The striking evidence is that Octopus's absorption into a group that gave it elephantine financial muscle led to nothing significant on the acquisition front. This had been one of the advantages cited most frequently by both Octopus and Reed that would flow from

Table 24: *Valuation multiples*

Date	Predator	Target	Turnover	Profits
			Purchase price expressed as multiple of historic results	
July 1987	Reed Intl	Octopus	3.4×	20.6×[1]
October 1986	Time Inc.	Scott Foresman	2.6×	NA
March 1987	News Corp.	Harper & Row	1.5×	26.3×
July 1987	BPCC	Harcourt Brace	2.0×	14.9×[2]
July 1987	International Thomson	Associated Book Publishers	2.5×	25.9×

1 22.5× if exceptional profits are excluded.
2 Withdrawn in July 1987.

the takeover. While it is true that in 1988 Reed's chief executive Peter Davis made an opportunistic attempt with his proposed merger with Pearson, thereafter nothing significant occurred, and the consumer books division became largely dependent on organic growth for its performance. But even that was not achieved, since, as we have seen, instead of expansion there was contraction.

For a definitive judgement on Reed's diversification into non-professional publishing, one must take one step back and consider in the first instance the price it paid for Octopus in August 1987, in relation to the valuations prevailing at the time. In table 24 the prices paid in a number of transactions are shown (a) as a multiple of turnover and (b) in relation to profits. Reed's aggressive pricing is at its most obvious in relation to turnover, on which measure it exceeds the four other examples shown, in some cases by a wide margin.

The profits multiple test is less clear cut, with Harper & Row and Associated Book Publishers apparently commanding higher ratings than Octopus. But then, the bulk of ABP's business was made up of highly valued legal publishing, while News Corporation could look forward to merger benefits and savings of the kind that arise when the two businesses involved share common interests. Neither set of circumstances applied to the purchase of Octopus by Reed, which can be said to have broken decisively into new high ground in the valuation of the different types of publishing making up the Octopus portfolio.

The question to which many have attempted an answer: 'How much did Reed overpay for Octopus?' does not lend itself to a ready answer. In the first instance, included in the purchase were the educational imprints, Heinemann Educational and Ginn & Co. They constituted one of Octopus's main attractions, and their subsequent performance has justified this enthusiasm and their retention. Critics of Reed occasionally forget this.

At the time, the Heinemann education division (including Ginn) had turnover approaching £30m and profits of £5.5m. If one were to take forward-looking valuations to reflect Reed's acquisitive enthusiasm of say 4.5 times turnover and 25 times profits, a value of £135m might have been attributed to the educational side within the £535m valuation given to the whole of Octopus. Deducting this total, together with the £96.5m realized from the disposals in 1997-8, leaves one with just over £300m unaccounted for, equivalent to close to 60% of the purchase price.

If this is accepted as being a measure of asset depreciation, albeit extremely rough and ready, some £100m may be explained by closures of activities to which a value had been attached in 1987 (Websters' non-Bounty turnover of £20m in 1987 and Mandarin Offset's £10m third-party business in 1987). The balance may be laid at the door of a decline in publishing ratings and general attrition in the value of businesses that were for the most part contracting and shedding margin.

While it would undoubtedly be wrong to look for a single explanation for this commercial catastrophe, the temptation is hard to resist. Some would draw attention to top management failure at Octopus in the aftermath of the Reed takeover. Others would single out the changed circumstances in publishing. But that the worm was in the apple from the start is not open to dispute. As Nicolas Thompson points out, the brevity of the purchase negotiations – seven days from start to finish – ruled out any serious due diligence. Reed's view of what it was buying was necessarily hazy, and post-acquisition surprises were assured.

From whatever angle one views the transaction, it can be stated (with the precious benefit of hindsight) that Reed paid an extremely high price for Octopus.

- 1998 Paul Hamlyn receives a peerage.
- 2001 Octopus Publishing Group acquired by Hachette.
- 2001 Paul Hamlyn dies leaving an estate worth almost £450m before tax.

Chapter 8

CHATTO, BODLEY HEAD
& JONATHAN CAPE

PEDIGREE AMONG LITERARY imprints is not all that counts. But it still scores. The creation in mid-1973 of Chatto, Bodley Head & Jonathan Cape marks the greatest concentration of literary excellence that the British publishing trade had witnessed up to then. Paradoxically, what drew the imprints together was rather mundane – warehousing and distribution needs. The exceptional quality of the combined lists came as a by-product – albeit material and one that ultimately proved to be of decisive importance.

In today's world, corporate empires are often created – and dissolved – with a swoosh. The story behind Chatto, Bodley Head & Jonathan Cape is very different. It is a case of evolution. But it would be wrong to assume that this was at all times unperturbed and unhurrying. The process was spasmodic and the pace came to be marked by distinct acceleration.

CHATTO & WINDUS

Somewhat arbitrarily, the story may be said to begin with the absorption in 1945 of the Hogarth Press by Chatto & Windus. The Hogarth Press, started in 1917 by Leonard and Virginia Woolf as a recreation, had become a small business and, after Virginia Woolf's death in 1941, an increasing burden to Leonard Woolf.

Its backlist was hugely distinguished: Virginia herself, Sigmund Freud, T. S. Eliot, Maynard Keynes, Lytton Strachey, Rainer Maria Rilke, Anton Chekhov. ...

Ahead of the merger, Leonard Woolf duly sought and was readily granted guarantees of editorial independence, and once the press was safely in the custodial care of Ian Parsons and Chatto & Windus, he was able, as J. H. Willis elegantly expresses it, to relax into the garrulous pleasures of old age – travel, conversation, autobiography. Leonard Woolf became a partner in the enlarged company and a director in 1953, when it was converted into a private limited company.

The Chatto & Windus list was no less distinguished, and included such names as Aldous Huxley, William Faulkner, G. M. Trevelyan, T. F. Powys, Norman Douglas, and F. R. Leavis. Its ethos seemed peculiarly suited to the

Hogarth Press. In his evidence to the Restrictive Practices Court in 1962, Ian Parsons, whose career at Chatto & Windus began in 1928, recognized that non-commercial motives sometimes governed publishing decisions. A case in point was the firm's series Phoenix Living Poets, about which he said, 'I happen to be very interested in poetry. I like publishing poetry and I do not mind losing money on it.'

Half an hour later he was explaining to Mr Justice Buckley that his pre-tax profit margins were 7% in 1958, 12% in 1959, and 8.5% in 1960.

A concern for the bottom line as well as for literary excellence was bound to appeal to such a man as Leonard Woolf: while setting his face against expansion for fear of diluting the quality of his annual publishing programme of about twenty titles, he at the same time rigorously kept the Hogarth Press in the black throughout the 1920s and 1930s, even if in some years the surplus was measured in little more than shillings.

JONATHAN CAPE

At Cape the post-war period witnessed the sad sight of a dominant creative figure overstaying his welcome. In the period up to 1939, Jonathan Cape had presided over the creation of a list that had started auspiciously in 1921 with C. M. Doughty's *Travels in Arabia Deserta* and then gone on to include such names as Arthur Koestler, Ernest Hemingway, T. E. Lawrence, Eugene O'Neill, Sinclair Lewis, H. E. Bates, and H. G. Wells. At the end of the war he was 65 and set in his ways. In 1953 he suffered a severe stroke, and thereafter his health was subject to ups and downs. Notwithstanding, he continued to occupy the position of chairman until his death in February 1960 at the age of 80.

This is not to suggest that no new publishing was undertaken in the fifteen years that marked the end of his reign. Most famously, *Casino Royale* appeared in 1953, and this heralded a hugely successful association with Ian Fleming. But with Jonathan Cape still firmly in the editorial saddle, reliance on existing Cape authors increased, and the list became more and more in need of reju-venation. His reluctance to part with any shares discouraged the entry into the firm of younger blood, and his consequent failure to identify an internal successor led to some desultory conversations with a number of other literary houses.

Jonathan Cape's successor as chairman was his co-founder G. Wren Howard. Aged 67 at the time, he fell into the category of a caretaker chairman; in that role, however, he was greatly supported and influenced by his son Michael, himself a director since 1950. Michael Howard was largely respon-sible for attracting into the firm Tom Maschler, who joined within months of Jonathan's death. Tom Maschler came to Cape in June 1960 from Penguin, where he had worked as fiction editor, having previously had short stints with André Deutsch and MacGibbon & Kee. Aged 26, he was charged with the task of reviving the Cape list. He was made a director in July 1961. About a year later, Tom Maschler in turn introduced Graham C. Greene, 26 years old, to Cape. Greene, a nephew of the writer Graham Greene, joined as Cape sales director from Secker & Warburg in September 1962.

Two key positions had thus in the space of little more than two years been filled by a couple of talented, ambitious young men, both as it happened with strong publishing/literary connections. The yawning editorial lacuna had been plugged by Tom Maschler, while the sales post, for which Cape had not until then felt any great need, had been created for Graham C. Greene.

At this point, some comment on Cape's share structure is required. Jonathan Cape held seven-twelfths of the shares, Wren Howard five-twelfths. While Jonathan Cape can be criticized for failing to secure his successor in the critically important editorial role – let alone hand over responsibility to such a person in good time – he was not improvident with regard to the eventual disposition of his shares. He had given to Wren Howard and his son, Michael, an option to lift their family holding to seven-twelfths of Cape shares. On his death, this option was promptly exercised.

This left 41.7% in the estate, for which a home needed to be found. Since the purchaser(s) of these shares had to secure the approval of Michael and Wren Howard, at no stage was there any danger of a hostile takeover or the emergence of an unwelcome new shareholder. Minority stakes in unquoted companies are not the easiest things to shift, however, and so it proved on this occasion. It meant that Wren and Michael Howard were bound to entertain a proposition put to them in 1962, under which three disaffected Michael Joseph executives, Charles Pick, Peter Hebdon, and Roland Gant, with financial backing from Sir Allen Lane and Norman Collins (of Associated Television), would obtain a major stake in Cape.

An embarrassment came with the publication in the press of articles which treated the share purchase as 'a done deal' and represented it as a takeover of Cape. The wartime admonition that walls have ears, particularly those in certain areas of the Garrick Club, had clearly been ignored. Then came official confirmation, with a press statement issued by Cape that spelled out the minority position that Wren and Michael Howard would occupy. A month later *The Bookseller* conveyed the startling news to its readers that there was to be no change at Cape after all. The explanation given in Michael Howard's history of the company for this about-turn was that the refusal on the part of the Michael Joseph trio to retain the services of Tom Maschler had proved unacceptable to the Howards. Thus ended one of the earliest known attempts at a management buy-in in publishing.

Shortly thereafter, Sidney Bernstein took a further step into the world of book publishing when Granada bought from the estate the 41.7% holding and was given representation on the board. A year earlier he had acquired MacGibbon & Kee. The friendly nature of this investment was demonstrated in 1964, when the Howards and Granada agreed to reduce their holdings so as to enable Graham C. Greene and Tom Maschler to acquire an initial stake of 7% each.

With this diversion out of the way, the path was clear for the new team at Cape to concentrate on publishing and selling. One of the most striking innovations, and one that took Cape on to the fringes of the educational market, was the Jackdaw series. *The Battle of Trafalgar*, published in December 1963, was the first in a catalogue that grew to more than a hundred titles, where historical material was packaged in a dossier. This can now be seen as a precursor of the interactive products of today. Publication in 1964 of John Lennon's *John Lennon in His Own Write* was further, somewhat surprising, evidence of the fresh approach at Cape. In the trading accounts, the cumulative effect was a rise in turnover from £250,000 in 1961 to more than £500,000 in 1964 and more than £600,000 in 1965.

Recognition of the role played by Graham C. Greene and Tom Maschler in this renaissance came with their appointment in 1966 as joint managing directors. At about the same time, significant adjustments were also made to the share register: the Howard family interests relinquished control with their stake being reduced to 45%, while Granada dropped to 30%. The balance was accounted for by Tom Maschler with 16.7% and Graham C. Greene with 8.3%.

In the second half of the 1960s, the firm was clearly in fighting form. Its own publishing programme was shortly to make it, in Anthony Blond's eyes, 'probably the busiest literary publisher in London'. Its management headaches were behind it with two youthful joint managing directors in place, having strikingly complementary skills. At the same time, under the watchful gaze of the Howards, especially Michael, the traditional values of the firm were being sustained. Under these circumstances, it comes as no surprise that increasing thought should have been given to exploring opportunities for growth through alliances. The term takeover was not part of the Cape vocabulary.

A first step along this road was made in 1967, with the formation of a joint venture with the poetry publisher Goliard Press. The decision had been taken in 1966 to invest some of the surge of profits from the previous year in support of poetry. Tom Maschler was given the job to investigate and his choice fell on a small press, the spare-time occupation of two people. In order to ensure the continuing editorial independence of Goliard, an essential prerequisite for both parties, the two sides were put on an equal footing so that no one party could be overruled. In Michael Howard's words, 'We realized that far from being profitable, the enterprise might well lose money for a time and we should have no power to prevent it; but it seemed to us worthwhile to support such dedication in the cause of poetry.' Shades of Ian Parsons before Mr Justice Buckley.

A much more substantial opportunity came on the horizon briefly in 1968 when Heinemann looked ready to sell Secker & Warburg. Again to quote Michael Howard, 'The firm itself was friendly and familiar especially to

Graham, and represented the kind of cultural amenity that deserves sympathetic preservation.' Nothing, please note, about 'enhancing the bottom line' or 'building shareholder value'.

In the event, Heinemann withdrew and the flirtation was over. This enabled Cape management to devote itself wholeheartedly to the serious matter in hand, a two-year courtship of Chatto & Windus.

CHATTO & JONATHAN CAPE

In April 1967 Michael Howard, chairman of Jonathan Cape, had initiated a discussion with Ian Parsons, chairman of Chatto & Windus, with marriage as its subject. In May 1969 the two firms were formally united. The two years that elapsed from start to finish do not merely epitomize the pace of a more relaxed business environment than that of today. They also illustrate the fact that the two firms did not at the time feel any pressing threat from outside forces, even though the much exaggerated American invasion was then at its most credible.

From the Cape side the moving force was Graham C. Greene, with the meetings taking place in his London flat in Albany; maximum discretion was achieved through the use of the tradesman's entrance in preference to the main door. It was Greene who was particularly aware of the advantages that scale allied to technology could bring. This covered such areas as the computerization of accounts and stock control. It made sense to contemplate combining forces in warehousing and distribution. Further possibilities were seen to exist in collaboration over marketing and even sales, mainly overseas.

Ian Parsons, for his part, may also have given some thought to his age – he was approaching 65. Tom Maschler recalls: 'At Chatto they were all feeling mortal and wanting to be part of a team.'

The two publishing houses were already well known to each other. Personal links existed. The kind of publishing engaged in by both firms had much in common. In the climate of today, such a profile would cry out for post-merger rationalization and rebranding. In the 1960s, in the offices of Chatto and Cape, it called for the creation of a structure that would guarantee the editorial independence of both parties. This had been a cardinal principle behind the union of Hogarth Press and Chatto & Windus, as it was in the formation of Cape Goliard. So also with Chatto and Cape. The extent to which acceptance of this principle coloured all discussions is illustrated throughout a long letter Michael Howard wrote to Ian Parsons in April 1969. A representative passage reads: 'It is probable that there will be ways in which our paperback series will complement one another and gain in marketing and promotion. But otherwise we do not see at present that there can be or should be any overlap on the editorial or sub-editorial areas.'

Those guaranteeing the preservation of the separate identity of the two firms were to be the two chairmen, Ian Parsons and Michael Howard, who became joint chairmen of the new holding company, supported on each side by three board members, Norah Smallwood, Cecil Day-Lewis, and Geoffrey Trevelyan on the one hand, Tom Maschler, Graham C. Greene and W. Robert Carr (Granada's representative) on the other. As to the name, it seemed only courteous that Chatto, founded in 1855, should take precedence over Cape, a 1921 upstart, notwithstanding that its business (turnover of £582,000 in 1968) was only three-quarters the size of Cape's (£796,000). Admittedly, there had been some give and take in the negotiations with the dropping of Windus from the masthead. (The last sighting of Chatto's colleague, W. E. Windus, identified by Ian Norrie as a minor poet, had been around 1875.)

The financial basis of the merger gave Cape shareholders 60% of the new holding company and Chatto shareholders 40%. And yet Michael Howard was able to announce 'in this combined company control will be 50:50'. This sleight of hand was made possible by the creation of two classes of shares: 800,000 voting shares divided equally between Cape and Chatto, and 200,000 non-voting shares that went only to Cape. For economic reality to intrude into the boardroom, it was furthermore provided that fifteen years would have to elapse, at which point the non-voters were to become enfranchised.

THE BODLEY HEAD

Four years after Chatto & Windus allied itself to Cape, the Bodley Head joined the fold. On this occasion, the merger led to the emergence of a key new share-holder: Max Reinhardt.

Max Reinhardt's background was cosmopolitan and romantic. Born in 1915 of Italian parents in what was then Constantinople, he was educated at the English High School in Constantinople, where his father, an architect, worked for Kemal Ataturk. His university days were largely spent in France. The start of the war found him in England, representing the family trading firm's interests and occupying space in the City offices of his accountants, Spicer & Pegler. After serving in the Royal Air Force during the war, despite the awkward possession of an Italian passport, he renewed his pre-war links with the accountants. When the firm sought to dispose of H. Foulkes Lynch, its publishing and accountancy training firm, he grasped the opportunity; he also accepted the condition that he should take on the loss-making printer, Stellar Press. The total cost came to £5000. The financial success of HFL Limited, which was to be kept separate from his other business interests, helped finance his venture into trade publishing, under the Max Reinhardt imprint. His friendship with Ralph Richardson and Anthony Quayle, who became fellow directors in 1948, gave his debut in trade publishing a theatrical bias, as did no doubt his marriage to his first wife, the actress Margaret Leighton.

In mid-1956, he was approached by the merchant bankers Henry Ansbacher, on Ralph Richardson's introduction, with a view to his joining in the purchase of the Bodley Head. This distinguished imprint had gone into voluntary liquidation in 1936 and had been saved from extinction by Sir Stanley Unwin the following year. Sir Stanley himself put up two-thirds of the money towards the cost of buying the assets, while Wren Howard and W. G. Taylor (of Dent) on a personal basis put up the balance. Sir Stanley took on the roles of chairman and managing director. By the 1950s he was looking to shed the burden, having restored the business to profitability.

Terms were agreed, with Max Reinhardt and three Henry Ansbacher partners having two equal shares, Max's contribution being largely satisfied by the injection of Max Reinhardt Limited. The sum paid was £72,000. Two years later, Max was able to lift his holding to 80%. Close links were retained with the merchant bank, with George Ansley of Ansbacher becoming chairman of the Bodley Head and 'Boy' Hart, a fellow director, also joining the board of the Bodley Head, in which he was a shareholder.

The subsequent development of the Bodley Head in the final years of the 1950s and throughout the 1960s was marked by a number of acquisitions, in the financing of which Ansbacher often played a role, and the creation of a broadly-based trade list. Charles Chaplin, Georgette Heyer, Alistair Cooke, and J. B. Priestley were among authors who featured prominently. The establishment of an outstanding children's list under Judy Taylor, with Anatole and Captain Pugwash to the fore, was a source of particular pride.

One development that deserves special mention in this history took place in 1962, the year that Graham Greene (the author) severed his links with Heinemann and chose the Bodley Head to be his publisher. His move was prompted by a botched attempt in 1961 at a merger of Heinemann and the Bodley Head (a design that had had his full support) and which left him feeling that Heinemann's owners, the Tilling Corporation, did not deserve his fullest confidence. As he explained at the time, 'I have had many years' experience of publishing, I am a director of the Bodley Head (he had been a board member since 1957) and a personal friend of Max Reinhardt.'

The Greene connection was further strengthened in 1969 when Sir Hugh Greene, former director-general of the BBC, took over the chairmanship of the Bodley Head from George Ansley; in addition to being the novelist's brother, he was Graham C. Greene's father.

As the Bodley Head's business expanded – sales in 1971 exceeded £700,000 – pressures on the support departments increased, existing warehouse and distribution arrangements needed enlarging and wider computer applications explored. Little surprise that the board should have given increasing thought to the merits of combining forces with other publishers sharing the same challenges. Chatto & Jonathan Cape was an obvious candidate. Its own merger had gone well: on the all-important issue of editorial independence the evidence from both partners had been thoroughly reassuring, and there were the personal family links already mentioned.

From Chatto & Jonathan Cape's point of view, the last four years had given management a taste for what volume increases could make possible. There was also the realization that additional scale was needed in order to bring some economies and efficiencies within reach. The Bodley Head list had much to recommend it to Chatto and to Cape, and the same family connections formed a natural bond. In short, the choice of the Bodley Head as a third partner had considerable attraction.

There were other points of empathy. One of these concerned typographical standards. For Ruari McLean, writing in 1951, 'Chatto & Windus have probably the longest unbroken record of excellence in book design of any London publishers still in business.' While Jonathan Cape may have been criticized for a certain sameness in design – Hugh Walpole thought the books came from some kind of intellectual factory – not everybody shared such views and the books became famously recognizable for the high quality of the creamy John Dickinson & Co. paper, their rich binding cloths and their typographic sobriety.

The importance attached by Max Reinhardt to quality in book production is demonstrated by his choice of two celebrated typographers, Will Carter in the 1950s and, from 1957, John Ryder, as his book designers. The Bodley Head historian, J. W. Lambert, was of the opinion that 'Ryder's combination of clarity, elegance, and visually durable impact has given the Bodley Head books their unmistakable quality'. And if any further evidence is required of Max Reinhardt's typographic credentials, there is the partnership he formed with Sir Francis Meynell when the opportunity of starting again the Nonesuch Press presented itself in 1953.

The merger valued the Bodley Head at 35% of the combined group and Chatto & Jonathan Cape at 65%. This corresponded closely to the turnover ratios for the 1972 calendar year, with the Bodley Head's turnover representing 36% of the whole (£814,000) and that of Chatto & Jonathan Cape 64% (£1,474,000). At an earlier stage in the negotiations a 42:58 split had been suggested by accountants Spicer & Pegler as a sensible basis. But as Max Reinhardt wrote at the conclusion of the negotiations to a fellow director, 'I know that we might have deserved a bigger share, but I don't mind so much; I was in a generous mood because it is really the quality of the partnership that is most important. As you will realize I was keen on the project and pleased that we have come to an agreement. I am quite confident in the long run it will be to the advantage of everybody.'

The merger of the Bodley Head with Chatto & Jonathan Cape was announced in August 1973 and the statement carried the now familiar assurance of editorial integrity. It was reinforced on this occasion with a stirring concluding flourish that would have warmed the hearts of the signatories of the *Declaration of Independence*: 'Each publishing house will continue to have complete freedom to publish the kind of books it wishes, under the same imprints as previously, responsible to nobody but itself and its authors.'

The composition of the boards served as a warranty. On the board of Chatto,

Bodley Head & Jonathan Cape, the renamed holding company, the pattern of joint chairmen was preserved, with Max Reinhardt joining Ian Parsons and Graham C. Greene (who had succeeded Michael Howard in that position in May 1970); the other directors with their affiliations were (a) from Chatto, Norah Smallwood, Hugo Brunner, Geoffrey Trevelyan; (b) from Cape, Michael Howard, Tom Maschler, W. R. Carr; and (c) from the Bodley Head, John Hews and Judy Taylor. Beneath the holding company were the three operating companies, each with its own board. Ian Parsons continued as managing director of Chatto (to be succeeded on his retirement at the end of 1974 by Norah Smallwood); Max Reinhardt and Graham C. Greene were managing directors of the Bodley Head and Jonathan Cape respectively, in addition to their responsibilities as joint chairmen of the holding company.

The pattern of shareholdings was greatly altered by the introduction of the Bodley Head into the group. It led to the addition of 538,460 new shares, bringing the total issued capital to 1,538,460 shares. Max Reinhardt as 80% owner of the Bodley Head received 430,768 shares and became thereby the largest single shareholder.

The summer of 1973 was an exhilarating one to have lived through. As Max Reinhardt recalls, 'We were all good friends, all very proud of our lists. To begin with it was perfect, we trusted each other.'

Underwriting this spirit of enthusiasm had been the modestly profitable trading experience of the three operating companies. Jonathan Cape, on sales in 1972 of £851,000, had profits of £25,000, Chatto on sales of £623,000 had profits of £11,000 and the Bodley Head on sales of £669,000 had profits of £27,000. Such comparisons should not, however, be scrutinized too closely because of different year-ends, and to some extent accounting practices.

In the event, the timing of the merger proved fortunate in that it took place ahead of the 1974-75 recession. On their own, some of these firms might have had difficulty coping. The greatest recessionary impact was felt in 1975, when all three moved into the red, with the group reporting losses of £216,000 on sales of £3,286,000; this represented an adverse swing of £420,000 from profits of £204,000 the previous year.

Management was not deflected, however, from its goal of exploiting the advantages of scale to develop the central services that the three firms saw as one of the main reasons for their participation in the group. A central sales and marketing organization had already been formed in December 1972; the Bodley Head list was taken on shortly after the merger. The main item of capital expenditure was the construction of the group's own warehouse and distribution centre at Grantham. During the course of 1974 and 1975 £420,000 was spent on land, buildings, and equipment, largely financed by a mortgage from the National Westminster Bank. The centre was opened by Michael Foot MP. Graham C. Greene recalls that the Sogat (Society of Graphical and Allied Trades) Father of the Chapel – shop steward in any other industry – confided to a somewhat startled Michael Foot that the warehouse was seriously overmanned but that he was quite sure that 'Mr Greene had plans'.

An important editorial initiative occurred in July 1975 with the incorporation of Triad paperbacks. An alliance was formed with Granada whereby the latter's sales force would carry, under the Triad paperback imprint, titles, agreed to by Granada, which the editors at Chatto, Bodley Head & Jonathan Cape put forward. With 17.5% of the shares held by each of the Chatto, Bodley Head, and Jonathan Cape companies (aggregating 52.5%), Granada's stake was 47.5%. At the time it was seen to be a sensible way of giving CBC more of a presence in an expanding market and one for which some in the industry – but not everybody – were forecasting explosive growth. It limited the trading risks and was also economical on capital, a resource to which CBC, as a tightly held unquoted company had restricted access.

As a result of these and other actions, the group emerged from the recession better placed than would otherwise have been the case to benefit from a healthier trading environment. There was a return to profit in 1976 and a marked improvement the following year, when pre-tax profits stood at £487,000 on turnover of £4,939,000; this represented a healthy margin of nearly 10%. The strategy looked as if it was working.

In trying to recapture the atmosphere of those days, Liz Calder recalls that when Tom Maschler recruited her she was given a somewhat backhanded compliment when he said that there was just one book that she had published at Gollancz that he regretted not having secured for Cape: *The World According to Garp* by John Irving. Liz's role at Cape was to publish books alongside Tom, who stood ready to challenge but not to overrule. And she experienced, as had Michael Howard before her, what it was to be carried along by Tom's literary enthusiasms and brilliant advocacy.

The next few years were hugely productive for both of them – and indeed for the group as a whole. If the Booker Prize is taken as a measure of success in fiction, 1981 was the apogee: Cape had the winner with Salman Rushdie's *Midnight's Children*; Cape also supplied two of the shortlisted titles and the Bodley Head one. Chatto stayed on the sidelines, having won in 1978. And when it came to paperbacks, Liz and Tom concurred: 'We felt we had such desirable books that we could – and did – maximize their potential, selling the rights to all the good paperback houses.' Typically, this did not include Triad paperbacks.

There was not much contact between the imprints, other than through personal friendships and at an annual picnic. The centralized sales operation was a pretty remote affair, with very little exchange of information. However, each imprint had a fortnightly sales conference with the head of sales, together with the UK and export sales managers, at which they presented their titles.

Liz Calder was the first woman to join the Cape board. She remembers Graham C. Greene as a benign and somewhat remote figure, much occupied by his other responsibilities, both inside and outside the firm. His outside duties included the Publishers Association, where he filled the demanding post of president in 1977-79. He was a trustee of the British Museum, he was on the board of the merchant bankers Guinness Mahon (one of his Guinness family connections), and a director of the brewers Greene King and of the Statesman & Nation, the publisher of the *New Statesman*. His internal responsibilities had much to do with administration, with him chairing the central services company and the warehouse subsidiary, as well as exercising control of the purse strings. On the editorial front, political biographies were one of his areas of particular involvement. In most publishing houses, the leading lights are intent on finding a Salman Rushdie (as Liz Calder had done), rather than making their reputation by cutting a couple of days off delivery times. Deep gratitude is felt, but not always acknowledged, when somebody of stature concerns himself with the humdrum.

A further vignette concerns the aura of a long-established and proud literary imprint. There is a certain resistance to change, reinforced by a hierarchical tradition symbolized by carpets in the directors' offices, linoleum elsewhere, from which Cape was not totally immune. This gave rise to a somewhat blinkered 'we've always done it this way' attitude.

The group approached the end of the 1970s in comparative comfort: the centralized services and warehousing were in full operation, there was a lot of editorial ebullience and Triad Publishing was moving ahead, albeit not at the speed or on the scale that some might have hoped. It is true that in the two years, 1978 and 1979, operating margins fell sharply from their 1977 high of 10% to 6.5% but with sales advancing rapidly the absolute levels of pre-tax profits remained pretty steady. When the recession of 1980 hit the UK publishing industry, a near-lethal combination of galloping domestic inflation and surging sterling, Chatto, Bodley Head & Jonathan Cape stayed triumphantly profitable. This was more than Penguin or Collins achieved at the time.

Underlying this relatively reassuring overall picture were some specific areas of concern. First, at the operating level, before contributions from Triad, all three companies were loss-making in 1980. Second, although there was a significant advance for the group as a whole in 1981, with Jonathan Cape swinging back into profit at the operating level, the other two companies were still in deficit. Third, there was the special case of Chatto & Windus, whose profitability at the operating level in the period from 1973 to 1981 had been undistinguished: three years in the black, six in the red, including the last three. The warning lights were flashing. Jeremy Lewis in his book of publishing reminiscences reported that Chatto, under the directorship of the indomitable Norah Smallwood, was at the time dying on its feet. A successor to Norah, who was in poor health but unwilling to retire, was a looming necessity.

Graham C. Greene can take most of the credit for having identified Carmen Callil as the appropriate successor to Norah Smallwood. This received the enthusiastic endorsement of the other joint chairman, Max Reinhardt.

With Carmen came an attachment in the shape of the feminist publishing house Virago, which she had founded in 1972. Harriet Spicer, originally Carmen's secretary, and Ursula Owen, who joined a little later, were then to form a powerful triumvirate. Carmen was greatly attracted to the prospect of running a long-established literary publisher of the quality of Chatto & Windus. She found the Bloomsbury links particularly seductive. At the same time she was hugely possessive of Virago, which she had reason to regard as her creation. From the start of the discussions with Graham C. Greene, it was therefore made clear that if she were to join the group to take charge of Chatto, Virago needed to be accommodated as well.

From the standpoint of CBC, Virago was seen as an acceptable addition to the existing imprints. It had a vigorous publishing programme: 43 titles in 1981, 52 planned for 1982. Its original publishing by then accounted for about half the business and reprints the other half. There was a prophetic touch to the fact that the first Virago title after it had separated itself from Quartet in 1976 should have involved the reissue of a Hogarth Press book, graced, more-over, with an introduction by Virginia Woolf: *Life as We Have Known It*, a collection of oral accounts by working-class women, edited by Margaret Llewelyn Davies. Virago was furthermore a profitable business, with operating profits in the year to 28 February 1982 of £55,900 on sales of £568,200. Also to be considered was the fact that its absorption into the group would add to the throughput of the central warehousing and distribution operations.

Within the Virago camp, the less than ego-building realization that in the purchaser's eyes the primary attraction lay in securing the services of Carmen disturbed the other two main shareholders, who feared that their interests and those of Carmen might diverge. Ursula Owen and Harriet Spicer were also concerned about the editorial integrity of Virago, a worry that should have been allayed by a swift glance at the history of the development of the CBC group. The original idea that had found favour with Carmen that Virago become a subsidiary of Chatto & Windus was consequently anathema to them. In the event, Virago was to enter the family as a sister company of the three publishing subsidiaries, notwithstanding its relatively small size, and, under pressure from the Virago executives, its position was publicly enshrined one year later in the holding company's name of Chatto, Virago, Bodley Head & Jonathan Cape.

Within Virago creative tension had become a way of life. This may have had something to do with the voting structure, which by 1979 was divided 46.2% to Carmen, 30.8% to Ursula and 23% to Harriet. Any two had the majority – or to put it the other way, no single shareholder was in control. (By the time

Virago was acquired by CBC, 15% of the capital was held by other share-holders, thereby reducing proportionately these percentages.) When the possibility of the sale of the company came up for consideration, the tensions inherent in Virago became converted into mutual suspicion. At one point the three main shareholders were taking separate legal advice. It also meant that the discussions extended over a period of a year, rather than one week, which Ursula Owen remembers had been Graham C. Greene's expectation.

LOOKING AT THE UP SIDE

But there was also a lot of common ground between them. For Virago, association with a much more substantial operation opened up the prospects of greater stability on several counts. It had been through a number of unsettling changes in the warehousing and distribution of Virago titles. As Carmen was to promise the authors once the transaction was completed, they would enjoy 'a full sales and distribution service throughout the world and a distribution and warehouse system of exceptional efficiency and other services too dreary to list here'. In addition, there was the potential open to a company that had scrimped and scraped all its life through being given access to enlarged financial resources. A further advantage to Virago shareholders was the unlocking of equity values and consequently the receipt of substantial sums in cash. This was, however, far from being the overriding consideration behind their agreement to sell.

The structure that was finally established was that Carmen Callil should become the non-executive chairman of Virago; Ursula and Harriet were made joint managing directors in succession to Carmen. Carmen for her part was to join the holding company board and become joint managing director of Chatto with Hugo Brunner; she received at the same time an undertaking that she would become sole managing director within two years.

Virago's asking price was not less than £300,000. CBC'S original thinking, as advised by accountants Spicer & Pegler, had been £150,000. In the event, the final price of £244,000 gave effect to the evidence of buoyant trading at Virago and to some hard bargaining on its part. Also, at Virago's insistence the great majority of the consideration was cash – £206,000 in two tranches. The balance was satisfied through the issue of 130,393 CBC shares valued at 30p; this corresponded to the level at which CBC shares had recently been traded. Carmen Callil argued forcefully that this was the relevant valuation rather than the much higher net asset value per share figure. Provision was also made for performance-related payments, with the vendors due to receive 40% of the gross profits in excess of £190,000 for the first ten months to end-1982 and 40% in excess of £230,000 for the full year 1983. This gave them, as it turned out, £85,000 for 1982 and a tidy £155,000 for 1983.

Financially, 1982 was Chatto, Virago, Bodley Head & Jonathan Cape's banner

Table 25: *Trading record*

Year to 31 December	1982*	1983	1984	1985	1986
Turnover (£000)	13,301	13,426	16,259	16,391	18,322
Gross profit (£000)	5705	5814	6816	6979	7274
Gross margins	42.9%	43.3%	41.9%	42.6%	39.7%
Operating profit (£000)	875	428	489	(89)	(90)
Net interest	+55	+5	−127	−319	−364
Pre-tax profit (£000)	929	433	362	(408)	(454)
Pre-tax margins	7.0%	3.2%	2.2%	(2.5%)	(2.5%)

*Includes Virago results for 10 months: turnover £676,000, operating profit £72,000.

year, with pre-tax profits rising to £929,000 on turnover of £13.3m. If Virago's results for the ten months that were consolidated following its acquisition are taken out of the figures, 1982 profits were 1.75 times larger than those of 1977, the previous year of peak profitability for the group.

The subsequent four-year record, however, makes chilling reading (see table 25).

On the revenue front, the near-40% increase in turnover in the period covered, representing a compound rate of growth of 8.3%, may look acceptable at first glance. However, when set against inflation running at 4.8%, it indicates an annual real rate of growth of a mere 3.5%.

Indeed, a recurring lament within the individual publishing houses, other than Virago, was the lack of volume increases that they were able to achieve. Responsibility for this comparative stagnation can be laid at the now familiar door of the group's limited involvement in paperbacks and heavy dependence on hardbacks.

The mid-1980s probably marked the low point in demand for hardbacks, with the institutional market contracting and the consumer increasingly shifting to soft covers. Of particular relevance to Chatto, Virago, Bodley Head & Jonathan Cape (CVBC) was the burgeoning of the B-format paperbacks, such as Pan's Picador imprint. While this admittedly offered opportunities in the form of subsidiary rights, and was potentially a valuable source of cash flow, in its impact on sales it was clearly not a substitute for direct ownership of paperback imprints.

The story of costs is best considered at two levels. First, the cost of sales expressed as a percentage of turnover (see table 26). Such costs were held broadly steady up to 1985. In 1986, however, a sharp jump in special sales, on which low gross margins were accepted, pushed the percentage up sharply.

Costs that are treated as being internal to the organization fall into two categories: selling and distribution costs, and administrative and editorial costs. Once again, these can be expressed as a percentage of turnover (see table 27).

Selling and distribution costs appear to have been kept under good control, and indeed to have been on an improving trend in the final two years. It is in

Table 26: *Cost of sales as percentage of turnover*

Year to 31 December	1982	1983	1984	1985	1986
	57.1%	56.7%	58.1%	57.4%	60.3%

Table 27: *Operating costs as percentage of turnover*

Year to 31 December	1982	1983	1984	1985	1986
Selling and distrib. costs	20.2%	21.2%	21.1%	20.9%	19.3%
Admin. and editorial costs	16.1%	18.9%	17.8%	22.2%	20.9%
Total	36.3%	40.1%	38.9%	43.1%	40.2%

the control of administrative and editorial costs that the real weakness lay. Such costs were on a steep upward curve, rising as a proportion of turnover by as much as 38% in the three years from 1982.

Much of the evident lack of sensitivity to the deteriorating performance of the group that this illustrates can be related to the issue of editorial independence. In the spirit of the assurances given repeatedly since the absorption of the Hogarth Press by Chatto & Windus in 1945, editorial and related departments were treated as no-go areas to anyone outside the individual houses. This had numerical as well as geographic consequences.

On the numerical front, it meant that if economies were called for, publishing managements would look 'every which way' before considering editorial. Geographically, creative freedom was seen as demanding physical divorce in different buildings, with the attendant overheads that that implies – all the more significant when the addresses are in the West End of London.

By the start of 1986, the holding company board had become sufficiently exercised over the trading performance of the group to call for wide-ranging cost savings and, even more significantly, substantial reorganization. This was to include the sharing by Jonathan Cape and the Bodley Head of such services as copy-editing, publicity, production, and rights. It also involved moving the two editorial departments under one roof.

The thoroughly revolutionary feature was the inclusion of nine editorial posts in the 26 redundancies that the reorganization originally called for. The state of shock that this provided is faithfully reflected in an apocalyptic address that the Bodley Head directors presented to the holding company board. 'We foresee that a move of the editorial department to 32 Bedford Square would virtually signal the end of the imprint: the practical result is that no agent or author is going to address any manuscript to any publisher other than Cape at 32.'

Reference to 32 Bedford Square is important. It is not a typographical error for 30 Bedford Square, which had been the home of Cape since 1925. In the middle of 1984, the decision had been taken to acquire a 25-year lease on the

Table 28: *Indebtedness*

Year to 31 December	1981	1982	1983	1984	1985	1986
Borrowings (£000)	(308)	(225)	(796)	(2272)	(2862)	(3425)
Cash (£000)	253	984	64	207	95	9
Balance (£000)	(55)	759	(732)	(2065)	(2767)	(3416)

adjoining building, 32 Bedford Square, with a view to having Cape move into it a year later. Bodley Head, for its part, would then leave its Bow Street offices to occupy 30 Bedford Square. The refurbishment of Number 32 was grand and lavish. In Liz Calder's retrospective judgement this was a very bad move, though at the time she applauded the outlay, while Ursula Owen says it gave the signal that overheads were out of control. It certainly represented a net increase in space and added significantly to group overheads.

Group operating profits, which had stood at £875,000 in 1982, had been converted into a loss of £89,000 in 1985 and one of £90,000 in 1986 (see table 25). This adverse swing was further reinforced at the net interest line with interest receipts of £55,000 in 1982 being replaced by net interest payments of £319,000 in 1985, and £364,000 in 1986. This proclaimed a massive weakening of the balance sheet.

At the end of 1981, the group balance sheet was essentially debt free – cash of £253,000 against borrowings of £308,000. The following year, in the wake of record results, the group had net cash of more than £750,000. In the ensuing four years there was a dramatic deterioration, year by year, with the 31 December 1986 position showing net debt of £3.4m, an adverse swing of £4.2m since 1982 (see table 28).

Where had the money gone? Nearly £370,000 had been spent on buying the company's own shares and £271,000 had been paid out to Granada in accumulated reserves in 1983, once the decision was taken that Triad should cease to trade. Additions to fixed assets were heaviest in 1984 and 1985, with expenditure over and above depreciation of £630,000. This covered, among other outlays, an extension to the Grantham warehouse and the big Bedford Square refurbishments. More generally, there was the industry-wide escalation in advances to authors; in 1985 alone, the group's increase in advances to authors amounted to £345,000. And then, of course, there was the drain represented by a decisive move into losses.

How did the group seek to manage this deteriorating financial position? The short answer is: slowly to start with. The increased presence of the group in Bedford Square and the embellishments that were undertaken were hardly calculated to set amber lights flashing. Furthermore, the number of people within the group who were in a position to recognize the significance of any such flashes had they occurred was severely limited. The publishing company executives were busy publishing, and on the holding company board there was a ready acceptance that, on financial matters, 'one could leave it to Graham'.

After all, Graham C. Greene's experience set him apart from the rest of them. There was also comfort in the knowledge that the accountants Spicer & Pegler were in the wings as auditors. This was particularly relevant to Max Reinhardt, whose friendship and links with them extended to pre-war days. He, moreover, had introduced them to the group and following the 1973 merger they had been appointed auditors to all the group companies.

Nonetheless, the periodic visits to the manager of the National Westminster Bank in Lombard Street – another introduction of Max's – quickly ceased to be a courteous formality. The 1983 year-end saw the company overdrawn for the first time to the extent of £700,000. A year later the overdraft had risen to £2.2m and by the end of 1985 to £2.8m. Bearing in mind that the peak borrowing period occurred in March/April, with the payment of royalties amounting to as much as £1m, it is hardly surprising that requests that the banking facility be increased became a feature of these visits undertaken by the two joint chairmen.

Belated attention was also directed to improving the working capital position. Stocks and work in progress, having outstripped the growth in turnover between 1982 and 1985, were sharply cut back during the course of 1986.

As far as capital-raising initiatives were concerned, 1986 witnessed the mortgaging of a property in New South Wales, which raised £200,000, and the sale of assets, which raised some £400,000. This included the aeronautical list of the Bodley Head's subsidiary, Putnam, and – more contentiously – the volume rights of Jeffrey Archer's first two books, *Not a Penny More, Not a Penny Less* and *Shall We Tell the President?*. Both books went to Hodder & Stoughton, which had already paperbacked them under the Coronet imprint. Also put up for sale by the Bodley Head were six Agatha Christie titles that were bought by Collins. There was talk in the trade of outright sales of rights to Penguin, affecting such authors as Virginia Woolf, F. Scott Fitzgerald, and James Joyce. This probably had its origins in the fact that CVBC had for a number of years treated its assets in somewhat the same way as a property development company treats its buildings: some are developed for inclusion in the investment portfolio, some are developed for the trading account, and some that are in the investment portfolio are occasionally shifted into the trading account. The analogy is imperfect, not least because of the permutations when a plurality of rights attaches to individual titles. As is acknowledged by Simon Master, who was appointed chief executive of CVBC in June 1987, active management of this kind had, by the time it was incorporated into Random House, given the portfolio a pronounced Emmenthal quality.

Easily the most important capital-raising exercise, however, came with the July 1986 rights issue. By early June, the bank overdraft had risen to £3.4m, despite management's best endeavours. This put CVBC uncomfortably close to its bank facility ceiling of £3.6m, particularly since the period of peak seasonal indebtedness had not yet fully run its course. Alarmingly, the National

Table 29: *Percentage of share ownership*

Year end	Issued shares (m)	Graham C. Greene (%)	Tom Maschler (%)	Max Reinhardt (%)	Granada (%)	Other main board directors (%)	Others (%)
1973	1.54	7.8	7.8	28.0	11.8	20.7	23.9
1981	1.54	12.5	12.5	34.6	21.1	14.4	4.9
1982	1.67	12.8	12.8	35.4	19.5	14.8	4.7
1983	1.34	15.9	15.9	44.0		18.4	5.8
1984	1.00	21.2	21.2	25.0		19.6	13.0
1985	1.00	24.6	24.6	25.0		17.8	8.0
1986	2.26	40.7	36.0	11.1		7.0	5.3

Westminster Bank declined at this point to increase the facility. A resulting cash flow crisis was only just averted by Graham C. Greene giving the bank a personal guarantee, following which the facility was raised to £3.8m. Having once obtained essential temporary short-term finance, the company was then able to go ahead with the rights issue, raising £923,000. When the money was received in mid-July, £600,000 was applied to repaying in full Graham's bridging loan.

A financial performance of this kind is bound to set up tensions. The experience at Chatto, Virago, Bodley Head & Jonathan Cape proved no exception. And yet, the suddenness with which harmony gave way to disharmony was remarkable. Much of this is captured in the share register.

The story is best taken from the time of the purchase for shares of the Bodley Head in 1973. This involved a rise of 50% in the issued capital to 1.54 million shares (see table 29). In the ensuing thirteen years, there were four transactions that affected this total. One has to wait nine years until 1982 for the first change brought about by the purchase of Virago and the issue of some 130,000 shares in part payment. They were valued at 30p a share. One year later, the company bought back for cancellation Granada's holding, which by then had risen to 325,000 shares, at a price of 35.3p a share. Another twelve months elapsed before the company again acquired a block for cancellation, this time 339,000 shares belonging to Max Reinhardt, paying 75p per share. And in July 1986 a massive rights issue more than doubled the issued capital, lifting the total by more than 1.25 million shares to 2.26 million shares; the subscription price was 78p.

Turning to the fluctuations of individual share-holdings, the starting-point in the middle of 1973 shows Max Reinhardt as the largest single shareholder, with 28% of the stock; Graham C. Greene and Tom Maschler each held 7.8% and Granada 11.8%. The other 'main board directors' with 20.7% were former Chatto & Windus shareholders – Norah Smallwood and Ian Parsons each with identical holdings of 5.25%, Hugo Brunner with 4.1%, and

Geoffrey Trevelyan 6.1%; with the exception of Trevelyan they were all working directors.

The residual 'all other' classification was largely made up of the Howard family trusts 12.1%, J. F. Charlton 4.1%, L. A. Hart 4.5%, and F. Levy 2.5%. The last three owed their presence on the share register to the earlier assimilation of Chatto & Windus (J. F. Charlton) and the Bodley Head (L. A. Hart, F. Levy). Charlton was a working director; Hart and Levy were Ansbacher partners. This left a thin tail of holders, speaking for 0.7% of the equity.

As table 29 shows, by 1981 Max, Graham, and Tom had all added to their stakes, such shares coming principally from outside the holding company board and to a lesser extent from their colleagues on the board. The sharpness of the fall in the 'all other' category, which went from 23.9% in 1973 to 4.9% in 1981, is in striking contrast to what often happens in private companies due to dispersions on the death of large shareholders and pressing personal needs for pools and yachts. And when such a company uses its shares to make acquisitions – as had been the case with Chatto & Jonathan Cape when it merged with the Bodley Head – the shares normally become spread that much more widely. Not so with CVBC.

The board decisions to cancel the two large lines of stock that were put up for sale suggest that a policy of tighter share ownership was actually being pursued. This served to reinforce an existing centripetal tendency flowing from the fact that when shares were presented for sale they were offered on a *pro rota* basis to existing holders. At the same time, there was no formal system in place to help 'deserving executives' to buy stock. This did not mean, however, that the share register was actually closed to new names. John Hews and Judy Taylor both initially acquired 1000 shares each in 1975; David Machin's stake, which eventually rose to 5000 shares, also had its start in 1975, as did Dennis Enright's and Tony Colwell's. In October 1986 divisional directors were invited to take up 14,000 of the unissued shares relating to the rights issue; seven new holdings were thereby created. All of this, however, adds up to small beer. There are no echoes of the generous dispositions made to enable Graham and Tom to become sizeable shareholders in Cape in their early days with that firm.

Hodder & Stoughton, albeit a larger and more diversified group than was CVBC, provides an interesting contrast. In 1993, when it was absorbed into Headline, 80% of the shares were held by descendants of the founder, Matthew Hodder – few having any direct involvement with the firm – while the remaining 20% was largely in the hands of employees. As a result, Hodder & Stoughton rejoiced in a shareholder list that stretched to 160 names.

At CVBC, readiness to see the equity base become more concentrated in terms of ownership, and even to contract in absolute terms, may be said to have inhibited the development of the group by making the raising of fresh equity capital more problematical. The onus fell on too few shoulders. Interestingly, Hodder & Stoughton ran up against similar difficulties for precisely the opposite reasons: the wide dispersal of its shares among individuals whose financial circumstances did not on the whole leave them with much headroom for subscribing to additional equity, effectively ruled out a rights issue when the need for more capital arose. One possible moral that emerges from these two tales is that both extremes are best avoided. Another might be that, in a cash hungry business, the need at some stage to secure access to outside equity funds is hard to sidestep.

GRANADA PULLS OUT

The disappearance of Granada from the share register in 1983 calls for some comment. By taking up its entitlements as shares came on offer, it saw its holdings rise in absolute terms from 182,000 shares in 1973 to a peak of some 325,000 shares by 1982, and this had lifted its stake from 11.8% to 19.5%. The decision to sell this holding coincided with its decision to withdraw from publishing through the sale, announced in March 1983, of Granada Publishing to Collins.

From the point of view of CVBC, the removal from the share register of what had become a large outside presence was regarded positively. Separately, there was by then some dissatisfaction with the Triad arrangements: results were not living up to earlier hopes, not least because of the failure of the imprint to achieve recognition. Following Collins's takeover of Granada Publishing, the relationship with Triad became that much more anomalous and, later that year, agreement was reached that it should be wound down. This presented CVBC with the opportunity to pursue other options, which culminated in the setting up in mid-1985 of a co-publishing agreement with Pan. This was on a 50:50 basis, involving the paperbacking under the appropriate Pan imprint of titles submitted by CVBC and accepted by Pan. CVBC's favoured plan that it become a fourth shareholder in Pan with Heinemann, Macmillan, and Collins had been rejected.

As to the main individual shareholdings, it is clear that a Siamese rule governed Graham and Tom's percentages which kept perfect step from one year to the next up to 1986. In that year, both of them greatly increased their holdings when they between them took up virtually the whole of the rights issue; the symmetry was broken, however, with Graham's position becoming greater than Tom's. For Tom, subscription also meant borrowing (with Graham's backing) much of the £450,000 required to take up his block of shares.

The faith that Graham and Tom had in the company clearly never wavered. Neither of them ever sold a share. And when the opportunity arose to add to their holdings they took it. There was also the little matter of the personal guarantee granted by Graham to the bank. Max, to whom the same request was made by the bank, turned it down. Graham's swift action had the huge merit of enabling the company to trade its way clear of some very nasty rocks.

The history of Max Reinhardt's shareholding is complex. His starting position of 28% (431,000 shares) put him well ahead of Graham and Tom's combined stake of 15.5% (239,000) shares. He built on this position over the next nine years to the point where in 1983 it had risen to 44% (591,000 shares). It was still well ahead of Graham and Tom's combined stake of 31.75% (426,000 shares). He was within six percentage points of securing an absolute majority. In March 1984, however, he sold more than half of his shares, thereby destroying an eleven-year pattern of accumulation and increasing dominance.

Max himself recalled 'being approached by the Cape people', who raised the question of what he proposed doing with his shares in the event of his death. Such shares would go to his two daughters, who were not likely to be interested in publishing. 'They asked me if I would agree to sell some of my shares. Very foolishly I agreed. I consulted Spicer & Pegler and they fixed a reasonable price.'

He was 69 at the time. The view of the board was that it would be in the interests of the company that such a stake be reduced on the understandable grounds that his shares could, at his death, come on to the market at an awkward time for the other shareholders. This is turn would create a risk that control might then pass to outsiders. The close shave experienced after Jonathan Cape's death served as a warning precedent. But this same board only a year earlier had chosen to magnify the potential threat posed by Max's holding by cancelling the Granada stake: this had had the effect of smartly lifting Max's equity interest from 35.4% to 44%. And Max, for his part, had been buying more shares as recently as 1982.

It was confirmed that Max would remain executive chairman of the Bodley Head and that he would continue as joint chairman of the holding company for a further five years at least. In recognition of that, a material increase in the fees paid to Max's family company for his services was also agreed, covering the ensuing five years.

The outward appearance of 'business as usual' was, however, deceptive. For whatever reasons, Max's action had alerted his fellow directors that he did not seek to wear a crown.

Hanseatic Leagues and Triple Alliances have a tendency to dissolve. So with Chatto, Virago, Bodley Head & Jonathan Cape. In this latter instance, however, it was not so much because outside threats became less apparent, rather it was as a result of the internal glue proving less effective. For 'internal glue' one can also read 'mutual trust'.

A snapshot of the trading experience in 1985 illustrates the shared problems of the publishing companies (see table 30). The analysis is admittedly complicated by a large positive 'balancing entry'; but even if such profits are allocated to the divisions, they remained firmly unprofitable. The single ray of sunlight was supplied by Triad, which by then was in its second year of being wound down.

Table 30: *Trading experience 1985*

	Turnover (£000)	Operating profit (£000)
Jonathan Cape	5984	(292)
Bodley Head	3349	(129)
Chatto & Windus	3026	(172)
Virago	1634	(5)
Virago Bookshop	151	(35)
Triad	1323	275
Balancing entry*	924	269
CVBC	16,391	(89)
Net interest		(319)
CVBC pre-tax profits		(408)

* The balancing item includes the Australasian company's turnover and operating profit.

The build-up of tensions that this slide into unprofitability prompted is well documented. Virago, as the newest recruit and the most battle-hardened, having had to live during its brief existence on its wits rather than its backlist, was particularly critical.

One issue that rankled with all the publishing companies revolved around the attribution of central overheads, which had the effect of giving them control over less than half the overheads they bore.

There were the deficiencies in central accounts which led to operating companies receiving news of large, unwelcome revisions to overhead allocations up to four months after the period covered.

'Costs out of control' was a frequent cry, which the statistical evidence, when it became available, did nothing to quieten. The critics were more scathing in their denunciation of rising administrative costs and more protective of advancing editorial costs.

A general feeling developed at Chatto, Bodley Head and Virago that the business was run for Cape. It was even suggested that the central sales force favoured Cape titles over others. There was firmer evidence that Cape men and women fared better when rationalization issues arose.

On the use of scarce capital, there was widespread condemnation of the 32 Bedford Square 'extravaganza'. At the same time, Chatto attracted criticism for 'a spending spree' on promotion and advances. Virago came in for criticism over its diversification into retailing. And so the list could be extended.

No business is going to be free of rivalries and discontents. If one has to choose a date that marks the moment when the dissatisfactions at CVBC began seriously to threaten its existence, it must be 11 July 1986. That was when Max Reinhardt conspicuously failed to support the rights issue. It occurred shortly after his decision not to join Graham C. Greene in giving a personal guarantee, when NatWest required additional security before increasing the group's banking facility, and represented an unambiguous vote of no confidence by one of the two joint chairmen. It also indicated that Max Reinhardt was prepared to see his stake in the business further eroded from 25% to a mere 11% of the equity.

Underlying that decision was no doubt concern over the financial state and prospects of the group. Spicer & Pegler for its part cannot have been a soaring fount of optimism. Most important of all, there was a loss of confidence, epitomised in Max's comment: 'Things were being done all the time without my being consulted. I had the feeling I was being pushed around.' Carmen Callil broadly concurs: her recollection of the holding company board was that things seemed to get done outside the minutes.

In the wake of the rights issue, centrifugal forces started to build up. Virago decided to free itself of the incubus of central charges which it did not regard as appropriate to its size or its business. In July it proposed a management buyout. In October, this was formally presented to the board by Ursula Owen and accepted in principle. By April 1987 negotiations had advanced sufficiently for *The Bookseller* to announce the imminent completion of the management buyout.

In this exercise Virago enjoyed the avuncular support of Robert Gavron, one of its early backers, who acted as a negotiator on its behalf. While the terms were not disclosed, it was indicated that sales and distribution would stay with CBC (the acronym to which it would have had to revert) and that Carmen Callil would retain her posts as non-executive chairman of Virago and managing director of Chatto & Windus. Ursula Owen recalls that in negotiations Tom Maschler was tougher than Graham C. Greene and that it was he who insisted on CBC retaining 10% of the equity. Intriguingly, the value placed on the CVBC shares that the Virago executives would be selling back to the company was set at 40p, little more than half the July rights issue price (but modestly up on the 30p valuation put on those shares when they formed part of the purchase package in 1982). Such a discount was justified on the grounds that CBC was a reluctant buyer.

The Bookseller articles also confirmed that the Bodley Head would be staying put. This may have come as something of a surprise to its readers, who could be excused for not having realized that separation had ever been contemplated. In fact, Max Reinhardt had tentatively explored the idea of removing the Bodley Head from the consortium. In this he was encouraged by Graham Greene (the author), who was nostalgic for the intimacy of earlier days, when the firm was run more independently and in a more personal way. In the end, extraction was judged to be too painful, presenting immense practical difficulties, and the idea was dropped.

The same *Bookseller* articles were scrutinized less for the news they carried on the subject of Virago and the non-news on the Bodley Head than for the light they might shed on a fifteen-line letter that had appeared in *The Times* on 24 March. In it Graham Greene took his nephew to task for treating rumours of changes at CVBC in a *Times* Diary comment four days earlier as pure fantasy. He went on to assure his nephew that if none of the necessary changes in the firm's administration were introduced, he – and he had little doubt other authors – would consider leaving the group.

For a company with cash flow problems, this was publicity it could well dispense with. Already, its bank's support the previous July had been less than wholehearted. Subsequently, the group's trading experience had remained difficult, Virago's separatist ambitions were not of a kind in themselves to inspire confidence, and Liz Calder's departure in August had been damaging. Worse still, at one point the press was reduced to hoisting Simon & Schuster, the most diffident groom in publishing history, into the position of possible suitor.

It requires little imagination to visualize the state of mind of the NatWest Bank manager in Lombard Street. As Michael Davie wrote in the *Observer* a year later, 'one brief letter destabilized the group. It had to raise capital from somewhere other than banks.'

Max Reinhardt's resignation as joint chairman on 31 March 1987 was something of a formality. Nonetheless, he retained his seat on the holding company board and remained executive chairman of the Bodley Head. He also explicitly renounced any ambitions to withdraw the Bodley Head from the group.

The suggestion that there is no such thing as bad publicity was exemplified in Cape's history, when Granada acquired a critical stake in the company after the well-publicized failure in 1962 of a management buy-in. The same can be said of the Graham Greene vs Graham C. Greene episode: shortly thereafter, Tom Maschler received a telephone call from his friend of long standing, Bob Gottlieb. At the time Gottlieb was editor of the *New Yorker*, but before that he had been editor-in-chief and publisher of Alfred Knopf. The question he asked was, if Si Newhouse – his boss and the Random House owner – were to come to London, would it be possible to meet. The reply sent back to Bob Gottlieb was positive, though little was expected to emerge from any such conversations.

It was duly arranged that Graham C. Greene and Tom Maschler, who between them owned 77% of the stock in the aftermath of the rights issue (against Max's 11%), would join Si Newhouse and Robert Bernstein for breakfast at the Connaught one Sunday morning early in April. Breakfast stretched to lunch and that afternoon Random House declared itself ready to pay £20m for the company; after taking into account £3m of debt, this valued the equity at £17m, equivalent to one year's turnover, and worked out at £7.64 a share. It was two to three times the value put on the company in some private estimates and nine and a half times the value that the rights subscription price of 78p implied. Board representation was promised to Graham and Tom, as well as attractive ten-year contracts.

Graham took Si Newhouse to 32 Bedford Square. As he sat in the lazy quiet of a Sunday afternoon, surrounded by the serried achievements of 65 years of publishing, Graham harks back with a sense of irony to Si's phrase, 'and nothing will ever be altered'. At the time, it confirmed him in his decision not to have pursued any British solutions – notably with Macmillan – where obvious duplications existed and rationalizations loomed.

Max Reinhardt remembers being greeted by Graham and Tom with the comment, 'You're a millionaire now!' Gratifying as that might have been, he was astonished that they should have negotiated the deal behind his back. The suspicions on the other side surface in Tom's explanatory comment: 'We were scared he would muck things up in any negotiations. We had just been sold down the river with the Graham Greene letter.' Max for his part points out that the novelist 'wrote the letter because he was really cross – and that he was not the sort of chap to consult anybody'. Max recalls reading it on 24 March, along with the rest of *The Times* readership.

The financial conclusion to a 20-year experiment in collaboration was hugely pleasing. It confirmed that valuable assets could still be created in a type of publishing that attached overriding importance to the quality of the list and took great pains at achieving elegance in the finished result.

Moreover, the price offered appeared to overlook the fact that CVBC had sadly provided convincing evidence that 'people who make money in literary publishing are rare' and that 'literary trade publishing is doomed to fail the profits tests of a quoted company'. These comments of Carmen Callil and Tom Maschler respectively reflect the publishing priorities spelled out by Ian Parsons and Michael Howard in the 1960s to which the imprints had remained faithful. They also provide one of the infrequent instances – some might say the unique occasion – when Tom and Carmen could be seen sharing common ground.

Speculation over the inevitability – or otherwise – of the end of a multi-faceted merger can be unproductive. What the story has shown is that the limited basis of the alliances left the group ill-equipped to face the changes in publishing as they developed in the 1970s and particularly the 1980s. Furthermore:

– having the editorial activities set up in separate fiefdoms shielded, for a long time, a large slice of costs from critical scrutiny;

– more important, it killed any possibility of establishing a strong direct presence in paperback publishing, precisely when trade publishing was becoming more and more dependent on paperbacks for its profits;

– simultaneously, the management of the share register, which served to concentrate and narrow the equity capital base, inhibited the group's development by increasing its dependence on borrowed funds;

– while asset disposals afforded some financial relief to a business that typically absorbed cash rather than generated it, self-evidently they provided no long-term solution;

– the central management structure was such that excessive reliance was placed on one man – Graham C. Greene – who at the same time pursued numerous outside business interests.

Graham C. Greene acknowledges that, had he proved a more forceful chairman, the outcome might have been different. But then he adds: 'Whether I'd have been the right person, given that I had acted for over 20 years as custodian of the style bequeathed by Jonathan Cape and Wren and Michael Howard, I'm not certain.' As a fellow Publishers Association Council member has put it, Graham is the industry's most accomplished committee man and publicist. Ambitious and determined, yes, but certainly not a banger of heads.

To many in the group it was inconceivable that they would fall prey to a predator, either domestic or foreign. The few who were shareholders remained adamant up to the last minute that the group's position as an independent British publisher needed to be retained. But then, as Ambrose Bierce has reminded us, adamant is a mineral that is soluble in solicitate of gold. So it proved in 1987 when it was plunged into a £17m solution.

• **May 1987** Purchase completed by Random House (through a subsidiary) of Chatto, Virago, Bodley Head & Jonathan Cape. Price paid: £20m, including some £3m of debt.
• **June 1987** Simon Master appointed chief excutive of CVBC, with Graham C. Greene remaining chairman.
• **July 1987** Buyout of Virago Press completed.
• **October 1987** Resignation from the board of Max Reinhardt.
• **February 1988** Name changed to Random House UK Limited.
• **April 1988** Resignation from the board of Graham C. Greene.
• **June 1989** Purchase of Century Hutchinson for £64m. Anthony Cheetham appointed chairman and chief executive of Random House UK.
• **October 1991** Departure of Anthony Cheetham. Gail Rebuck appointed chairman and chief executive.
• **March 1998** Bertelsmann announces purchase of Random House Inc. for a reported $1.3bn.

Chapter 9

WILLIAM COLLINS

THIS IS HOW A DIPLOMATIC David Nickson conveyed the news to *Printing World* in the summer of 1979 that Jan Collins had ceased to be executive chairman of William Collins and was to become non-executive chairman: 'It is entirely a restructuring at board level and there is no significance behind it. I do not think this will affect our policy in any way.' It must rank as the publishing industry's equivalent of the newsflash 'small earthquake; few dead'. If one is looking for a date that marks the start of Collins's protracted slide into bondage, the choice of 3 August 1979 would certainly be among the strongest.

A sense of the past is usually desirable when seeking to understand change. In the case of William Collins, a firm that was founded in 1819 and remained under family management and control for 162 years, it is essential. The briefest possible synopsis of its history can be reduced to a list of six near-identical names: William Collins I, born 1789, founder of firm in 1819, died 1853; William Collins II, born 1817, head of firm from 1853 to his death in 1895; William Collins III, born 1846, head of firm from 1895 to his death in 1906; William Collins IV, born 1873, head of firm from 1906 to his death in 1945; William Collins V, born 1900, head of firm from 1945 to his death in 1976; and W. Jan Collins, born 1930, head of firm from 1976 to 1981.

The strength of the Collins genes is readily apparent, with the average life-span of the first five William Collins amounting to 70 years (their ages ranged from 60 to 78). Typically, they took command in their late 30s, with the result that they each reigned for an average of 31 years (the 11-year reign of William Collins III being the principal exception).

This pattern of family continuity is noteworthy but not unique. What is remarkable is that Collins became the largest independent publishing house in Britain while still under family control.

In looking at clues that might help to explain the firm's achievement, family genes come to the fore once again, specifically the happy accident that resulted in a succession of printer-publishers surfacing in each generation. Many members of the family made their careers within the family firm. The Collins name was not confined to the chairman of the day. Their strengths were not identical but all were called upon to display industry, commitment, and, ultimately, business acumen. A subtle filtering system meant that few who lacked such qualities achieved positions of authority.

The tone of a firm is set at the top. In this respect, the single-minded concentration on the firm's interests and activities by the family members occupying the leading positions was hugely influential. While members of the Collins family undoubtedly contributed effort and time to outside activities, by and large those who survived the filtering process fashioned their careers within the framework of the family firm. The main exception to this came in the 1930s, when Sir Godfrey Collins, younger brother of William IV, entered politics and, ultimately, the Cabinet as Secretary of State for Scotland. Generally, though, the firm was not weakened by 'the call of public duty' acting on the more ambitious members. This was a family business run by full-time executives and not by absentee proprietors. William Collins V was knighted for export achievement, not for political services or donations.

Succession planning was a feature of William Collins. This is in contrast to other companies, where succession takes the form of a board game operated by the incumbent chairman/chief executive. In publishing, the supreme example was Penguin under Sir Allen Lane.

Not so at Collins, where advance planning prevailed, whose visibility was enhanced by a postwar attachment to a triumvirate structure. In the 1950s and 1960s, when Sir William Collins (Billy Collins) was the most prominent figure in his capacity as the publisher-salesman chairman, he had as co-proprietors at main board level his brother I. G. Collins (Ian Collins) in charge of finance, administration, bible, and reference publishing, and his cousin W. Hope Collins, Sir Godfrey's son, in charge of manufacturing and children's publishing. In terms of shareholdings, Ian and Hope overshadowed Billy.

The three were of the same generation. The potential danger that this presented was recognized and action was taken. In 1967 Jan Collins, Ian Chapman, and David Nickson (now Lord Nickson of Renagour) were all appointed to the holding company board and simultaneously made managing directors of the main operating company. This was another triumvirate, but of a different generation. The death later that year of Hope Collins provided confirmation of the foresight displayed in these appointments. Then, four years later, Ian Collins retired.

When Sir William Collins died in September 1976, not only was his successor identified, but so was the triumvirate that was to replace the one in which he had been the outstanding figure. Furthermore, Jan Collins's assumption to the chairmanship was thoroughly predictable.

– There was the historical inevitability reflected in the list at the start of this chapter of the earlier heads of the firm.

– There was the day-to-day evidence of a man of great industry, whose whole working life had been spent in William Collins, thereby sustaining the tradition of single-minded devotion to the family company.

– Finally, there was the formal anticipation of his role, his ascent marked by the main board appointment in 1967 and the vice-chairmanship of the main operating company in 1971.

The first point that needs making is that the picture provided so far of a company whose top management was united in its objectives and harmonious in its relationships has to be qualified. At its simplest, Collins was a Glasgow printing and publishing company that had diversified into London. Before the war, Sir Godfrey Collins had been assigned the task of starting a publishing office in London, and after the war Sir William Collins had made an outstanding success of this outpost.

By the 1960s publishing in Glasgow encompassed the more humdrum schoolbooks, dictionaries, bibles, and children's books, while London undertook the more glamorous trade publishing and an increasing amount of children's books. Furthermore, London was where the paperback revolution was taking place. The jealousies that were bound to surface from this publishing division were magnified by the supplier/customer relationship, with all manufacturing, warehousing, and distribution centred in Glasgow and little scope given to the editors to buy their print needs outside the group.

When Glasgow looked south it saw a collection of long-haired publishing eccentrics. When London looked north it saw a crowd of troublesome, obdurate printers. Author Philip Ziegler, who was editor-in-chief at Collins from 1979 to 1980, summarized the position: 'It's hard when the tail starts to outgrow the dog.'

These differences were enshrined at board level, where Ian Collins and Hope Collins represented the Glasgow interests and Billy Collins those of London. There were some periods of open warfare. Philip Ziegler remembers one occasion when Ian Collins and Hope Collins refused to leave Billy's office until he abandoned a book they regarded with particular distaste, declaiming passages that gave special offence. On that occasion, Glasgow won the day.

While tensions exist within all firms, those within Collins were rendered that much more intractable for two reasons. In the first instance, the disequilibrium in terms of financial performance between London and Glasgow seemed destined to become ever more pronounced. Publishing in the 1960s and the first part of the 1970s experienced sustained growth. In manufacturing, on the other hand, the days when a small army of Glaswegian lassies in the printery and the bindery at Cathedral Street could be deployed as the workload dictated were well and truly over. Union demarcation rules and a narrowing of differentials in pay took care of that. At the same time, competitive pressures leading to the installation of modern equipment and consequential increases in capacity made it harder and harder for Collins's own publishing to provide the necessary throughput on a sustained basis.

The second aggravating factor lay in the management structure. As we have seen, the earlier triumvirate of William Collins, Ian Collins, and Hope Collins was shadowed in 1967 by a second trio of Jan Collins, Ian Chapman, and David Nickson. However, apart from being of another generation, they differed from the older trio in the important respect that only one member was a proprietor. What was lacking, therefore, was the glue that shared ownership often brings to partnerships.

Any expectation that the younger trio would be able to operate for a while in the shadow of the senior was defeated by the death later that year of Hope Collins and the retirement of Ian Collins in 1971. Billy Collins's increasing isolation was relieved, however, by the presence of his wife, Priscilla, known as Pierre. Lady Collins was not only a woman of considerable intellect and great strength of character, she was also a powerful figure within the firm, being head of the high-profile religious list.

The young triumvirate had ridden to power on the introduction of a computer program, sanctioned in 1965, which gave the company such novelties as management accounting and budgeting. This in turn invited greater clarity in executive responsibilities and subjected received opinions to increased scrutiny.

The cause of the younger directors was furthered in 1968 with the appointment to the holding company board of Mark Collins, Jan's younger brother. Since 1962 he had been in charge of Fontana and had overseen the rapid development of the paperback side. His elevation to the Collins board did not, however, mean that the trinity of younger directors had become a quaternity.

At this point one should hark back to the image presented at the start of this article of a family company pursuing a smooth succession path as one generation gives way to another. Here again reality was different to appearances.

Well before Billy Collins's death in 1976, frictions had emerged, principally between Jan Collins on the one hand and Ian Chapman and David Nickson on the other. The irony was that all three had started off with the firmly held ambition precisely to avoid a repetition of the boardroom battles of the kind they had observed between their seniors.

In terms of management style, many of the points of dispute were paradoxically linked to the lengths to which Jan's conscientiousness took him. While he was respected for his strategic insight – his development of Collins dictionaries being a case in point – he was represented as being a poor delegator and a bad communicator. The chaos that often ensued was said to have come close to breaking the nerve of his more organized and decisive fellow directors.

Such issues were far from being swept under the carpet. In 1974 Ian Chapman and David Nickson faced up to Jan and told him that they did not believe he had the makings of the next chairman and advised him to stand aside. This exchange took place at a time when Billy Collins was abroad on one of his foreign tours. It was regarded as an act of treachery and served to consolidate Jan's position rather than weaken it. Following the death of Ian Collins in 1975, an event that focused renewed attention on the future ownership of the company, a more conventional attempt at finding a way out of the management problem was made, using the consultants, McKinsey. They failed, however, to come up with a solution that was acceptable to Jan, Ian, and David.

This period of intense uncertainty coincided with the final years of Billy Collins's life. The natural conservatism of a man of his age meant that he was reluctant to endorse change, the consequences of which were bound to be unpredictable. Furthermore, he may well not have accepted all the criticisms of Jan, being swayed in this by his wife, whose support of Jan was unswerving and unqualified. In short, he was not prepared to initiate any action that would mean a move away from the natural line of succession. He therefore passed up the opportunity to set in train any of the filtering processes that had been used by his forebears.

It would be wrong to suggest that the only points of contention were those that related to style of management. The future of the manufacturing business in Glasgow was a recurrent object of analysis and one that generated strong emotions. The Glasgow-based directors tended to be protective. Billy Collins's own position was conservative, influenced by his sense of responsibility for the workforce in Glasgow, where many were second-generation and some third-generation employees. By contrast, Mark Collins was unremittingly sceptical of the advantages that were expected to accrue to a publisher having its own production facilities.

The quest for a resolution of these problems posed by manufacturing took one turn that had far-reaching consequences, the recruitment of George Craig in 1975 to head the manufacturing and distribution sides of the business. He was an accountant by training, whose previous experience had been in Procter & Gamble and Honeywell. His organizational experience and his communication skills in a strongly unionized environment were highly relevant to Collins's needs.

On the death of Sir William Collins in September 1976, Jan Collins took the chair. To the outside world – and indeed to almost all within the firm – this was exactly as expected. That it came as no surprise did not mean, however, that it was the occasion for buoyant prophecies. Philip Ziegler, who was an editorial director of the general trade publishing division during the 1970s, recalls that, even before Billy died, it was easy enough to predict that this succession 'wasn't going to work happily'.

For those outsiders who took the trouble to study Jan's first chairman's statement to shareholders in the 1976 accounts, published in April 1977, the signs of coming conflict were already visible. The chairman revealed that his initial task had been to plan and implement a new organizational structure to meet the company's needs for future growth. He wrote: 'My own role is that of overall chairman with an interest in all areas of the company with a special interest in the American company, children's, bible, and reference division, and the manufacturing division and finance.' This reads like an impossible workload for a company chairman. It suggests a marked disinclination to delegate. It also shows the scars of the earlier no-confidence motions of his fellow executive directors.

Table 31: *Collins operating performance*

Year to 31 December	1976	1977	1978	1979
Turnover (£000)	49,030	53,756	60,631	65,098
Pre-tax profits (£000)	5221	3149	3345	(255)
Pre-tax margins	10.6%	5.9%	5.5%	–
Earnings per share	29.7p	15.8p	20.1p	(0.2p)
Net dividend	4.2p	4.7p	5.2p	–

A more subtle piece of evidence of boardroom divisions came with the appointment of non-executive directors. While this complied with best company practice, it was noticeable that each member of the managing triumvirate had in effect 'his man' on the board: Jan's choice was Sir James Blair-Cunynghame, chairman of the Royal Bank of Scotland, Ian's was Sir Charles Troughton, former chairman of W. H. Smith, while David Nickson had selected Robert Smith (now Sir Robert Smith), chairman of Scottish United Investors.

Whatever the management pressures within the company, trading influences increasingly dictated events in the three years after Billy Collins's death. Their effects are best illustrated in a simple table (31) of Collins's operating performance.

Underlying these figures were a number of factors that were peculiar to Collins and a number that were general to the industry. Among the former, the single most important was the move completed in early 1977 of the distribution centre and office block to Bishopbriggs, six miles outside Glasgow. Since 1972 the whole of the manufacturing had been transferred there. The total cost in buildings, new plant, and equipment had been £17m – but after grants and tax allowances this had been cut to £5m. More than 2500 employees were employed at Bishopbriggs. The resulting increase in productive efficiency resulted in a substantial increase in capacity. The management line was that this provided the company with a strong base from which to develop and expand its manufacturing and distribution operations.

Of lesser importance was the challenge arising out of the purchase of the World Publishing Company from the Times Mirror Group. This had taken place in 1974 and was an initiative with which Jan was closely identified. The intention was that its bible, reference, and children's book publishing would complement and supplement Collins's existing activities in the United States. In addition, the ambition was that the Bishopbriggs manufacturing division would benefit from print orders from the USA for the King James' Bible (one title not subject to the US manufacturing clause).

The main outside influences, which were general to the industry, were domestic inflation, at a time of immense union power; and sterling appreciation, propelled by its status as a petrocurrency. In 1977 UK inflation was

13.5% and there was a 6.5% rise in sterling against the dollar. In 1978, inflation was 8.3% and currency appreciation 12.4%; in 1979 inflation increased to 17.4% and currency rose 10.5%. in 1980 the inflation rate was 15.5% and sterling appreciated 8.1% against the dollar.

For an industry such as book publishing, in which about 30% of sales were typically exported, this was a catastrophic combination. For a company such as William Collins, which was also massively involved in production, the outcome was even more severe: from being a soaring opportunity, the increased manufacturing and distribution capacity took on the characteristics of an albatross. It also undermined part of the rationale for the purchase of World Publishing, whose trading performance was in any case proving deeply disappointing.

Emphasis on what went wrong has the considerable demerit of drawing attention away from what went right. In the fourteen years between 1962 and 1976 the company had experienced an uninterrupted rise in turnover from £6.2m to £49m. Pre-tax profits over the same period had advanced from £693,000 to £5.2m, with only one break – in 1974, the year of the country's three-day week. Profit margins at the end of the period were in excess of 10%, as they had been at the start. By any standards this was a remarkable achievement. There were some who might have concluded that the dissentions on the Collins board illustrated the benefits of 'creative tension'.

However, when things started to turn awry, as they did in 1977, when there was a 40% drop in profits, top management had had little experience of dealing with an overall deterioration in the business. While this was a challenge that most other British publishers faced, for Collins the position was aggravated by its exposure to manufacturing. Most important of all, at a time that called for decisive leadership, the board was in disarray.

The pressures for action built up as the economic environment deteriorated: even though in 1978 reported profits were ahead of a year earlier, the extent of the recovery was modest, and results in the second half of the year fell below expectations. It was in the first six months of 1979, however, that trading took a decisive turn for the worse.

The full extent of this deterioration was only made public on 7 September, with the release of the half-year results, which showed losses of £828,000, against profits the previous year of £1,234,000. At board level the trend had been known well before that date, even though the precise figures had still to be established. This major setback had given rise to a whole range of alternative and competing proposals involving the restructuring of the board and the reallocation of executive responsibilities. The one point to which everybody subscribed was that the triumvirate structure had to be abandoned.

After a little while the battle lines became clearly defined. On the one hand there was Jan, whose favoured solution centred on his remaining a full-time chairman, while a new chief executive would be brought in from outside the firm. His candidate had already been chosen, as had several other new directors. This would have been accompanied by the departures of Ian Chapman, David Nickson, and possibly George Craig. Jan's proposals gained little support from the existing board. On the other hand, it was said to have the backing of family shareholders representing up to 50% of the voting capital. In the event of the board turning down this proposal, there was an expectation that these family shareholdings would be offered for sale, leading almost inevitably to the loss of the company's independence.

The other side was united in its belief that Jan should cease to exercise executive authority. There were many permutations to the schemes that were contemplated which would achieve that result, with some directors favouring one solution and others another, such views being subject to change as developments unfolded. Eventually, agreement was reached that had the support of the directors, not counting Jan at that stage.

It carried about it a distinct aroma of compromise. Jan was to stay as chairman, but in a totally non-executive capacity. Ian Chapman, who was not prepared to serve as group managing director while Jan remained chairman, albeit non-executive, was to continue as deputy chairman and was to take on responsibility for all the Collins book publishing interests, both in the UK and overseas. David Nickson was to assume the role of group managing director, while remaining vice-chairman. Robert Smith was to be made joint vice-chairman.

David Nickson's acceptance was heavily hedged: he made it clear that his was a temporary appointment, not least because of his recent appointment as chairman of the Scottish CBI. David's own favoured solution had throughout been that Ian Chapman should become chairman.

Ian Chapman, for his part, was in the position that his contract was due to expire at the end of December 1980. At that point he could either take retirement, having reached the age of 55, or commit himself to a new contract. This in effect introduced into the agreement yet another imponderable, which would crystallize a little over a year hence.

At a full board meeting on 3 August 1979, the proposal was accepted with Jan's concurrence. In the light of his earlier position, this outcome was far from being predictable. Provision had indeed been made for other eventualities. Had he withheld his agreement, an extraordinary general meeting would have been called at which a resolution would have been put to remove him from the chair and for Mark Collins to be elected in his place.

While the existence of such alternative arrangements may in itself have been a spur on Jan to accept the proposals, a more telling argument was almost certainly the erosion of shareholder support. Within the 50% figure quoted earlier of family holdings that he was in touch with, two trusts set up in 1950-1 accounted for some 33%: Stoke Albany Trustees Limited, named after Sir William and Lady Collins's house in Northamptonshire, with their children and grandchildren as beneficiaries, had 17.3%; while Crossburn Trustees Limited held the shares of Ian Collins, amounting to 16%.

The trusts had in common two trustees who were Collins's professional advisers: Hobart Moore, of accountants Moore Stephens, and Alan Rees-Reynolds, from the solicitors Joynson Hicks. The trusts were so constituted that a majority of three out of five issued shares were held by Hobart Moore (two shares) and Alan Rees-Reynolds (one share). Stoke Albany's other trustees were family members or connections, with two votes between them: they consisted of Peter Lewis, son-in-law and chairman of the John Lewis Group; Michael Lloyd, Lady Collins's younger brother; Lady Collins herself and Jan Collins. No family representatives were trustees to the Crossburn Trust.

Ultimately the company's professional advisers among the trustees decided to back the members of the board other than Jan. They took the view that this was the best way for the trusts' investment in Collins to be protected and nurtured. In so doing, they also ruled themselves out of being a party to actions that would have cost Collins its independence, i.e. the offer of shares to an outsider.

The aftermath of the board's decision to deprive Jan Collins of executive authority saw a flurry of management initiatives.

Specific measures included:
– the sale of the freehold of 12-15 St James's Place for £3.6m, thereby helping to reduce the balance-sheet gearing (net debt as a percentage of shareholders' funds) from a disturbing 63% at the end of 1978 to a more manageable 50% at the end of 1979;
– some 600 redundancies and job savings, of which about 470 were in the UK, largely in manufacturing;
– in UK publishing, the concentration of three separate children's units into one;
– disposal of the loss-making World Publishing Group in three separate transactions;
– in Australia, heavy stock write-offs and sharp staff cutbacks.

For 1979 as a whole, a pre-tax loss of £255,000 was recorded, with second-half profits failing to offset the first-half loss of £828,000. Both interim and final dividends were passed.

In the first half of 1980, the group managed a return to modest profits, despite continuing adverse inflation and currency movements. The prospects were judged to be sufficiently encouraging to justify a symbolic return to the dividend list. In the event, the seasonally important second-half profits were sizeable at £1.9m. These were struck, moreover, after some £150,000 of exceptional charges and despite a currency that continued on its perverse upwards path. The final dividend that the board declared went well beyond the level of a token payment.

Legacies remained, nonetheless, from the earlier management upheavals. Among some of Jan Collins's supporters, notably his mother, there was a deep sense of injustice done to him and considerable resentment *vis-à-vis* those who were seen as the perpetrators.

There were also other more dispassionate considerations. One that influenced Jan was the belief that, as the family involvement in the management of the company declined, so the justification for family members having the bulk of their personal assets tied up in the firm was reduced.

Furthermore, there was the looming threat of Robert Maxwell. Every time a death occurred in the family, the heirs and/or the trustees of the estates involved were courted by Maxwell. His stated objective was to acquire control, and to that end he was building up a holding in the voting shares at a speed that he clearly wished to see accelerate. The argument of Jan and his fellow shareholders went as follows: 'Might it not make sense to secure the future ownership now, in case an accident were to pitch the company into Maxwell's lap?'

Indeed, in mid-1980, a group of investors – part-family, part-institutional – made tentative moves to find a corporate home for approximately 25% of the voting capital. Flies were cast over Longman, Trafalgar House (at the time owner of Beaverbrook Newspapers), and International Thomson, all of which declined to rise to the bait.

From the autumn of 1980, Jan was made aware of a developing boardroom view that the 1979 compromise was not a long-term solution to Collins's management difficulties. One recommendation that had David Nickson's support was that Ian Chapman should become chairman.

This no doubt acted as a stimulus on Jan and his family to take further soundings of potential purchasers. Through Lady Collins's friendship with Dolly de Rothschild (Mrs James A. de Rothschild) contact was made with Lord Goodman. On 11 March 1981 a small dinner party was given by Paul and Helen Hamlyn to celebrate Rupert Murdoch's fiftieth birthday. The scene was set in their Chelsea house in Old Church Street. As Paul recalled, Arnold Goodman, one of the guests, took Rupert aside to ask if he might be interested in certain family holdings that were looking for a good home. The initial response, 'Why do I want to be in book publishing?', heralded some close questioning of his host over the ensuing weeks.

And then, on 19 April 1981, Hobart Moore died.

At this point, it is desirable to explain more fully the background to the William Collins share structure. In 1949 the holding company had been incorporated and was made public through the issue of 297,000 ordinary shares, 28.8% of the then issued ordinary capital of 1,030,000 £1 shares (later to be split into 4.12 million 25p ordinary shares). In subsequent years, the ordinary capital was increased entirely through free bonus issues of ordinary 'A' non-voting shares. By 1981 the issued capital consisted of 4.12 million 25p ordinary shares and 9.68 million 25p non-voting 'A' shares.

The quotation in 1949 was obtained primarily with a view to simplifying valuations for estate duty purposes. Subsequent bonus issues in non-voting shares were a device to enable ordinary shareholders to raise capital in order to finance personal expenditure or to pay inheritance taxes, without having to deplete their voting shareholdings. The quotation was emphatically not a facility for the company to raise capital. It was a financial convenience to minimize the dangers of dilution to family control. Continuity of family control was further buttressed by the establishment of the two trusts mentioned earlier. In an interview in 1969 given to the *Times* columnist Pooter, Sir William Collins vowed to fight off any industrial takeover and pointed to these trusts as a means of securing family succession.

But the death of Hobart Moore gave the lie to these hopes. The voting balance within the Stoke Albany Trust (17.3%) had shifted to Jan's faction. It enabled them to assemble a group of investors whose collective holdings constituted a critical mass, likely to attract a suitable predator. This package totalled 1,168,037 ordinary shares (and 435,941 'A' shares), the constituents of which were Stoke Albany Trustees with 711,820 shares; Jan Collins's beneficial holdings of 66,812 shares; and shares held by Jan as trustee amounting to 111,500 shares, which included, ironically, some shares held in a trust in which Mark had a life interest. This left 277,905 shares held by other members of the family, notably James Collins, who had inherited from his father Hope Collins.

All told, this represented 28.35% of the issued voting capital.

Heavily guided by Lord Goodman, the choice of purchaser had fallen on Rupert Murdoch.

While News Corporation was by that date a substantial business, its turnover in its previous financial year had been £500m (Aus$1bn); Collins's £65m of turnover would have made a meaningful addition. Collins would not have run the risk, therefore, of disappearing into a footnote to the accounts.

Furthermore, in January 1981, Rupert Murdoch had also acquired the loss-making *Times*. This had the effect of softening his image of a buccaneering Australian intent on nourishing man's baser instincts. As Michael Leapman records in his book *Barefaced Cheek,* Jan's enthusiasm overflowed: 'Following News International's acquisition of Times Newspapers, it was clear to me that we could not hope for a better purchaser.'

From Murdoch's point of view, one consequence of his *Times* purchase was that he had become part of the establishment, an experience that appears on later reflection to have disagreed with him. William Collins also had the advantage of an establishment aura, deriving from such features as Hatchards' three royal appointments and Collins's own privileged position as publisher of the bible. More significantly, it was seen as an outstanding turnround situation.

NEWS INTERNATIONAL BID

On 13 May 1981 News International announced that it had agreed to acquire from members of the Collins family and related interests 1,168,037 ordinary shares and 435,941 ordinary 'A' shares at 200p and 150p respectively. When added to the 83,400 ordinary shares already held, this gave News International a total holding of 1,251,437 ordinary shares.

This represented 30.4% of the ordinary capital, a level at which it was obliged under Stock Exchange rules to make a bid for the whole company, on the same terms.

The previous day, ahead of the 13 May annual general meeting, a board meeting had taken place. It had been a long-drawn-out affair due to the fact that the chairman, Jan Collins, had been hugely delayed. Finally, late in the evening, he arrived and announced to an astonished board that he had sold his shares to Rupert Murdoch as a first step towards News International's purchase of the company. He was voted off the board and Ian Chapman was chosen to succeed him. Ian's first action as chairman was to recommend that shareholders stay closely attached to their shares, pointing out at the same time that this was not a bid that the board had sought.

On News International's terms, the whole of Collins was being valued at £22.75m, equivalent to 0.4 times Collins's 1980 turnover.

The dramatic aspects of the bid were numerous and ensured it a degree of interest that was out of proportion to the scale of the battle:
– the bid was unheralded and unwelcome;
– the newsworthiness of the bidder was beyond dispute;
– the target company had been in the same family's ownership and control for more than 150 years;
– the current company chairman and his mother were joint conspirators in setting up the bid;
– the chairman's younger brother was fighting in the opposite camp; and
– it was left to the new chairman, whose blood links with the Collinses were nil, to take the lead in defending the family traditions.

The News International offer document appeared on 10 June. In Rupert Murdoch's letter to shareholders he doffs his cap to 'the mutual benefits that we believe can accrue from the association of our newspapers with an eminent book publishing group and the potential assistance we would be able to offer Collins's management arising out of our extensive experience in the communications industry worldwide'. Nothing terribly meaty there.

A much more interesting document is Collins's rejection, published two weeks later. The core argument centres on a profits forecast for 1981 of not less than £4m, a virtual doubling of the 1980 results, and a forecast net dividend of 7.5p, which compared with 3p in 1980 and a previous peak of 5.18p in 1978. This was expected to be covered 2.6 times.

Subsidiary points included the fact that the News International offer fell below the balance-sheet net asset value of the shares, which itself was understated through the absence of any valuation for the copyrights and licences held by Collins. That the bid was a cash bid also meant that investors who accepted would crystallize taxable capital gains. And then there was the comforting fact that the market price of Collins's ordinary and 'A' shares at 230p and 158p respectively remained above the prices offered, and had done so from the start.

The overall argument, persuasively presented, was that Rupert Murdoch had lighted on an undervalued situation, a company that was in the midst of a major profits recovery. He had made an opportunistic and cheeky bid. Management, for its part, was intent on preserving the company's independence, and this also fitted in with the hopes of many of its authors as well as those of the Scottish lobby.

Two days later, Robert Maxwell sold his holding of the ordinary shares, which had been built up to 388,100 shares (9.4%) to Rupert Murdoch at a price of 225p. This lifted News International's stake to 41.1%. The sale followed Maxwell's assurances made to Ian Chapman a few hours previously that he would not sell to Murdoch, assurances that had the ring of truth in them given the strained relations between Maxwell and Murdoch.

Curiously, this sale also coincided with:
– the purchase by Maxwell's company, BPC, of News International's loss-making Eric Bemrose gravure printing group;
– settlement of a long-standing commercial dispute over the printing of the *Sunday Times* colour supplement by BPC's Sun Printers;
– undertakings made by News International to BPC for the continued production of the *Sunday Times* and the *News of the World* colour supplements. The City Takeover Panel leapt into action with a view to establishing whether there was any link between these other agreements and the Collins transaction, entailing favourable treatment not available to other Collins shareholders. This would have constituted a breach of the takeover code. No stone was left unturned in the search for compromising evidence (notarized documents would have done), all hedgerows were subjected to minute scrutiny and, on 10 July, the full takeover panel was able to announce to the waiting world that such suspicions were baseless and that the honour of the two protagonists and of all their advisers was intact.

By paying 225p for Maxwell's stock, News International automatically increased its offer to all ordinary shareholders. Some days later, News International grudgingly increased the price to the 'A' shareholders to 163p, 8.7% up on the original 150p offer. At that point the whole of Collins was being valued at £25m. With the prices of the Collins shares still standing above these adjusted offers, Murdoch was still unable, however, to add further to his holdings by way of purchases in the market.

One intriguing aspect of News International's offer document of 10 June had been News International's recognition that it might not secure control, in which event it gave Collins management notice that it would be content to hold on to its shares and remain the largest single shareholder. Collins for its part responded by indicating that in that event it might offer News International a seat on the board.

As the battle progressed, with Collins recommending rejection at every change in the terms and News International thwarted in its attempts to add to its holdings through market purchases and giving no inclination that it might improve further on its offer, such an outcome looked increasingly likely. On 20 July News International rested its case, ending up with 1,740,800 ordinary shares (42.25%) and 767,236 'A' shares (7.93%).

Collins pronounced itself hugely satisfied with the outcome, invited News International to propose two directors for appointment to the Collins board and declared that it 'looks forward with confidence to working with them'. Thus a battle, where the odds had been heavily against Collins, ended in victory for the company. Ian Chapman had won his spurs in triumphant fashion. The one shadow, and a long one, was the realization that Rupert Murdoch had a piece of unfinished business on his hands.

The board was duly enlarged with the addition of two News International representatives, Rupert Murdoch himself and Sir Edward Pickering, his long-serving eyes and ears in Britain. News International gave an undertaking that it would not take advantage of the Stock Exchange provision which permits a shareholder with a stake of more than 30% to raise this by two percentage points a year, without being required to bid for the rest of the shares. In the situation in which Collins then found itself, it would have taken News International less than five years to achieve control in this fashion. Such action, however, would have made a nonsense of all the warm expressions of mutual esteem and promises of future co-operation that marked the end of the take-over battle. Ian Chapman in his letter to shareholders in the 1981 accounts was able to write, 'The support I have received from my colleagues on the board has been enormously encouraging and strengthening, and I particularly welcome the helpful contribution that is being made by Rupert Murdoch and Sir Edward Pickering.'

In terms of trading, however, one immediate casualty was the plan for Pan (one-third owned by Collins) to be warehoused and distributed from Bishop-briggs. Space had already been set aside to receive Pan's stocks. Heinemann and Macmillan, the other two owners, jibbed at the link, however indirect, with News International. In the event, Pan was taken into Macmillan's Basingstoke distribution centre.

A considerably more significant development, however, was the purchase of Granada Publishing in March 1983 from the Granada Group. This was made possible by a rights issue, the first in William Collins's history. Previously raising money by way of rights was not a realistic option: the Stock Exchange would not have accepted a capital-raising exercise that was confined to non-voting shares; but a rights issue in voters and non-voters would have presented the family shareholders and the family trusts with the impossible task of recon-ciling, first, the objective of maintaining the existing level of control and, second, the need to respect the rules of investment prudence which limits the number of financial eggs one puts into one investment basket, regardless of whether or not the family hen is still laying.

The Granada purchase can be said to have marked the moment when Collins slipped the family moorings.

The acquisition of Granada cost a total of £7.9m and the rights issue raised £6.3m. News International had no trouble subscribing in full to its entitlement of new ordinary shares at 220p and 'A' shares at 175p, and the issue was a resounding success. Granada's attractions to Collins were considerable: first came its publishing strengths, with three-fifths of its sales in paperbacks; second, there was the scope for having the printer at Bishopbriggs supply its needs (Ian Chapman recalls that Granada's annual paperback output of 14 million units corresponded almost exactly to the 15 million volume gap in print orders at Bishopbriggs); third, the excess capacity in distribution stood to be eliminated.

An event took place in June 1983 which further illustrated the changed circumstances at Collins. Mark Collins, the family director who had fought hard and conspicuously against the bid by News International, resigned. Three months earlier he had been appointed executive chairman of Collins's retail subsidiary Hatchards, having previously been managing director of Collins Publishers. There were few who thought that this represented promotion.

Mark Collins, who subsequently helped launch the eponymous publisher Collins & Brown, feels today that he had served his purpose at Collins and that it was time for him to move. His departure meant the end of any direct family involvement at senior level; ten years previously there had been eight Collinses in the company, four of them main board directors.

On the trading front, were one to have held an audit five years on from the May 1981 bid, it would have revealed a pretty healthy situation: 1986 turnover of £144.4m, against £63.7m in 1980, the year immediately preceding the bid: pre-tax profits of £15.5m, compared with £2.2m, giving margins of 10.7% against 3.5%. Earnings per share of 32p were nearly six times the 1980 level of 5.5p (adjusted for bonus and rights issues). Such results were rightly ascribed to effective management initiatives taken in a very much more friendly economic environment with sterling and inflation having both fallen dramatically.

In the stock market, the company was valued at £135m at the start of 1987, compared with £25m, which was the value of News International's raised bid in July 1981.

From one point of view, this amounts to a powerful argument in favour of failed bids, where the defence has to live up to its promises. From another, it puts into relief the benefits when the unsuccessful bidder, having retained his interests, acts as a supportive financier. The remarkable feature about the Collins situation was that News Corporation's support did not stop there.

In March 1987 News Corporation bought Harper & Row Publishers, the US house with major publishing interests spread across trade (including children's and religious), professional (notably medical), and college textbooks. Harper & Row had had several years of indifferent performance and was widely seen as an interesting recovery proposition. It was also one of the few remaining independent US publishers of any size.

The first predatory move was made by the entrepreneurial Theodore L. Cross, well known for his successful operations in the field of publishing. On 11 March he bid $34 a share for the 94% of the shares he did not already own, thereby valuing the company at some $150m. Two days later, Harcourt Brace Jovanovich bid $50 a share, valuing the company at $220m. Both bidders had indicated that they would not pursue a takeover if Harper & Row rejected their bids. At this point, Harper & Row revealed that it was in discussion with 'a considerable number' of companies, and analysts took note of the fact that management's previously expressed wish to remain independent had been dropped from company statements. In other words, an auction was under way.

On 30 March News Corporation showed its hand with an offer of $65 a share, which had the recommendation of the Harper & Row board. It valued the company at $300m, 1.5 times 1986 turnover of $202m, 26 times pre-tax profits of $11.4m and 51 times net earnings of $5.9m. The News Corporation offer was nearly double Ted Cross's sighting shot.

The successful outcome of Murdoch's bid owed much to the price he had been prepared to pay. It was also the preferred result from Harper & Row's point of view. Collins – and Ian Chapman in particular – were well known to the Harper & Row management, and these links were behind their decision to invite Collins to act as a white knight. A consideration that also influenced the Harper & Row management was the fact that rationalization measures and integration measures would be less severe than with some of the other bidders, given the fact that neither News Corporation nor Collins had much in the way of an existing US book publishing base.

For the News Corporation/Collins partnership, however, some of the very factors that helped it win Harper & Row added to the challenge that it faced: if there were no easy head office savings and warehousing and distribution economies to be had, the underlying profits turnaround had to be that much more profound. From the outset, therefore, it was recognized that Collins, having the professional expertise, would provide the top management. At the same time, it would own half the business.

The first part of the plan was implemented immediately, with Ian Chapman and George Craig being appointed joint chief executives of Harper & Row in May 1987, as soon as the News Corporation acquisition was finalized. An action team incorporating Collins executives was set up and a number of wide-ranging measures was proposed. Following their approval at Harper & Row board level, their implementation fell largely to George Craig, who had taken up full-time residence in New York.

The second half of the plan, which involved Collins acquiring a 50% stake in Harper & Row, had to be postponed for tax and legal reasons. Collins was therefore given the option of buying half of Harper & Row some six months hence at News Corporation's cost price. This says much for the happy trusting relations that prevailed at that time.

On 2 September 1987 Collins duly announced first-half results which revealed a pre-tax profits advance of 22% and a similar increase in earnings per share; that it would be exercising its option on 50% of Harper & Row at a cost of £95m; and that this would be financed by the second rights issue in its history, to raise £113m.

The subscription terms were one new ordinary share at 761p for every two held and one new 'A' share at 637p for every two held. News International confirmed that it would be taking up its full entitlement worth nearly £24m.

Collins was able at the same time to reveal some of the results of the work undertaken by the action team that had been put into Harper & Row. Annualized cost reductions and revenue improvements had been identified and were being implemented, worth $15m. These fell under eight headings and included such matters as cutting back on agency arrangements, sharpening buying practices, and eliminating head office excesses. What was not quantified was the advantage that 'global publishing' was hoped to bring. This was something that Collins had attempted in the 1970s with the purchase of World Publishing, but the timing was wrong and the choice of company unhappy.

Rupert Murdoch had proclaimed at the time of the March takeover, 'We have the opportunity to develop a truly international publishing network.' Ian Chapman in his September letter to shareholders announcing the rights issue had described the situation as 'a once in a lifetime opportunity'. He might have added that the quest for a 'global' publishing capability had two years previously involved them in detailed discussions with NAL (subsequently bought by Pearson), and that at a dinner in Overtons restaurant with Rupert Murdoch towards the end of 1986, he had identified Harper & Row as the ideal candidate for acquisition 'if it were ever to become available'.

The rights document described the management structure for Harper & Row. News International and Collins were to have equal board representation and Rupert Murdoch and Ian Chapman were to be the first co-chairmen. The intention was also spelled out to appoint in due course a chief executive officer of Harper & Row Publishers, at which time Ian Chapman and George Craig would cease to have executive responsibilities.

In the event, however, George Craig resigned from his position as group managing director and vice-chairman of William Collins in March 1988, citing 'certain differences of approach'. Shortly thereafter, he was appointed president and chief executive officer of Harper & Row, the company in which William Collins continued to have a 50% interest and on the board of which Ian Chapman remained as co-chairman.

George Craig, recruited in 1975 from outside the world of books to take charge of the manufacturing and distribution divisions, had been made a Collins board director in 1976. He had fought his corner, resisted divestment suggestions involving on one occasion R. R. Donnelley as a possible buyer of the printing interests, and helped lay the foundation for Collins's distribution side becoming recognized for the efficiency of its operations. In 1977 his chartered accountancy background earned him additional overall financial responsibilities on the departure of the then finance director.

In the wake of the boardroom changes in 1979, Craig emerged as the managing director of all Glasgow operations, and in April 1983 he was made group managing director. Announcing this appointment, together with that of Charles Allen as group managing director of Collins Publishing, Ian Chapman explained that they were made 'in order to assist in longer-term succession planning'. George Craig was also said to be assuming 'a wider role in the general management of the Collins Group'. The strong impression that he was being identified as heir apparent was further reinforced in 1984 with his appointment as vice-chairman.

What happened subsequently to sour the atmosphere is hard to tell. One factor appears to have been the reservations some non-executive directors had over George's lack of publishing experience. More generally, it may have had much to do with the clash of ambitions between two men, Ian Chapman and George Craig, who had divergent timetables.

Whatever the reasons, strained relations at the top became public knowledge within the firm from about 1986 and this inevitably filtered into the trade. George Craig's secondment to Harper & Row in early 1987 was seen by some as a neat organizational solution for Collins: George would be in New York and largely running his own show, while Ian would remain based in London. In practice, however, it solved nothing. Collins duly became a 50% owner of Harper & Row and both companies continued to expand internationally in trade publishing. As one Collins observer put it, 'All that happened was that the warheads took longer to land.'

It has to be said that company histories are littered with struggles of this kind. Nor is it by any means certain that the companies suffer as a result. Indeed, such clashes may actually help to enhance performance to the extent that they expel complacency. The reason that they need to be drawn attention to in a history of Collins is that they formed part of the official justification for Rupert Murdoch's second bid for the company.

NEWS CORPORATION'S BID

The announcement on 17 November 1988 that News Corporation, through its subsidiary News International, was bidding for the shares of Collins that it did not already own came as a considerable surprise. Two months earlier Collins had released its half-year results, which had been pretty well received. Admittedly, it was noted that the 62% improvement in pre-tax profit was explained by a £6.7m contribution from the half-interest in Harper & Row, while operating profits of Collins's businesses were £1.7m lower. These were struck, however, after exceptional stock write-offs of £1.2m that harked back to under-provisions the previous year. Most importantly, the interim dividend increase of 15.4% carried buoyant implications, which were reinforced by the chairman's comment: 'I look forward to the months ahead with great confidence.'

In investment circles, the element of surprise came with the timing of the bid, rather than with the bid itself: the presence of Rupert Murdoch with a near 42% voting interest was always recognized as potentially destabilising, but at the same time welcomed as a spur to Collins's management to perform. This they seemed to be doing. For Ian Chapman, the surprise ran deeper. Marmaduke Hussey (now Lord Hussey of North Bradley and at the time chairman of the governors of the BBC) had been a non-executive director of Collins since June 1985; as he recalls, 'Ian had total trust in Rupert. Time after time Ian said that Rupert had assured him that he would never make a bid for the company unless it was an agreed bid.'

In contrast to the first occasion, when the defence document held the attention, in the second bid it was the other way round, with the offer document attracting the most intense analysis. The tone was aggressive. Specific points centred on:

– the decline in Collins's first-half operating profits;
– the departure in the preceding twelve months (subsequently corrected to eighteen) of eight key executives;
– Collins's refusal to distribute and sell Harper & Row titles in the UK.

General points included:
– Collins's failure to exploit to any significant extent the great potential offered by the Harper & Row acquisition;
– the poor staff morale;
– the need for stronger direction to regenerate confidence and develop new initiatives.

At the same time, News International took credit for encouraging and supporting a major capital expenditure programme in Scotland, a number of acquisitions and two rights issues, plus the initiative leading to the purchase by Collins of half of Harper & Row.

Aside from the decline in first-half operating profits, which was factual, the most telling specific criticism related to staff defections. In February 1988 Sonia Land had resigned her position as finance director (which did not carry with it a seat on the main board). George Craig, group managing director and vice-chairman, had left in May 1988. Eddie Bell, managing director of the Collins General Division, had resigned in October 1988.

Eddie Bell had joined George Craig at Harper & Row, and Sonia Land, after a spell with a venture-capital group, had become the first woman director of News International.

As far as the more general criticisms were concerned, it was necessary to pinch oneself in order to be reminded that News Corporation had had board representation since 1981 and had not chosen to voice its disquiet. It is hardly surprising, therefore, that investors looked outside the offer document for the real reasons behind the bid.

Sonia Land recalls the conversation she had in New York with Rupert Murdoch that immediately preceded this second bid, in which he admitted to being uncertain as to whether he should sell his shares in Collins or buy the lot. This indecision is also taken up in the article written by William Rees-Mogg (Lord Rees-Mogg) for *The Times* of 3 January 1989. In the course of a telephone conversation on New Year's Eve, during which Rupert Murdoch reviewed the course of the bid, he stated that he had originally been willing to sell or buy Collins, but that he had wanted to buy out Collins's stake in Harper & Row. In the event, the arguments that Collins and Harper & Row made up a superb combination of publishing strengths carried the day. But to benefit from such strengths, a 41.7% voting interest and a 21% overall equity interest in Collins, plus a 50% holding in Harper & Row, bred managerial and financial inefficiencies: powers of appointment and dismissal were muted and cash advantages were confined to the dividends to which Murdoch's holdings entitled him. As News International finance director Peter Stehrenberger conceded, the fact that the acquisition of Collins would give Murdoch access to the entire cash flow 'was not something we had overlooked'.

What he might have added was that News Corporation, having spent $3bn three months previously on Triangle Publications Inc., publisher of *TV Guide,* was travelling down the slippery path that almost brought the whole group to its knees later in 1990. Already in the autumn of 1988 the US credit agency, Moodys, had downgraded some News debt. Little surprise, therefore, that Murdoch felt the need to clarify his interests in book publishing. 'My advisers tell me this is the only way I can validate my investment' would be his refrain.

To manage the bid, he chose Sonia Land.

From the outset she played a strong hand with considerable verve.

Her detailed knowledge of Collins's business at a managerial level was of impeccable quality, having been obtained during her years in the key position of finance director. It was only in February 1988 that she had resigned.

While George Craig was neutral, being the servant of both News and Collins, he gave moral support. 'I know that the publishing management is demoralized,' he told the *Sunday Telegraph* correspondent.

In having Rupert Murdoch as her boss, Sonia Land was representing the interests of a corporate heavyweight.

Most significant of all, the bid was being launched from an impressive platform – 41.7% of the voting stock. (The disposal of some 30,000 shares in 1984 had reduced the News holding from the 42.25% it ended the day with in 1981.) This was appreciably higher than the 30.4% platform from which the first bid had been launched.

The News International bid valued the Ordinary shares at 640p and the 'A' shares at 535p. Immediately preceding the offer they stood at 543p and 453p, respectively. The whole of Collins was being valued at £293m.

In his rejection of the bid, Ian Chapman commented: 'We can see why this looks to be a good deal for News, but it's a lousy one for William Collins.' A

City research note of the same date drew attention to the fact that the bid prices were well below the levels at which shareholders – including News International – had subscribed for shares in the Collins rights issue a mere fourteen months previously. In addition, comparisons with some other publishing transactions, such as Reed's purchase of Octopus in July 1987 and Maxwell Communications's purchase of Macmillan in the USA in November 1988, suggested that the basis of valuation of Collins was at an extremely low level: the News bid was equivalent to about nine times Collins's profits and this was less than half similar calculations for Octopus and Macmillan. News International, for its part, pointed to the fact that it already had a near-majority stake in the voting shares and consequently that there was no reason for it to pay a premium for control.

The defence had two principal options:
– to persuade institutional shareholders to stay put by demonstrating how derisory the offer was on a valuation basis and in relation to the company's prospects, or
– to identify another purchaser who would value the business more realistically and carry the day or, at the very least, force News to improve on its bid.

In the 1981 bid, Collins's profits forecast in effect won the battle for the company. In 1988, when the defence set about working on projections, the signs looked promising: after all, Collins had just produced some reasonable half-year figures and had made a strong statement for the important second half, buttressed by a sizeable interim dividend increase – all of this endorsed by the directors, including, of course, Rupert Murdoch and Sir Edward Pickering. In practice, the task was greatly complicated by the privileged position enjoyed by News, which left Collins, the target company, in a position of dependence on the predator for much of its defensive armour.

John Clement, appointed group managing director for publishing in mid-1987, recalls that the 1988 profits forecast covering Collins's own operations (but never released) 'was certainly not gloomy and would have met the reasonable expectations of the City'. The spotlight, however, was on Harper & Row – which, as a turnaround situation, 'had more juice to it' than a comparatively mature Collins.

Forecasts for Harper & Row and valuations of its assets needed, however, to be endorsed by the Harper & Row board. The defence experienced difficulties in getting responses to queries and, wherever there was an element of conjecture, a conservative interpretation now held sway at Harper & Row. The defence's efforts culminated in a meeting in New York on 15 December. Collins was supported by its advisers, Schroders and Lazards. News had Charterhouse. At the meeting, the release of information by Harper & Row under questioning from the Collins camp was cut short, however, by the legal opinion that the News team had just secured. This was that, under US Stock Exchange rules, no disclosures were permissible that went beyond what had already been revealed to shareholders. This view was subsequently endorsed by further legal opinion. That was the moment that the Collins board, for all practical purposes, lost the use of a profits forecast in its defence.

It also spelled the end of its efforts to preserve its independence. It had to fall back on its second option which was to find an alternative buyer with more realistic views on pricing. While approaches were received from several large international groups, the only serious enquiry came from France.

Groupe de la Cité and William Collins were already in contact with each other at a trading level, thanks to a lexicographic partnership, the Collins-Robert (in France, Robert-Collins) bilingual dictionary And it was John Clement – with impeccable Anglo-French connections, since he had started his publishing career at Gallimard – who had been heavily involved in the development of the joint venture. What could be more natural than to turn to one's friends in a time of crisis?

Groupe de la Cité was at a very early stage of its development, having emerged at the start of 1988 from a 50:50 fusion of publishing interests belonging to CEP Communication (which contributed to the new company such well-known names as Larousse, Nathan, and its subsidiary Robert) and Générale Occidentale (which injected business publishing assets through Presses de la Cité, trade publishing through Plon, Presses Pocket, and its 50% interest in the major book club group France Loisirs). At the time, the share ownership of Groupe de la Cité, which had been floated on the Paris stock market, was 38% CEP Communication, 38% Générale Occidentale, and 24% institutional and private investors. Behind CEP was the French media group Havas, with 48%.

The newly formed Groupe de la Cité had just acquired a toehold in UK publishing with the purchase in September 1988 of Grisewood & Dempsey. It was a perfectly reasonable assumption that it would be eager to extend this. On that basis, Collins presented an extraordinary opportunity to a management bent on international diversification.

Nonetheless, it was a spirited act for a continental group, in existence in its present structure for less than a year, to enter into a contested takeover in a foreign land and one in which its declared rival, a man of formidable reputation, enjoyed a 41.7% head start.

In the event, the emergence of a white knight and his subsequent withdrawal took place within the space of fifteen days.

The afternoon of 22 December 1988: at 1.14 p.m. the Stock Exchange electronic news screen carried William Collins's announcement that it had received an approach 'which may lead to offers being made, at a level appreciably above the level of the News International offers, for the whole of Collins'.

At 4.52 p.m. the Stock Exchange news service reported News International's reaction, which was to state 'categorically that it will not accept any competing offer in respect of its 41.7% voting stake in Collins. News has been a major shareholder in Collins for over seven years and wishes to retain its shareholdings for the longer term. News is not interested in selling.'

The identity of the potential bidder was not revealed, but the article in the *Financial Times* the following day relayed publishing analysts' speculations that it might be Hachette or Presses de la Cité. On the cold-to-hot scale, this ranked very warm.

One has a sense of the frustrations experienced by the defence in the comment by Schroders that this was 'negotiation by megaphone. He [Murdoch] is shouting his public response across the room, rather than sitting down around a table and talking about it.'

On 29 December Schroders announced that 'the potential offeror' intended to make offers subject to a significant number of Ordinary shareholders undertaking irrevocably to accept the offers. The indicated prices were 880p for each ordinary and 735p for each 'A' share, a 37.5% improvement in both cases on News International's terms. The offer had the recommendation of the Collins directors. The statement went on to say that 'the potential offeror wishes to discuss the merits of the offers with News International, particularly in view of its joint ownership with Collins of Harper & Row'. One implication was that the offeror, whose identity still remained officially hidden, was ready to cede back to the News group Collins's half-interest in Harper & Row.

The following day, the white knight was revealed to be the Groupe de la Cité, and on the same day News International raised its own offer to the same level as that of the French group. News reiterated that it would not sell its stake and was not interested in discussions.

Meanwhile, the hunting trip undertaken on behalf of Collins by its brokers to garner irrevocable acceptances of the white knight's offer was producing limited results, even though the institutions were given an escape clause, in the event of a higher offer emerging from one source or another. The rock-hard inflexibility of News to contemplate discussions, let alone sales, acted as a deterrent. In addition, the length of time that the French group chose to remain anonymous was not helpful. In the event, holders of around 16% of Collins ordinary shares gave such undertakings. Groupe de la Cité had been hoping for something closer to 40%, which would have put it on a par with News.

An even more important development had been a telephone call from Rupert Murdoch, who was in Australia, to Christian Brégou, président directeur général of the Groupe de la Cité. The details of the conversation are unrecorded, but it is believed to have been short. Neither man is a linguist but the message that Rupert Murdoch was conveying to Christian Brégou to 'keep off my patch' lent itself to a few crisp, colourful expressions in basic English.

4 January 1989 saw Groupe de la Cité announce that it would not proceed with its offer as proposed. Furthermore, its readiness to improve on those terms so as to come to an agreement with News International, covering both the valuation of the business and the disposition of the stake in Harper & Row, had been spurned. Groupe de la Cité was, therefore, withdrawing.

On 6 January the Collins board unanimously recommended acceptance of the News offer. On 23 January Ian Chapman resigned as chairman and chief executive, being replaced as chairman by Rupert Murdoch and as chief executive by George Craig.

Chapter 10

CURRENT TRENDS AND ISSUES

THIS CHAPTER SETS OUT to consider a number of the issues that were previously raised, some of which will have emerged from the accounts of individual publishing groups, and to give them a more timely assessment. Any up-date of this kind extends into some discussion of possible future developments. There are in addition specific sections on the outlook for books in the Chinese market, the scope for print on demand, the growth of self-publishing, and changes in the provision of finance. The concluding section touches on valuations of publishing businesses.

CONGLOMERATION AND LITERARY STANDARDS

The impact of conglomeration on literary trade publishing was the subject of analysis in Chapter 2. Nearly ten years later, the subject retains its topicality.

Once again, the Booker Prize can be called into play to provide 'independent' evidence in a debate that is inherently subjective. The passage of time now makes possible a neat division of the period since the establishment of the prize in 1969 into three: twelve years to the end of 1980, eleven years to the end of 1991, and twelve years to the end of 2003. A table of Booker winners and of those short-listed reveals publishing houses falling into four broad divisions – those with a consistent record, those whose fortunes have waned, those that have been ascendant, and fourthly a long tail that offers no pattern, often based on solitary sightings (see table 32).

For consistency, Jonathan Cape is outstanding, achieving eight, thirteen, and seven showings and within these figures two, three, and one Booker Prize winners. It is notable how Cape has not been diverted from this steady path of excellence by several changes in its corporate shape and in its ownership: 1969 was the year it joined forces with Chatto & Windus and 1973 when Bodley Head was added; in 1987 it became American-owned when Random House bought the combined group, while in 1998 ownership swung back to Europe with Bertelsmann's purchase of Random House. Cape's experience is mirrored by that of its publishing sibling, Chatto & Windus, albeit at a lower level of achievement, with five, seven, and four entries and a Booker Prize winner in each of the first two periods. Somewhat the same comments can be made of

Table 32: *Booker Prize showings since 1969*

	12 years to 1980	11 years to 1991	12 years to 2003
Consistency			
Jonathan Cape	8 (2)	13 (3)	7 (1)
Faber & Faber	3 (2)	7 (2)	7 (2)
Chatto & Windus	5 (1)	7 (1)	4
Hamish Hamilton	3	5	4
William Heinemann	4 (1)	4	2
Secker & Warburg	1	7 (1)	4 (3)
Duckworth	4	2	2
HarperCollins/Flamingo	3 (1)	2	2 (1)
Allen Lane/Viking/Penguin	2	5	4 (1)
Hodder & Stoughton/Sceptre	2	1 (1)	3
Eclipse			
Michael Joseph	5	–	–
André Deutsch	3 (1)	3 (1)	–
Hutchinson	2	1 (1)	–
Bodley Head	2	1	–
Weidenfeld & Nicolson	3 (2)	–	–
W. H. Allen	3	–	–
Ascension			
Macmillan/Picador	3	2	9 (1)
Bloomsbury	–	2	6 (2)
Fourth Estate	–	–	3

Note: Brackets relate to titles that received the Booker Prize (now known as Man Booker); they have been included in the unbracketed figures of short-listed titles

William Heinemann and Secker & Warburg, which also have in common ownership by Random House, but since the later date of 1997.

Publishing houses within media groups that can lay claim to consistency of a more modest character are Allen Lane/Viking Press/Penguin within the Pearson empire, Hodder & Stoughton/Sceptre, now part of retailers W. H. Smith, and Collins/Flamingo, part of News Corporation.

Among the independent publishing companies, the reliability of Faber & Faber is as remarkable in its way as that of Jonathan Cape, while Duckworth merits a thoroughly honourable mention. As will emerge later in the section on independent trade publishers, the correlation between literary excellence and profitability is not necessarily high.

The sad little list of houses that have suffered an eclipse include Penguin's Michael Joseph (which is explained by a change in the character of the imprint, away from the literary and into the popular). W. H. Allen and André Deutsch have literally or virtually ceased to trade, while the Bodley Head imprint is now reserved for children's titles, a rare instance of rationalization within Random House. Hutchinson, also part of Random House, has developed along more popular lines. The non-show of Weidenfeld & Nicolson, part of Orion since 1992, which Hachette acquired (as to 70%) in 1998, is attributable to a period of under-investment in fiction, though the imprint retains its literary character.

For growth stories, one needs to turn in the first place to two new entrants, Bloomsbury, launched in 1987 and still an independent company, and Fourth Estate, which started trading in 1984 and was acquired by Harper/Collins in 2000. While the success of Bloomsbury and to a lesser extent Fourth Estate, in capturing the Booker judges' attention is indeed noteworthy, it is as nothing compared to that of Macmillan's trade paperback imprint, Picador: in the eleven years to 2002, it had a title in the short list in eight of those years, one of them as winner of the prize. On only three occasions, therefore, did it fail to supply a finalist. That this owes much to – is directly attributable to – the Picador editor, Peter Straus, who joined Macmillan in 1990 from Hamish Hamilton, is reinforced by the fact that Picador, founded in 1972, was not in consideration for the first twenty years of its existence. Peter Straus's decision in July 2002 to join the literary agency Rogers, Coleridge & White is commented on later in the section on literary agents. His departure from Picador puts to the test the strength of the literary momentum within an imprint once the inspirer is no longer there.

What might be termed a growth story in the making is provided by HarperCollins, the very house that presided over the extinction of such names as Fontana, Grafton, and Unwin, and agreed a management buy-out of Harvill. Victoria Barnsley, fresh from her creation of Fourth Estate, is a forceful champion of the commercial – as well as literary – advantages that distinctive imprints can offer.

The most numerous category in the Booker short list is the residual fourth, with nineteen imprints represented, many with one entry and none more than two over the life of the prize. At this point the inclusive nature of the prize's rules calls for consideration. Any UK publisher may enter up to two full-length novels (as well as a list of five further titles out of which the judges will be required to call in from eight to twelve titles). These rights attach to recognized imprints, with the vital consequence that when a Cape or Hamish Hamilton for example changes ownership, their absorption into Random House and Penguin respectively in no way extinguishes their eligibility for the prize. These rules also have a 'democratic' fall-out. Since works of unknown or little-known authors are unlikely to be selected by the big fiction houses for submission, they have to wear the colours of the smaller houses or even experimental imprints to have any chance of recognition. This was demonstrated in the 2002 Man Booker, when *The Life of Pi* by the Canadian-born Yann Martel won the prize. Canongate, as publisher, was an improbable source on several counts. In the year 2000, on turnover of £2.2m, pre-tax profits were vestigial at £23,000, while subsequent interviews with Jamie Byng revealed the publisher of a burgeoning literary imprint rich in expletives. This had the obvious merit of adding to the Man Booker Prize's newsworthiness, but did little to further one's knowledge of the publishing process. The 2003 Man Booker included within the short list two small publishers (Tindal Street Press and Atlantic), but then reverted to form with Faber & Faber securing its sixth win with D. B. C. Pierre's *Vernon God Little*. Canongate was not, however, to be totally denied a place in the limelight, having previously bought the US rights.

Among unusual finalists, there was in 1994 Jill Paton Walsh's *Knowledge of Angels*, self-published in the UK by Green Bay and accompanied by a cloud of bitterness over the failure of established UK houses to recognize its merits, including Weidenfeld & Nicolson, publisher of her two previous novels for adults. Conglomeration was said to be at the heart of this blind spot. The criticism was dulled by the judges' choice that year: James Kelman's deeply inaccessible *How Late it Was, How Late*, written in Glaswegian vernacular and published by Secker & Warburg, at the time part of the Reed Elsevier conglomerate.

Among poor individual losers, special mention goes to Salman Rushdie, when *Shame* failed to win in 1983, as recalled by Martyn Goff in *A Celebration of 30 Years of the Booker Prize for Fiction*. For corporate poor losers, Orion stands out when the firm staged a rival party on the night preceding the Booker dinner, in protest at Vikram Seth's *A Certain Boy* having been overlooked in 1993.

From this analysis of the Booker Prize finalists and winners, several generalizations seem justified:
– the consistency with which some ten literary imprints have contributed titles to the shortlist *throughout* the 35 years of Booker's existence;
– the way that changes of ownership have not influenced one way or the other such imprints' success rates;
– the fact that two other imprints have been able to force their way in among the consistent contributors (Bloomsbury and Picador);
– the evidence repeated over and over again that membership of the Booker finalists' club is open to all writers;
– the lack of any indication that concentration of ownership within publishing leads to homogenization – i.e. diminution of editorial quality and variety. This does not extend, however, to book design, as witness Penguin's sad little announcement in January 2003 that it was setting up a central text-design department, with standard templates to be used for most titles.

One final area of enquiry concerns the degree of support given to new writers. The Whitbread Book Awards, among which a prize for the first novel has been included since 1981, may be used to throw some light on the subject. Over the period of 21 years, Hamish Hamilton has had three winners (the first in 1981, the most recent in 2000), while Picador, Faber & Faber, Macmillan, Secker & Warburg, and Jonathan Cape have each had two. Of the remaining eight prize novels, four were published in the 1990s (Viking, Bloomsbury,

Black Swan (Transworld), and Chatto & Windus) and four in the 1980s (Constable, Heinemann, Pandora Press, Salamander Press).

This listing has much in common with the Booker listings, with the same imprints consistently dominant. As between conglomerate publishers and independent houses, the former are if anything more in evidence in the Whitbread results than in those of the Booker. The evidence, limited as it is, does not support those critics who view the withdrawal of support for new fiction writing as a necessary consequence of greater concentration in publishing.

Looking backwards in order to make a judgment on the future often seems wrong-headed, or at best perverse. What the past does seem to indicate is that, in a period of unprecedented change in British publishing, literary fiction as seen through the lens of the Booker Prize has held to a remarkably steady course. This is an encouraging augury.

PROFITABILITY OF THE LARGER GROUPS

Since the mid-1990s the trading results of a number of the large trade publishing groups have been such as to elicit the question 'What is it that they are getting so right?' Table 33, which presents the results of three companies, provides the best – albeit highly imperfect – view of trade publishing at that level. They reveal a pattern of strong underlying margin improvement. The main weaknesses in terms of analysis are:
– the omission from the table of Random House, the largest trade publishing group in the UK; its performance is, however, commented on in the text;
– the inclusion within the Penguin Group of the north American and Australasian results; total sales of Penguin's UK based businesses, including Dorling Kindersley, account for less than 40% of world-wide group sales;
– the inclusion within Hodder Headline of the educational and academic businesses, which make up about 25% of group sales;
– the HarperCollins figures incorporate the whole of the book interests of News Corporation. The results of HarperCollins Publishers are also shown, since the company covers the majority of HarperCollins's UK businesses. The disparity in profitability is largely explained by the earlier implementation of margin-enhancing measures taken in the US company.

While, for reasons of coverage and definition, direct comparisons between the groups may be unwise, within individual companies' results, year to year comparisons appear to be largely justified.

Penguin's operating margins were heavily influenced by the purchase in May 2000 of Dorling Kindersley, which resulted in the consolidation in the year 2000 of £125m of turnover and zero profits, in 2001 of £146m of turnover and losses of £7m and in 2002 of £160m of turnover and £8m profits. Excluding Dorling Kindersley, operating margins in the three years were 12.5%, 12.9%, and 11.7% respectively. Penguin's 2002 results were struck after exceptional costs of £10m.

Table 33: *Trading record within media groups*

	1997	1998	1999	2000	2001	2002
*Penguin (£m)**						
Sales	525	523	565	755	820	838
Operating profits	58	48	65	79	80	87
Operating margins	11.0%	9.2%	11.5%	10.5%	9.8%	10.4%
(excl. D.K.)				12.5%	12.9%	11.7%
Hodder Headline (£m)						
Sales	93*	102*	–	116‡	128‡	137‡
Operating profits	8.7	10.0	–	16.0	18.0	20.0
Operating margins	9.4%	9.8%	–	13.8%	14.1%	14.6%
HarperCollins (A$m)†						
Sales	946	1087	1224	1634	1907	2059
Operating profits	16	55	77	141	205	224
Operating margins	1.7%	5.1%	6.3%	8.6%	10.7%	10.9%
HarperCollins Publishers (£m)†						
Sales	130.8	122.0	124.3	135.7	150.0	184.6
Operating profits	3.3	5.1	6.4	6.8	8.0	11.6
(adjusted)				8.0	9.1	14.0
Operating margins	2.5%	4.2%	5.1%	5.0%	5.3%	6.3%
(adjusted)				5.9%	6.1%	7.6%

*Year-end 31 December.   †Year-end 30 June.   ‡Year-end 31 August; excluding Helicon 2000 to 2002.

Hodder Headline's remarkable 40% margin improvement between 1998 and 2000 straddles its acquisition by W. H. Smith in May 1999. It is partly explained by the £2m saving achieved when it ceased to be a stand-alone publicly quoted company; this relates to costs such as audit fees and Stock Exchange listing charges. In terms of trading benefits, the affinity felt by W. H. Smith's public for Hodder Headline's products is worth stressing. This is exemplified in a conversation that Michael Pountney, then book buyer for W. H. Smith, had with Tim Hely Hutchinson in 1986. To the question 'At what market is your new company aimed?', the answer was 'Yours'. That the mutual regard between customer and publisher remains warm was illustrated in the W. H. Smith Book Awards 2003: of the eight categories put out for public vote, Hodder Headline featured in the shortlists of all but two, and in a couple of cases came out top.

HarperCollins stands out with easily the most dramatic improvement in margins over the period covered – admittedly from very depressed levels – both in respect of the global results of News Corporation's book publishing interests and of those of HarperCollins Publishers. In the narrative attached to the annual accounts of the UK company, the exclusion of exceptional items gave adjusted profits in 1999/2000 of £8.om and margins of 5.9%, adjusted profits in 2000/2001 of £9.1m and margins of 6.1%, and adjusted profits in 2001/2002 of £14m and margins of 7.6%.

In the case of Random House, its UK trade publishing interests date from the 1987 purchase of Chatto, Virago, Bodley Head and Jonathan Cape (Chapter 8), which was followed two years later by the acquisition of Century Hutchinson. A key event in the history of the group was its move out of loss into modest profit in the year to 30 June 1994, when it achieved operating margins of 2%. These had risen to 5% by 1996 and stood at 8% in 1997, by which time Reed's trade publishing division, comprising William Heinemann and Secker & Warburg, had just been acquired. By 1998, when Random House itself was bought by Bertelsmann, margins had reached 10%. This change of ownership entailed the addition to the Random House group of Transworld, whose own profitability had been exemplary: in the year to 30 June 1999, the last time that Transworld's figures were publicly available, operating margins were a healthy 13%, while over the five previous years they had averaged a remarkable 16.5%.

For the Random House group as a whole (made up of the UK operations as well as of those of the Australasian and South African subsidiaries), operating margins in 1999/2000 were 11.5%. In the year to 30 June 2001 on sales of £202m and operating profits of £23m, margins remained steady at 11.5%. Following a change in the year-end to 31 December the calendar year 2002 saw operating margins of 12%. Random House's pattern of profitability reflects, as the chief executive, Gail Rebuck, explains, the continuing policy of diversity within a federal structure (some thirty separate imprints), combined with focus within imprints, where micro-management of individual titles is the rule. One might add that management appears to have made the most of the cost savings and sales enhancing opportunities stemming from the succession of mergers and acquisitions that have largely shaped the company.

One way to explore the reasons for the rise in profitability of the larger trade publishing groups is to relate results to declared objectives. In Pearson's 1997 report to shareholders, the Penguin strategy was set out: 'Pearson's new management started to change some of its economic approaches to publishing. They began signing multi-book deals to build relationships with authors, aiming at bestselling books which will bring long-term revenues, focussing on popular literary fiction, philosophy, science, and business.' While some of the claims to novelty are overstated – after all Stephen King had been for many years a multi-book bestselling author nurtured by Viking Penguin since 1979 – what was new was that the strategy was being implemented in the UK in the immediate aftermath of the collapse of the Net Book Agreement in 1995.

That development lifted books into the classification of products suitable for year-round promotion. This freedom to discount was of obvious relevance to existing book retailers, chiefly the chains, with Waterstones and W. H. Smith in the van. It also coincided with the flowering of the electronic retailers, notably Amazon.com, the one that has proved lastingly successful. Most important of all, perhaps, in terms of their direct and indirect impact, the large supermarkets discovered in books a new marketing tool that offered good margins. They had not previously been a natural home for books, though own-label ranges of the cookery/life-style kind had periodically featured. Now, however, pricing freedom was opening up to them opportunities involving quantities that had considerable promotional potential.

The influence that supermarkets exert, both on prices at the retail level and on the related discounts secured from the publishers, is magnified by their purchasing practices: by joining forces and channelling their orders through merchandizing wholesalers, to whom they concede part of the discount, they save on management time, but also secure maximum leverage in negotiations with their suppliers. Cork International (whose ranges include pet accessories and hair accessories) is currently dominant, supplying books to motorways and supermarkets, notably Tesco, Morrison, and Safeway. In the case of straightforward thrillers and romances, more that half the initial print run of a mass paperback can be taken up by the supermarkets. One important drawback in respect of those paperbacks that fall outside the top bestseller category and of many hardbacks: publishers' experience is of a high level of returns – 30% to 40% not being exceptional.

Julian Monaghan, book-buyer for Sainsbury, with responsibility also for DVDs, computer games, and music, is intent on lifting the profile of books 'simply because the margins are good; while Sainsbury cannot increase the amount people physically eat, they can increase purchases of non-food items and use the margins to plough back into their food lines'. With supermarkets increasing the size of their outlets and widening the range of items sold, he anticipates further growth in supermarkets' role in the book business – currently 5% by value of the total consumer market. The fact that books enable supermarkets to provide their customers with fresh offerings every month strengthens, as Gail Rebuck notes, their long-term position in such outlets.

Tim Hely Hutchinson of Hodder Headline, an early advocate of the abolition of retail price maintenance, quantifies some of the changes thus: a 'successful' paperback can now be expected to sell 50% more copies than before abolition. In hardbacks, a multiplier of ten can be used so that, for example, a Christmas bestseller will be achieving sales of 50,000 against 5000 previously. His assessment of the rise in the market share (units) of supermarkets in leading popular trade titles is startling: now, 15-20% plus, previously less than 5%. An oblique view into the extent to which supermarkets feature as customers of the major publishing houses is provided by BookScan's calculations of the average discount on the recommended retail price, the higher the discount, the greater the likely involvement. In 2002, Hodder Headline stood out with a figure of 22.9%. This was followed in descending order by the Hachette Group (Orion chiefly) with 17.7%, HarperCollins 17.1%, Random House 16.1%, Pan Macmillan 15.9%, Time Warner 14.9%. Penguin brought up the rear with 13.5%, providing thereby a reminder of the benefits that possession of a deep backlist can provide.

The abolition of the Net Book Agreement has added to the advantages that accompany scale, whether in publishing or in retailing. For the publisher, scale is defined as market share, calculated according to sales value; there was a time when market share was more closely equated to numbers of new titles published. A significant percentage figure gives the publisher automatic entrée to the Waterstones, W. H. Smiths, Tescos of this world and guarantees that his/her offerings will be considered by the retail chain when the latter comes to choose the twenty or so titles it is prepared to promote over say Christmas – or indeed its monthly choice. Negotiations are then conducted at two main levels: size of discount on the cover price granted by the publisher to the retailer and promotional support to be given by the publisher. The absence in the UK of the equivalent of the US Robinson Patman Act, which prohibits – in practice discourages – discriminatory discounts, under which one outlet is privileged by the publisher over another, ensures that in Britain such negotiations have a peculiarly tangled character. For illustrative purposes, a retailer having agreed to take (on a sale or return basis) 100,000 copies of a book, secures a discount of perhaps 60%, rather than something closer to a now standard 55% for that type of title. The next stage sees the publisher's sales representative return to discuss with his marketing department the degree of promotional support that the publisher is prepared to give that particular title. This may have three strands to it: (a) consumer advertising on radio, buses, underground hoardings; (b) aids at the retail outlet such as dump bins, stickers; (c) of increasing significance, what are sometimes known as 'catalogue' promotions. Aside from securing a listing in the retailer's own catalogue, this term shelters payments made for a key position in the store, whether it be a window slot or proximity to the till or presence on a table carrying the heading 'Choice of the Month'. They also rejoice in the suitably unattractive term 'bung'.

The happy conclusion of such negotiations heralds the birth of a bestseller. This view finds support within marketing departments: Lucy Ramsey, senior publicity officer at Headline, noted in the course of an interview with *Publishing News* that she had 'never worked for a company before where people say 'we're going to make this a bestseller' and it really happens'.

It is axiomatic that large companies need large sales to sustain their operations. The experience since 1995 teaches that these are realized by concentration of effort. This translates into the objective of 'getting more out of less' which in the first place calls for a reduction in new title output. Random House can be said to have led the field in the pursuit of economies in the mid-1990s, with a reduction of new titles of 40% from some 1500 annually. After the incorporation of Transworld into the group, new title numbers rose again to the 1500 level, where they now stand. At Headline and at Hodder the number of new titles has been cut back over the last five years by about one third from 600 each to 400. The Penguin General Division under Helen Fraser has seen a reduction from around 350 to 250. HarperCollins in the UK has reduced its overall annual output of titles by some 20% over three years to 1400 and has as its longer-term objective a figure of 1000. Such reductions are achieved in a number of ways: some by raising the prospective sales levels, in terms of units or revenues, beneath which publication will not be contemplated; others by stipulating that any new general title that cannot sustain a promotion budget of say £20,000 falls out of consideration; and then there is the method that bears directly on the pockets of the editors themselves by including credits for falls in the numbers of new titles commissioned in their year-end bonus calculations.

Nowhere is the doctrine of concentration more in evidence than in marketing and promotional programmes. Helen Fraser recognizes that at Penguin 'our marketing spend used to be spread thinly. Now we're concentrating extremely hard on some 10% of titles, giving those with big potential the maximum budget'. Such selectivity, by its own weight, as it were, discriminates against titles whose appeal is less strident, for whose publication exceptional proselytism at the weekly editorial selection meetings is therefore required. Those successful among second runners, then stand, however, to be carried along to some extent in the wake of the bestsellers and will also benefit from the more wide-ranging publicity campaigns.

This emphasis on front-list bestsellers has as one consequence an increase in competition for big-selling authors. Leaving aside the writer of the title that unexpectedly becomes a runaway success, the popular author is courted by all the major houses, leading to substantial advances, stimulated by his or her agent's endeavours. This makes also for some mobility as between publishers, recent examples being the move of Dean Koontz, Headline's highly successful author over many years, to HarperCollins in a three-book deal, and that of Vikram Seth from Orion to Time Warner's Little Brown imprint.

The deflation in new title numbers has, however, helped to moderate the consequences of such inflationary advances to big name authors. As a percentage of turnover, the overall sums distributed by a publisher to all its authors may not have risen. There seems less agreement about trends of expenditure on publicity and marketing. One estimate has it that, prior to the abolition of the Net Book Agreement, such outlays as a percentage of turnover were typically in the 5% to 5½% range. Now, taking into account all the marketing costs discussed earlier, the percentages are said to have risen to 6½% to 7%, clearly a substantial advance in absolute terms. Others point to rises that have more or less kept pace with the increase in turnover. What is beyond dispute is that all of this money is being spent much more intensively.

So much for what might be seen as indirect economies. Many of the direct savings relate to manpower, often in parallel with significant reductions in new title output. These reductions come twinned with such questions as 'Is there a need for the same number of editorial staff, are there savings to be made in production, design, copy-editing? Can sales teams be combined/streamlined, in response both to the more concentrated buying procedures of book chains and the smaller number of titles in reps' bags? The position of HarperCollins is particularly interesting: while in the midst of a continuing programme of staff reductions, it is establishing a structure of 'creative publishing villages' under which the five divisions which now make up Harper General Books have their own dedicated design, publicity, and marketing staff. This is a rare instance of rationalization deferring, in some measure, to decentralization. At Random House, where the bulk of the new title cuts date back several years, recent staff reductions have been confined to those deriving from the merger of May 2001 of the Random House and Transworld children's divisions. Hodder Headline disturbs the symmetry of the argument since its rising margins over the last six years owe nothing to any substantial manpower reductions.

A more subtle advantage that scale brings concerns purchasing power. In the experience of two independent trade publishers, on absorption into large groups they found their print bills reduced by more than 25%. And, more generally, where sharply increased unit sales are achieved on the back of reduced title numbers the impact on margins can be material.

Warehousing and distribution costs also stand to benefit from greater concentration of sales. The Pearson group in the UK is going one better and looking to achieve major economies across all its book publishing activities in the UK, combining warehouse and distribution of both Penguin and Pearson Education at Magna Park, Leicestershire. This is due to become fully operational in June 2004. It is also the occasion for centralizing customer services and credit control operations. The Penguin Group's chairman and chief executive, John Makinson, adds that 'this will enable us to invest in systems that improve the accuracy, speed, and efficiency of our supply chain', a comment that holds good as an objective that is being pursued by all major trade houses. Underlying these improvements are usually significant staff reductions.

A third ingredient in the achievement of expanded margins has been in companies' withdrawal from certain fields. HarperCollins's sale in August 2002 of its business publishing list to Profile Books was prompted by a decision to avoid specialist imprints. Penguin's withdrawal from the Wainwright walking guides had a similar rationale. A couple of minnows embedded in two very large groups. Two transactions which may have more to do with the shortened time horizons of the larger groups are Penguin's disposal to Yale University Press of the Pevsner architectural series in 2002 and Macmillan's sale to Oxford University Press of the Grove reference list in 2003.

There is no doubting the financial benefits that the large trade publishing groups have secured from the abolition of retail price maintenance of books. How much is in response to action taken at the retail end and how much to initiatives taken by the publishers themselves is uncertain. Some publishers choose to put the responsibility on the retailer, citing expanded discounts and onerous marketing commitments. It is well to remember, however, that a number of the large firms started de-netting titles ahead of the abolition of the Net Book Agreement. That aside, an additional spur to action has been the lack of sustained growth in the UK market.

For the future, scope no doubt exists for further economies, whether it be in the pre-press or supply chain areas, though in some cases 'the easy bit' may well have already been done. But, as Helen Fraser succinctly puts it, 'one's bosses don't allow one to stay put'. Against this, when margins start approaching the 15% mark, the question must be asked whether long-term considerations are being sacrificed to short-term priorities. What is certain is that the heightened dependence on a handful of bestseller titles, year in year out, has increased the speculative element in large-scale trade publishing.

INDEPENDENT TRADE PUBLISHERS

The choice of five independent trade publishers is necessarily highly selective – being made from a universe of perhaps two thousand (see table 34). Furthermore, one of them, Fourth Estate, is no longer independent. They do, however, have in common a high profile in the trade and exhibit both interesting similarities and contrasts. Among independent literary houses within trade publishing, they have increasing scarcity value, with John Murray now forming part of Hodder Headline within W. H. Smith and Harvill Press absorbed into Random House. The firm of Gerald Duckworth demonstrated in 2003 how the extremes of despair and hope can be experienced in the space of four weeks: after being placed into administration in April, the assets and goodwill were acquired in May from the administrator for £460,000 by Peter Mayer in association with his small US family-owned publishing house, the Overlook Press, which he started with his father in 1971.

Fourth Estate

From the 1 April 1984 date when it commenced trading, Fourth Estate started slowly building up its business. After eight years, turnover had grown to £1.2m; acceleration then occurred and five years later in 1998 it exceeded £5.1m and by the year to 31 March 2000, the last as an independent house, it stood at £7.25m. By the mid-1990s, it had demonstrated its editorial skills with a succession of bestsellers, fiction and non-fiction, that had secured prizes, positions in short lists, and unit sales in the hundreds of thousands. This earned its travellers the easy entrée to the big retail chains and the company the accolade of Publisher of the Year in the British Book Awards of 1997. In July 2000, HarperCollins, one of the three largest trade publishers in the UK, decided it could not contemplate a future without the backing of Fourth Estate and successfully bid for the company.

Moving from the editorial achievements to the financial record: in sixteen

Table 34: *Independent trade publishers*

	1995	1996	1997	1998	1999	2000	2001	2002
					(£000)			
Fourth Estate (year-end 31 March)								
Sales	2292	2185	3770	5134	7346	7257		
Operating profit	38	(105)	133	209	270	16		
Margins	1.7%	–	3.5%	4.1%	3.7%	0.2%		
Canongate (year-end 31 December)								
Sales		1259	1426	1764	1935	2209	2676	4482
Operating profit		54	(27)	41	(81)	46	(1)	185*
Margins		4.3%	–	2.3%	–	2.1%	–	4.1%
Profile Books (year-end 31 March)								
Sales			606†	1008	1371	1574	2094	2307
Operating profit			(40)	53	58	20	62	59
Margins			–	5.3%	4.2%	1.3%	3.0%	2.6%
Faber & Faber (year-end 31 March)								
Sales		11,678	10,013	10,648	11,038	11,173	11,912	12,510
Operating profits		997	423	(72)	77	273	(1393)	(540)
Margins		8.5%	4.2%	–	0.7%	2.4%	–	–
Bloomsbury (year-end 31 December)								
Sales	11,371	13,655	13,705	15,231	20,863	50,676	61,140	68,016
Operating profits	1207	1557	1859	2277	2926	5380	7876	8780
Margins	10.6%	11.4%	13.6%	14.9%	14.0%	10.6%	12.9%	12.9%

* After write downs for stock and work in progress of £286,000.   † 17 months.

years it made operating profits in only six, achieving its peak level in 1999 with operating profits of £270,000 (giving it an operating margin of 3.7%). In its last year of independence, operating profits had dwindled to £16,000 and at the pre-tax level there was a loss of £60,000.

The cash-hungry nature of fiction- based trade publishing is amply demonstrated in Fourth Estate's experience. In thirteen out of sixteen years, money was raised through the sale of shares and/or the issue of convertible loan stock. Bank borrowings, however, did not feature at all until 1990. Subsequently, the total fluctuated in response to injections of equity capital: in 1999, the balance sheet was debt-free, but in 2000 bank borrowings stood at £727,000, a record year-end level for the company.

Dominating Fourth Estate's financial history is an event that took place in January 1991 when the Guardian newspaper group invested £164,000. This gave it an initial 9.8% stake. Thereafter, financial support was granted almost annually, thereby inflating Guardian Newspapers' equity interest: in 1996 it owned 50% of the company – and had two directors on the board – and at the time of the sale to HarperCollins its stake stood at 42%. This degree of financial support was of crucial importance in enabling Fourth Estate to spread its publishing wings with such success in the 1990s – but at some cost: it ceased to be independent in the fullest sense of the term, while the founders' interests suffered steady dilution, partly offset by the allocation of attractive share options.

The decision by Guardian Newspapers to withhold further financial support for what was their solitary book publishing interest (taken following the appointment in January 1997 of Bob Gavron as chairman of Guardian Media Group) presented Fourth Estate with a critical situation. In the short term, existing private shareholders invested further. But this was no long-term solution. There was the realization that the company's cash requirements as it strove to compete on level terms with the other well capitalized groups with long-established book publishing interests looked like accelerating. The cash outflow in the year to March 31, 2000 came to £896,000, up from £521,000 the previous year and more than mopping up the record financing of some £900,000 in the financial year 1999.

The sale price of £9.0m in relation to turnover in 2000 of £7.25m, indicated a multiple of 1.2 times; if £1.1m of bank debt is excluded, HarperCollins was paying the shareholders £7.9m for the business or 1.1 times turnover. For a company that was barely in profit at the operating level, the terms look thoroughly respectable – even without reference to the write-offs that HarperCollins saw fit to make following the acquisition.

The missing ingredient in this analysis is that HarperCollins's main objective in bidding for Fourth Estate was to secure the services of Victoria Barnsley. Other comparable instances within trade publishing are the merger of Allen & Unwin and Bell & Hyman in 1986, when Rayner Unwin was determined to have Robin Hyman as chief executive, and the purchase in 1982 of Virago by Chatto, Bodley Head & Jonathan Cape, when Carmen Callil was needed to run Chatto.

Canongate

For the purposes of this analysis, Canongate's history may be said to start in 1994 when the company was acquired by Jamie Byng and Hugh Andrew (managing director of the Scottish publisher, Birlinn) for £150,000. From the start, it set out to be a trade publisher, seeking out original books and avoiding passing fashions.

Sales grew steadily from £1.3m in 1996 to £2.7m in 2001, an annual rate of 16%, at which point it was publishing 102 new titles, three-quarters fiction. It had a staff of sixteen. The year 2002 witnessed a 67% jump in turnover to £4.5m on the back of Yann Martel's *Life of Pi*, which won the Man Booker prize and sold in hardback that year 106,000 copies.

Operating profits in the period up to 2001 swung between modest profits and modest losses. In 2002, there was a move into significant profit. In the balance sheet, net cash outflows from operating activities occurred each year, including 2002. This was compensated for by share issues, raising £66,000 in 1998 and

£351,000 in 1999. Among the investors was Sir Christopher Bland, stepfather of Jamie Byng, and Byng himself. Bank borrowings throughout were on an upward path. In 2001 Jamie Byng also extended a personal interest free loan to the company of £98,000. (If one were to look for a precedent, there was Graham C. Greene's action in 1986, when his personal guarantee was needed before NatWest would agree to an increase in the Chatto, Virago, Bodley Head & Jonathan Cape banking facility.)

Similarities with Fourth Estate's publishing experience (a Booker finalist) were further reinforced when Canongate was voted Publisher of the Year in the British Book Awards for 2002. David Graham, managing director since March 2000, gave £5m as a sales target for 2003 in an interview with *The Bookseller* in February 2003. With the publication of *Life of Pi* in paperback, coupled with sustained sales in hardback, this hurdle will have been comfortably cleared.

David Graham is convinced that 'as a small company, the only way to make it work is to select a small number of titles and to give each huge effort'. From 102 titles (hardback and paperback) published in 2001, the following year saw a reduction to 73 and the current medium-term objective is to trim this further to some 60. The task of selection has up to now been Jamie Byng's. At a time in the life of the company when backlist sales could do with further development, the challenge of nourishing an innovative front list from one year to the next is considerable. The maxim that success – which has raised Canongate's standing among agents and retailers alike – breeds further success can of course be invoked.

On the financial front, the management of cash stands to benefit from the appointment in July 2003 of a full-time finance director. The year-end balance sheet in 2001 can be said to have highlighted sharply such a need, with trade debtors exceeding trade creditors by over £1m. On the same date, bank borrowings were at a then record level of £605,000. And there was also the publisher's loan of £98,000. The year 2002 presented the company with a financial challenge of a different character – that of dramatic success. The demand that followed the Man Booker Prize award to Yann Martel on 22 October was met by raising the printing from 20,000 copies to 300,000 by year-end; this meant shifting production to a printer that had the necessary capacity, but one with whom Canongate at that stage had no credit arrangements.

A marked feature is a high overseas content to sales, amounting in 2002 to 40% (£1.8m). This is made up of exports, accounting for 25%, of which two-fifths to the USA, where Canongate has benefited from its link with Grove/Atlantic. This has provided them with a channel into the US sales and distribution network of Publishers Group West. The connection with Publishers Group West is now being made direct. In addition, over 15% of overseas sales relates to rights income. Canongate has consistently laid much stress on the purchase of rights (world volume rights wherever possible) and their vigorous exploitation. An unusual accounting feature, whereby rights revenue is carried gross into the turnover statistics before deducting authors' shares, inflates the overseas percentages (thereby also affecting debtors).

In considering Canongate's further development, management's determination to keep a tight control on costs – there are for example no plans to increase staff numbers by replacing Compass Independent Book Sales with a dedicated domestic sales unit of their own – will undoubtedly help the group ride out inevitable fluctuations in activity. The nature of Canongate's list also helps to insulate it from competitive, inflationary advances. Nonetheless, fiction publishing's cash-absorptive characteristic will remain a reality.

One historical curiosity is an article that appeared in *The Bookseller* of 27 October 2000, announcing the takeover – presented as a merger - of Canongate by Grove/Atlantic. This never happened. But were financial constraints to reassert themselves, the similarities with Fourth Estate's history as a small independent trade publisher could be carried one step further were such a agreement to be 'revisited'.

Profile Books

While in many respects Profile Books presents a sharp contrast to Canongate, the similarities are those of a youthful trade publishing house built on the ambitions of an entrepreneur backed by his own and family money and intent on creating a business step by step more or less from scratch.

One of the differences is that Andrew Franklin already had behind him a publishing career extending over eleven years at Penguin, the last six as publishing editor of Hamish Hamilton. Another was that he set out to create a non-fiction house, having observed that 'most small independent publishers who publish fiction make a loss – not something I would wish to pursue'.

Some six and a half years after Profile's launch, sales for the year to 31 March 2003 had grown to £2.4m. The breakdown bears to some extent the stamp of Andrew Franklin's previous publishing experience in that it included the Penguin author, Francis Fukuyama, as well as the Economist publications, for which he had been responsible. Together, they provided at an early stage a flow of backlist sales. Alan Bennett became one of their authors some two to three years after the firm was launched, an unusual instance of a high-profile writer moving to a small, young firm.

By 2002, new titles published were running at an annual rate of around 35 – plus 10 in the Economist series – in such fields as history, biography, current affairs, travel, and business. In August 2002, Profile acquired HarperCollins's general business books list, covering some 70 backlist titles; this is expected to add another 10 titles to the annual publishing programme and the overall impact on group sales points to an increase of some 15%. It is no disadvantage that the list should already be well known to the Profile Books editor, Martin Liu, who previously worked at HarperCollins, and who is responsible for Profile's business-book titles. For Victoria Barnsley, the rationale of the disposal was simple: 'business books are very difficult in the UK and the reason we sold the list is because it's not making enough money'. Freed from its share of a major organization's overheads and ensconced in an environment where the scale and the publishing priorities are congenial, the list has every chance of proving its worth.

On a more general note, the ground seems fertile for transactions of this kind, usually involving large media groups as sellers and smaller independents as buyers. One other example involves Penguin, which in December 2001 sold the Pevsner architectural guides to Yale University Press and in April 2002 announced the purchase of the 49% stake it did not already own of Rough Guides. The former was generating sales of some £300,000, the latter sales of £10m. The symbolism of this double transaction was highlighted by the fact that the Rough Guides staff began life at Penguin by occupying the very office space that the Pevsner staff had just vacated. For Yale, which had already acquired in 1992 the Pelican History of Art, the purchase represented an excellent fit. Financially, there was the hugely advantageous arrangement whereby the Building Books Trust (the charity set up in the early 1990s, the brain child of Andrew Franklin) funds the costs of updating and revising the guides.

The challenges faced by small trade publishers in getting their wares into retail outlets were made much of by John Murray in discussing the sale of John Murray Publishers to W. H. Smith. The traditional solution – pending the achievement of sales that would support a dedicated sales force – is for the books to be carried by the sales force of another firm, which itself stands to benefit from an expanded catalogue. Profile Books moved in January 2002 to Faber & Faber, having previously been sold through Signature and before that Fourth Estate. Profile's overseas sales account for a relatively subdued 20%, thus reflecting the domestic bias to many of its books. Foreign rights are sold through agents.

Financially, one remarkable feature that sets it apart from Fourth Estate and Canongate is its consistent profitability since 1998. (For the year to 31 March 2003 the company reported operating losses of £1900, the results having been adversely affected by asset write-offs following the purchase of the HarperCollins list. Pre-tax profts, however, remained positive at £5700.) Another lies in the balance sheet: zero debt and year-end cash balances, with interest receipts boosting pre-tax profits. At its inception in May 1996, the company raised £315,000, one half from among members of the family and one half from other private investors under the EIS (previously known as the Business Expansion Scheme). The purchase in mid-2002 of the HarperCollins business list was financed through the issue of new shares taken up by existing shareholders, which raised £197,000.

While the financial record owes much to prudent management, it also reflects the nature of the publishing undertaken, with the company largely escaping the twin scourges of fiction publishing – speculative advances and competitive discounts.

Faber & Faber

Faber published its first volume of poetry in 1925, appropriately by T. S. Eliot. Its position as the premier independent literary publisher in Britain remains unchallenged, but has become increasingly lonely, while its financial history over the seven years 1996/7 to 2001/2 provides no basis for complacency. With this as background, management has applied itself to restoring the company to profitability.

One of the first steps was taken in mid-1998 when majority control (80%) of Faber & Faber Inc. was sold to Farrar Straus (now part of Holtzbrinck). In February 1999 the company closed its own warehouse at Harlow and moved warehousing and distribution to Macmillan. In 2000/1 there was a substantial write-off of unearned advances.

In October 2001 Stephen Page was appointed chief executive, prior to which he had had thirteen years publishing experience with Longman, Transworld, Fourth Estate, and HarperCollins, the last two as sales director; at HarperCollins he combined this role with that of marketing director.

Since his appointment, there have been some further initiatives affecting support services. One relates to significant investment in computers aimed at giving management greatly improved management information, plus the flexibility to exploit copyrights in electronic format. The company takes a cautious view, however, of the likely demand for e-books. Another is the decision to move Faber's warehousing and distribution from Macmillan to TBS; an important consideration was the provision by TBS of warehousing information tailor-made to Faber's needs.

In respect of publishing, the profile inherited by Stephen Page was: fiction over 50% of sales; poetry/theatre/music/film 25-30%; children's books and general non-fiction 20%; backlist sales running at 40%. His three-year objective is to raise the children's proportion to perhaps 10% from 7% currently and to increase general non-fiction. The poetry/theatre/music/film sector is singled out for a reduction in its percentage, the effect of which stands to be softened, however, by a rise in projected group sales.

In common with the actions of many of the publishing houses discussed so far, sales growth is linked to greater concentration in the publishing programme: over the next two years, the intention is that the number of new titles published annually should drop by 20% from 230 to around 190. At the same time, promotional expenditure as a percentage of turnover, currently some 7%, stands to be increased, while the pricing of books will be adjusted where possible to compensate for the upward movement of discounts.

One feature that distinguishes Faber from a number of other houses is the degree of importance management also attaches to the non-financial advantages that should flow from the implementation of this strategy. For Stephen Page, one of the attractions is the windfall of time for thinking that applying the same overhead to a reduced number of titles will produce. This goes hand-in-hand with an awareness of Faber's special position in the culture of this country – tellingly exemplified in the role it fulfils of literary agent for the estates of W. H. Auden, T. S. Eliot, Louis MacNeice, and Ted Hughes. There is a commitment to culture – and for that matter to standards of production – that sets limits to decisions made purely on commercial grounds. At the same time, it would be quite wrong to dismiss out of hand the financial advantages that this reputation brings to the publisher: an enhanced ability to exploit world rights, whenever secured, and foreign rights; a position in the market-place such that 'there is no sense at Faber that we cannot sit at the top table at all the traditional outlets'; and let us not overlook a slush pile of unusual quality.

Financially, net cash outflows have been a feature in each of the last seven years, barring one when additional shares were issued, raising some £600,000, and the Faber & Faber Inc. transaction which brought in $1.1m (spread over two years). Typically, recourse has been had to bank borrowings; at 31 March 2002 they stood at £797,000. No dividends have been declared since 1998.

The underlying credit rating of Faber & Faber can be said to be high in the light of the deep pockets of its two main shareholders, the Faber family, through Geoffrey Faber Holdings, and Valerie Eliot, T. S. Eliot's widow, with 45% and 49.3% respectively. This family presence has given the company a solid foundation, notwithstanding the disappointing trading experience. It should be added that, with the firm's continued independence remaining a fundamental tenet, provision is likely to have been made by the proprietors for most eventualities. Meanwhile, the objective of a return to profit – and incidentally to the dividend list – must remain a high priority. In this respect, Faber & Faber stands to benefit from Stephen Page's business background which extends across the literary and the commercial sides of trade publishing and emphasizes the selling and marketing roles.

Bloomsbury

Bloomsbury is an instance of a publisher that has had large-scale ambitions from the day it was formed in September 1986. For the founder, Nigel Newton, and his three co-founders, David Reynolds, Alan Wherry, and Liz Calder, all of whom had already distinguished themselves in separate publishing firms, humble beginnings around the kitchen table held few attractions: they were united in wishing to create a substantial firm from the start and this translated into an initial publishing programme of a hundred titles and the achievement of turnover of £5.2m in 1988, the company's first full twelve-month publishing period.

A key decision, taken at the outset, was to aim at a stock market listing. This meant that, when Nigel Newton and David Reynolds set about seeking finance, equipped with a professional five-year business plan drawn up with the help of Price Waterhouse, they were able to command the attention of venture capital firms. In the event four of them put up £1.65m (Caledonia Investments, Equity Capital for Industry, Legal & General Venture Capital, Baring Brothers Hambrecht & Quist). In addition, Newton and Reynolds contributed in total £100,000. In terms of shareholdings, management retained 50% and the venture capitalists held 50%, with Nigel Newton in possession of a casting vote in the event of a deadlock. (Management's stake is now of the order of 6%, rising to around 10% on the exercise of outstanding options.)

The publishing profile was unequivocally that of a hardback trade publisher dedicated to literary fiction in the first instance, followed by non-fiction and reference. Its literary credentials were established at an early stage, with the company contributing its first title to the Booker Prize short list in 1989; the next four years saw Bloomsbury feature in three more Booker short lists. The publishing programme continued to gather pace – 160 new titles in 1989 – while turnover rose to £7m that year and to £8.5m in 1993. Throughout the period, Bloomsbury was in profit at the operating and pre-tax levels, barring the start-up year.

The decision to obtain a stock market quotation in 1994 was in response to this good trading record, the need to offer the venture capital providers with an exit, a market environment judged reasonable for publishing flotations and, perhaps most important of all, Bloomsbury's own expansion plans. The original capital had been put to full use; this had been supplemented by bank borrowings. To embark on the next phase of development, more permanent capital was required, all the more so as, in the establishment of three new divisions – paperback, children's, and home reference – the company would be denying itself cash benefits from the sale of paperback licences. The £5.5m raised, which served to repay the venture capitalists' loan stock, also included £3.1m of new money; this helped finance the launch of these three new divisions in the summer of 1995.

Having demonstrated their ability to create a profitable business, much of what management have since done has been aimed at reducing the volatility inherent in their type of publishing, without, however, prejudicing growth.

Central to this is the build-up of sales from the backlist (defined as titles from previous financial years); by 2002 they were in excess of 60%. In that respect, the development of the reference division has played an important part. This has included the creation and exploitation of electronic lexico-graphic databases, notably the *Encarta©World English Dictionary* launched simultaneously by Microsoft in electronic format and by Bloomsbury in book form in August 1999, and the English Language Teaching dictionary database where Bloomsbury's role is that of author, published in March 2002 as the *Macmillan English Dictionary*, filling a serious gap in Macmillan's ELT range. *Business – the Ultimate Resource*, presented as a definitive reference source for businessmen, was published in 2002, with Perseus having bought the US rights; by April 2003, it had secured six language deals and ten electronic deals. One of the attractions of the A. & C. Black acquisition of May 2000 was that publisher's reference list, most notably *Who's Who*, of which the first on-line version was licensed in 2002. While such reference works demand heavy investment (the immediate impact on the profit and loss account is softened by capitalizing the costs which are then written off over a period of up to ten years), Bloomsbury is careful to secure partners ahead of any major outlay, thereby reducing the speculative risk. The revenue streams that a database can generate are numerous: they include sales of the printed version, plus the related territorial and electronic rights, as well as sales from up-dating the printed and electronic versions and other spin-off works and licences for on-line usage. In 2002, reference turnover came close to £13m (19% of the whole).

For a British trade publisher to have a well-rounded business, once it has achieved a vertical hardback paperback capability, its thoughts will normally turn to the US market. In Bloomsbury's case, August 1998 saw the establishment in New York of a sales office. Two years later it included two full-time commissioning editors and in 2001 a children's publishing presence was added. From the start, St Martin's Press (in whose building Bloomsbury's New York office is situated) has carried Bloomsbury titles in the USA. By 2002 simultaneous publication in the UK and the USA had become an established feature. US trade sales that year (not including exports from the UK) came to £3.8m (6% of group turnover). In 2003, a total of 51 children's titles for publication in the USA is planned, against 37 the previous year. The entry into the US market has been intentionally cautious, but the long-term objective to achieve a presence comparable to that secured in the UK is undoubtedly challenging. The presence since January 2002 on the Bloomsbury board of Michael Mayer, president of a US venture capital firm, may herald a change of pace.

The determination to squeeze the maximum out of the copyrights the company controls has been a feature from the start. A rights department, now equal in size to Bloomsbury's domestic sales office, has progressively widened its scope, with foreign rights, whenever feasible, handled in-house, and with its brief broadened to include merchandizing and film rights relating to children's titles. In its quest for world volume rights, Bloomsbury is in the same camp as the major houses. In 2002, rights income of £3.5m represented 5% of group turnover.

Its purchase in April 2003 of Berlin Verlag gives Bloomsbury a useful presence in Germany, consisting of a medium-size literary house, with sixteen staff and a publishing programme of some forty new titles a year, and having a similar profile in adult publishing. It also represents a further step towards the goal of worldwide publishing.

The development for which Bloomsbury is now best known is the Harry Potter phenomenon, which started in the autumn of 1997 with the publication of J. K. Rowling's *Harry Potter and the Philosopher's Stone*. Further titles have been published in hardback in 1998, 1999, 2000, and June 2003; paperback editions of the first four titles have appeared in 1997, 1999, 2000 and 2001. Bloomsbury holds English-language volume rights world-wide barring the

USA, where the publisher is Scholastic. In 2000 it also acquired from Warner Brothers certain merchandizing rights.

The Harry Potter era should not, however, be allowed to obscure the pre-Potter period: by 1997, ten years after Bloomsbury's launch, turnover had reached £13.7m, operating profits £1.9m, and operating margins 13.6%. After servicing its debt, 1997 pre-tax profits of £1.35m gave a margin of 9.9%, which had risen steadily since 1990, when it stood at 1.6%. In the context of a notoriously uncertain business – and with support from backlist sales inevitably developing only slowly – this was a considerable achievement.

To return to Harry Potter, in the period 1997 to 2002 the most visible direct impact has been the contribution to the near five-fold rise in turnover and operating profits. Outside estimates are that Harry Potter titles will have accounted for up to 40% of group sales. The profile of the company has been raised throughout the world. More prosaically, it made Bloomsbury the principal book supplier of several UK supermarkets on several occasions. Financially, it hugely accelerated the move into a cash-positive position. It provided the wherewithal to invest further in the reference sector – without recourse to share placings or bank borrowings – and facilitated expansion by acquisition – indirectly in the case of A. & C. Black where Bloomsbury's well-rated shares were used as finance, and more directly with a number of niche purchases for cash in 2002/2003. At the end of 2002, the group balance sheet contained net cash balances of £18.6m.

The experience in 2003 with the publication of *Harry Potter and the Order of the Phoenix* dwarfs all that has gone before it. The single UK statistic of total consumer market sales of 2.6m units in the course of eight days is perhaps the simplest proxy for an unprecedented publishing phenomenon.

The interest in Bloomsbury's position in British trade publishing extends well beyond the financial achievements to date. In a number of respects, it is out of step with many other publishing houses, whether large or small.

It is pursuing a policy of growth that does not rely on more concentrated publishing – new titles for 2003 of 750, compare to 729 the previous year – nor on related staff cuts. The history of trade publishing is in some respects an account of the unexpected and this gives management pause to any mechanical title-pruning.

Diversification remains an objective, through the development of electronic content and reference, as a means of reducing volatility in the overall business and enhancing the quality of earnings.

Bloomsbury is committed to the support of backlist sales, an objective that is given an extra edge thanks to the character of its publishing. While other houses will provide similar assurances, these are weakened where there is a very visible emphasis on commercial front-list publishing, having only limited shelf life.

Finally, Nigel Newton is outspoken in his view that medium is the optimum size in trade publishing. A repetition of the J. K. Rowling phenomenon might of course test this opinion to breaking point.

LITERARY AGENTS

The expansion of the role of literary agents ranks as one of the most arresting developments of the last thirty years in trade publishing. This has been a direct consequence of some of the issues discussed under the heading of publishers' profitability. It also reflects the agility and ingenuity of small units staffed by well motivated professionals.

The numbers in themselves are striking. In 1939, the UK *Writers' & Artists' Year Book* listed 56 firms of literary agents. By 1974 this had risen to 78; but the next 29 years to 2003 witnessed a more than doubling to 161. The acceleration can also be seen in the number of agencies founded: 20 in the 1970s, 31 in the 1980s, 49 in the 1990s and, so far into the first decade of the new millennium, ten. Looked at another way, of the 161 firms listed in the 2003 *Year Book*, 37% have been set up since the start of 1990.

One point that this demonstrates is ease of entry into the business: a small office (the dining-room at a pinch) and a telephone being all that is required in terms of equipment to start. But for the agency to be more than a pastime, the agent needs to have contacts with and knowledge of authors and publishers. This condition is readily satisfied by men and women working in publishing houses, hence the number of agencies that have been set up by ex-publishers. While such a background is not an essential requirement – Andrew Nurnberg, founder in 1975 of Andrew Nurnberg Associates, came into the business straight from university by buying a majority stake in a small agency specializing in Dutch translation rights – it forms the classic pattern.

To explain the explosion of numbers, several forces have been at work within the publishing industry, encompassing the two poles of dismissal and resignation. As to the former, the continuous changes within publishing houses, often in the wake of mergers or in response to altered trading conditions, have released skilled editors onto the market. Soured by their experiences, what more natural course could there be than to put to use many years of experience and to do so in an agreeably novel way as their own masters? For some of these, literary agency is seen as a new career, for others it takes on the shape of a gentle curve of diminishing activity as a prelude to complete retirement. One dispirited author, after a searing experience at the hands of a conglomerate, found the sight of such editors becoming literary agents tantamount to observing Herod retraining as a child-minder.

More intriguing than those who lose their jobs in publishing are those who resign their posts. The desire to escape from the corporate straitjacket of administrative responsibilities, where the individual has been promoted to positions of ever greater grandeur, dictates the move. A case in point is Peter Straus, who left his position as editor-in-chief of trade publishing at Pan Macmillan in September 2002 and joined the Rogers, Coleridge & White agency.

In 1995 Hilary Rubinstein declared that a literary agency offered the participant 'a better life, albeit a less decent living'. And in 2002, when Peter Straus moved from publishing to agenting, he suffered a sharp drop in salary. Such evidence notwithstanding, it may be becoming less true that the man who makes his career as an agent rather than as a publisher is donning a hair-shirt in financial terms.

The argument is two-fold. On the one hand, agents' value to publishers continues to rise. The hard-pressed commissioning editor welcomes the opportunity of purchasing titles which have the backing of respected agents. This accelerates the publishing decision in the publishing house and advances the publication date, both valuable attributes given the importance attached to swift results, particularly in houses subject to the financial disciplines of large media groups. There is in addition the assumption by agents of many of the editorial tasks once undertaken by publishers. Carole Blake describes the editorial role of agents as having changed out of all recognition since she set up her firm in 1974; at that time, some agents barely read the manuscripts before passing them on to the publisher, safe in the knowledge that the latter's editorial resources were comprehensive. The shift of roles was dramatically illustrated in 2002 when the Ed Victor agency recruited Philippa Harrison, purely in an editorial support role, on her retirement from running Little Brown.

At the same time, the value of literary agents to authors is being enhanced. As Andrew Nurnberg expresses it, 'the agent has become the author's true anchor in life' – for which role he is prepared to surrender 10% to 15% of his volume royalties. In the past, he might have had as 'my publisher' the Jonathan Capes, Max Reinhardts, Billy Collinses of this world. While this level of contact can still hold true for the smaller houses, it no longer applies to the larger. Then there is the consideration, in the words of David Godwin (who founded David Godwin Associates in 1995 after twenty years in publishing, the last five as publishing director of Jonathan Cape) 'one of the prime functions of an agent is to have the whole picture in his head'. This means that 'every agent is in the business of developing different revenue streams on the same book'. The aversion felt by agents towards the sale of world rights – unless the author has a pressing need for funds – is grounded on the belief that more can be secured by licensing rights separately. Self-interest enters here as well, since the agent's percentages apply across the board. This includes commission from the sale of television and film rights, whereas the publisher's direct interests normally stop with the printed word.

The role of agents, always crucial, has grown in complexity and importance. Aside from the obvious issue of advances, there are such matters as publishers' marketing commitments on publication and protecting authors' interests where the granting of exceptional discounts upsets traditional royalty calculations. There is also the greatly expanded field of non-volume rights.

The majority of agencies remain very small and make a virtue of their ability to operate at a cottage industry scale. This is greatly helped by the established practice of using other agents as sub-contractors. An agency that itself does not handle in-house foreign rights, for example, can pass the business on to other firms that have particular strengths, sometimes confined to individual countries, sometimes much broader. The price they pay is to hand over half the 20% commission that would otherwise go to them (80% going to the author). Similarly, one agency can sub-contract the film and television rights to another agency, foregoing in this instance half of the 15% commission.

It would however be wrong to imagine that publishers as a matter of course leave to agents the task of finding buyers for non-print rights. One famous example from the past is Faber & Faber's retention of all rights to the literary productions of T. S. Eliot, thereby ensuring for the publisher a massive stream of income from the staging of *Cats*. More topically, Bloomsbury has as one of its objectives the securing of world rights, including film and merchandizing. To that end, it formed in 2000 a partnership with the Hollywood firm, Creative Artists Agency, to sell film rights in selected Bloomsbury books to Hollywood studios and television producers.

A number of agencies have found it desirable to extend and strengthen the range of services they offer authors. One argument is that the one-stop literary agency, whether it be British or American, has a better hold on bestselling authors published by major international media groups. This has involved the establishment and/or strengthening within firms of a dedicated television/film division, of a more extensive foreign rights capability, and for some participants of a globetrotting life style. The Ed Victor and Belinda Harley agencies recently agreed to pool back-office resources as regards administration and subsidiary rights and, where appropriate, to develop projects together. Curtis Brown, Britain's largest independent agency, with turnover in 2001 of £4.2m, started representing actors in 2002 in furtherance of its objective to play a wider role, taking on clients across all media. The most extreme instance, however, of catholicism came in November 2001, when CSSStellar, the quoted sports and entertainment agency and events organizer, paid an initial consideration of £11.6m for Britain's largest independent literary agency, Peters Fraser & Dunlop (turnover £6.6m).

With personal attention to authors' needs as the main justification for the existence of agents, the advantages of scale require careful assessment. There is the looming danger of duplicating the very weaknesses of publishing houses from which the agents' clients have fled. At the same time, increased profitability is a justifiable objective. An agency may seek to achieve this by upgrading its portfolio, as it were: restricting new clients to those from whom several books may be anticipated; refining the list of existing authors, by shedding those whose creative vein is approaching exhaustion; concentrating energies on productive authors in such a way that work done on the front list will stimulate revenues from the backlist.

Moving away for a moment from the agency's profit and loss account to its balance sheet, the payment in 2001 of £7m to Curtis Brown by Disney in lieu of expected future revenues from A. A. Milne titles drew attention to the copyright benefits that accrue to agents. The intellectual property assets of some of the longer-established firms could attract some predators, both within the industry and outside it.

To the question, is this still a growth industry, the answer needs to be qualified. In the first instance, the penetration of the market is approaching saturation point: some 25 years ago 50% perhaps of writers of trade titles had agents, now this is variously estimated at 90% and over; exceptions typically include poets and writers in niche subjects – A. & C. Black's nautical list, for example. Secondly, for some authors the contribution that an agent can make to their careers is limited: for many titles, non-volume rights are irrelevant so that 'having the whole picture' can mean no more than that encompassed by books for which the publisher may be at least as well equipped as the literary agent. Set against this is the reality that the literary agent has become the essential conduit for a writer wishing to be published commercially. Increasingly, publishers will consider only those titles that come to them via agencies. (In the USA the situation is even more extreme than in the UK.) The role of the agent as the author's negotiator is unlikely to diminish in importance in an environment free of retail price maintenance – rather the reverse. And then there is the promise of continuity that small trading units innocent of hierarchical structures offer the author.

While the credentials of literary agencies as a growth sector are somewhat less secure than before, the participants continue to have before them the prospect of well-sustained demand for their services. A decent living is a realistic expectation.

SELF-PUBLISHING

The seemingly relentless efforts of so many publishers, whatever their size, to reduce the numbers of titles published and to trim their lists generates varying degrees of despair and frustration among aspiring authors. But, to take an analogy from nature, when the flow of a stream is impeded, the water quickly finds alternative channels, so authors are encouraged to find other publishing routes – namely through self-publishing. This quest has been greatly helped technically by developments in the fields of electronic transmission and digitization.

The use of the world-wide web to by-pass the traditional publishing/ printing process altogether was famously demonstrated by Stephen King when he made available in the year 2000 *The Plant* in on-line instalments via his own web-site. At the same time, he invited those downloading the instalments to pay him $1 per instalment. The failure of the numbers to meet his target – attributed to dishonour rather than lack of interest – led him to abandon the venture at Chapter 6.

In the USA a striking instance of advantage being taken of the internet to promote a self-published book is provided by Stephen Wolfram's *A New Kind of Science*: priced at $44.96, 1197 pages in length and weighing 4½ pounds it achieved bestseller status in the USA in June 2002. In this case, the targeted audience of scientists was peculiarly receptive to internet publicity, leading to vigorous debates on internet chat sites.

Today's average self-publisher is in a very different position to that of Stephen King. He is driven by the closed doors of publishers (and for that matter some literary agents). For a firm such as Book Guild, some four-fifths of whose annual output of 90 titles falls into the self-published category, 20% of its authors have already been published commercially. Carol Biss, chief executive and main shareholder, sees herself as supplying a full publishing service, once a title has been accepted (the cull is largely aimed at the pornographic, the racist, and what is described as the unreadable). Book Guild has the use of ten freelance editors, employs two full-time publicity officers, and has its own sales manager. Typically, production is undertaken by short-run litho printers, with runs of at least 500 copies. For anything less than 100 copies, use is made of print on demand.

On average, the cost to an author is in the region of £7000 to £8000, a substantial outlay that in itself acts as an additional filter. Royalties are set at 30% of the cover price; should a second printing be justified, Book Guild assumes the financial risk and the royalty drops to 20%. The shared interest that Book Guild (with its publishing overheads) and its authors have in achieving sales sets it well apart from old-style vanity publishers. Nonetheless, Book Guild discourages authors from seeing publication as a potential source of profit. Indeed, few cover their costs. Exceptions can arise, as when paperback rights are sold, two instances having involved Arrow and Penguin.

There are many lesser variations on the carriage-trade standards of Book Guild. In the USA, for down payments ranging from $1600 to as little as $99, authors are invited to get their manuscripts professionally laid out and bound. Xlibris, which describes itself as a strategic partner of Random House, offers varying levels of service, with copy-editing and marketing as options. Critically, production is linked to print on demand, thereby obviating inventory risks. The financial promise of self-publishing is something they do not shy away from, as witness the February 2003 announcement that they had just paid out their millionth dollar in royalties. They also encourage writers with historical parallels, citing Walt Whitman and Virginia Woolf as fellow self-publishers. In the case of Virginia Woolf, she was even said to have been reduced to buying a printing press in order to achieve publication. Her husband, Leonard Woolf, who described the launch in 1917 of the Hogarth Press as therapeutic for his wife and a hobby for both of them, would have demurred.

The ultimate in self-publishing opportunities comes with the internet, something that writers of scholarly journals were the first to discover. The absence of revenues mattered little to them. The loss of editorial control was of concern, however. One hybrid method involves the Open Publication Licence under which anybody is free to copy and redistribute a book so published, but any alterations have to be spelled out and credit given to the original author. Free electronic copies are made available on the internet, but at the same time regular printed copies are sold through bookshops and Amazon.

While it is easy to exaggerate the importance of self-publishing, one significant development is the weakening of the pejorative connotations that the term previously attracted. In publishing circles, this has the practical benefit that some houses will now as a matter of course consider for commercial publication self-published titles, particularly those that have already achieved significant sales in their first incarnation. Writing in *The Bookseller*, Stephen Phillips singles out Macmillan's US subsidiary, St Martin's Press, as a case in point. Self-publication thereby becomes not simply an end in itself but a back-door entrance into mainstream publication for the rejected author.

Under the joint stimulus of technological advances and a less accommodating environment within traditional publishing, self-publishing looks set to develop further.

PRODUCTION

Technical advances in the production of books often go by leaps and bounds. One such leap is digital printing, prompting John Holloran to predict that 'this technology will be all over publishing in the next decade'. After a long career in printing, which included McCorquodale as managing director and BPCC as chief executive, he is now chairman of the distribution company Marston Book Services.

The time-scale is important: 'in the next decade'. This helps to explain the diversity of views currently expressed by printers and even more so by publishers as to its impact. With the lack of consensus in part linked to the fact that the technology is itself undergoing rapid change, this does mean that technical objections raised one day may lose their justification the next.

For the modern publisher, text origination has been greatly simplified, now that computer-literate authors submit their 'manuscripts' on disc, using word-processing software. The publisher edits the text and adds what is required in terms of graphics and artwork, at a cost of around £1.75 a page – down from £4 to £5 a page when typescripts or manuscripts were what the author presented to the publisher.

The format of choice for sending print-ready work to printers is the portable document format (PDF). Such files can themselves be transferred to a disc, or more generally retrieved and placed electronically on the recipient's PDF site. The material is electronically scanned for storage in digital format at a cost of perhaps 10p a page for text and an additional £40 to £60 (depending on complexity) for a full-colour cover. On these figures, the publisher incurs a charge for the digitization of a 320-page paperback of under £100.

A point to remember is that this is a one-off cost to be spread over the period that the title retains its status of a publication available on demand. Against this, the printer may well charge an annual rental of around £10 for holding the file, this being negotiable, depending on the status of the customer. Another consideration is that digitization can be a prelude to the development of strategies for e-book publishing and on-line content syndication – not simply for print on demand.

Most digital presses used in book production are sheet-fed. The pages are printed sequentially. In recent years, marked improvements have been made in the speed of printing. Quality issues have centred on colour reproduction on digital presses, which in the view of many has typically fallen short of what is achievable with litho. David Armstrong of Page Brothers makes the point that to achieve good results on a cover you really need a run of 200 to 300 – but that creates an inventory and undermines the rationale of digital printing. Also, the fidelity of scanning means that the blemishes of a used copy are lovingly reproduced (unless corrected); this can be more than just an irritant, as in musical scores where inadvertent dots can lead to surprising notations. There was a time as well when the range of papers suitable for digital printers was restricted. These are two areas that have benefited from technological advances, but not to the extent of silencing all critics.

To the question, 'What are the unit print on demand production costs in relation to, say, traditional offset litho, and for what priced books and in what quantities is print on demand economic', there is a bewildering range of answers. Taking a 320-page demi-royal paperback, with printing costs of 1p a page for text and a further 60p for the full-colour cover, unit production costs to the publisher amount to £3.80. That in turn implies a cover price of £12 to £13 as a minimum. Currently, a unit cost of £3.80 would be twice as expensive as with offset litho on a print run of 1000. But if demand for this title is at a rate of say 300 copies a year or less, the high digital manufacturing charge needs to be set against (1) the virtual absence of warehousing costs – particularly telling in the case of publishers who have not invested in their own warehouse/distribution centres, (2) the financial benefits from having no capital tied up in stocks, (3) the speed of delivery thereby shielding the publisher from customer fatigue in cases where a reprint would otherwise be called for, and (4) the freedom from returns and stock write-offs, which can range from perhaps 5% for academic books up to 40% for trade.

To take an example from the USA, on an offset print run of 2000, production of a 300-page paperback with a colour cover might cost $2.00 a unit; printing 200 copies digitally could cost between $3.02 and $5.10 a unit. At the same time, the 'carrying costs' saved, on warehousing, finance, etc., can be estimated at 55 cents per annum per unit. No assumptions are made about possible write-offs on the offset printing. These figures are quoted in Jeff Nock's article, 'Digital Printing', in the March 2002 issue of *LOGOS*.

When the book in question has features such as colour illustrations or photographs, or special cover requirements, the calculations are more complex and the cover price implicit in the production costs for a viable publication that much higher – and at this stage in the development of the technology probably prohibitive. For illustrative purposes, unit manufacturing costs of a 96-page four-colour academic book might be of the order of £12.50, more than six times the £2 cost based on a litho printing.

At its factory in Eastbourne, Antony Rowe Limited, the short-run Chippenham-based printer, has also been developing rapidly its print on demand business. Starting in January 2001, print on demand now accounts for approaching 15% of group turnover. The factory itself is situated directly alongside the offices and warehouse of Gardners (the largest book wholesaler in the UK with turnover in 2001/2 of £130m), which currently accounts for one quarter - and rising – of turnover. This includes orders originating with Amazon. As a snapshot of the business, the factory has dealings with 300 publishers; over 40,000 units were printed in the month of March 2003, with an average print run of eight; they hold digital files on some 10,000 titles.

Interest in the opportunities that digital printing presents is currently concentrated within two widely separated fields of publishing, the academic and the literary. It does not touch the more commercial trade titles: the great advantage that print on demand provides publishers through the elimination of inventories carries with it the sting of invisibility. Print on demand denies titles a physical presence in retail outlets, and as Ralph Bell, chief executive of Antony Rowe, expresses it, print on demand in its purest form involves the sale of the book in advance of its manufacture.

So far, the academic embrace of such opportunities is undoubtedly the more whole-hearted. Since 2002, Cambridge University Press has followed a policy of digitizing all new academic monographs, plus a selection of out of print titles. At the end of 2002, it purchased for its own print factory a digital press. Its digital printing programme is predicated on achieving quality comparable to litho (the reproduction of black-and-white photographs has presented difficulties) and costs spread over the life of a title that are not more than 10% higher than if the work had been printed litho in one run, representing their calculation of those inventory, finance, and freight costs that print on demand enables them to avoid. Taylor & Francis is an early convert, having announced in 2001 its intention of digitizing the whole of its academic backlist (then amounting to 15,000 titles); normally, some 1000 titles would have gone into limbo, being declared out of print. At PalgraveMacmillan, new college and academic titles are automatically converted into electronic format and offered through print on demand. Pearson Education in the UK launched in 2002 print on demand publishing for 2000 previously out of print titles, while in the USA Pearson Education has developed its own in-house digital print facility.

Reference books, such as directories, where textual changes occur continuously, fit well into the print on demand model. The same applies to loose-leaf legal and tax publications. The bespoke opportunity that digitization offers educationalists – through the selection of chapters from several sources for a particular course for a limited number of students in any given year – has potential.

In literary publishing, the small specialist publisher, Carcanet Press, might be said to have been formed with print on demand in mind. In the words of its editorial and managing director, Michael Schmidt, 'good books of poems remain 'front list' in the teeth of time'. With this as an objective, print on demand is being used in a number of ways:

– To prolong the life of titles that would otherwise have required a reprint of at least 500 copies, but for which there is demand of perhaps 50 or less copies a year. The scale of change is seen in the reduction in annual totals of titles conventionally reprinted litho from 60/70 previously to 10 currently.

– To bring out-of-print titles back into print, such titles being destined for oblivion had they remained dependent on pre-digital technology.

– To enhance the profitability of north American sales by supplying that market through a US digital printer on whose PDF file the book is downloaded. This saves most obviously on freight and export costs. It may also lead to lower production costs – Michael Schmidt's experience in the past of US printing – and it certainly speeds up delivery.

The sometimes fine dividing line between print on demand and short-run litho printing is familiar territory to Antony Rowe since their Eastbourne and Chippenham plants supply the two markets respectively. For Penguin Classics, short-run printing is the preferred choice: in the light of their predictable pattern of steady but slow sales, the individual titles' warehouse bins are automatically replenished once stock is close to exhaustion. The task of managing the list is thereby simplified, while the litho printing costs on the numbers involved are less than would have been the case with print on demand.

In North America, digital printing would appear to be encroaching more than in the UK on short run litho work: in 2002 Quebecor's digital book module was aimed at print runs of 1000 and under, while the Perseus Group's own print on demand plant was set up to cater for the titles that sell during the course of the year less than 600 copies; on average, it prints 100 copies per title, but goes down to as low as 10.

In an interesting trans-Atlantic development, Biddles in the UK and IBT Global in the USA have signed a digital book agreement under which Biddles has taken over IBT Global's UK digital book production arm and henceforth will produce and distribute in the UK books and journals published by clients of IBT Global. The reverse applies in the United States. The work, largely made up of academic, legal, and scientific books and journals, is transmitted on PDF files with no concessions being made for differences in spelling. Other instances are on the increase of UK printers equipping themselves with digital print on demand capacity, one being Butler & Tanner.

What now appears certain is that digital printing has moved well away from its experimental stage to the point where it is a valid alternative to traditional production processes. Subject to the contractual arrangements with his authors, the trade publisher of low-volume titles now has open to him a number of options:

– on new titles, reducing a litho print-run from say 2000 to 1000 and relying on print on demand to accommodate any demand in excess of 1000;
– doing as above and raising the price of the books supplied through print on demand;
– to rely from the start on print on demand;
– to supply the domestic market as in the past, but to switch to print on demand for export markets, notably the US market;
– to extend the life of the backlist, by digitizing moribund titles and having them available on demand;
– to scour out-of-print lists and resurrect those judged capable of at least a trickle of sales on a print on demand basis;
– the use of print on demand for book proofs as a sales tool;
– to profit from the convenience of digital fulfilment, including the monthly receipt of any funds that are owed.

The rate at which technical advances are made is such that a reasonably safe assumption is that the quality problems that still affect print on demand will lose strength, thereby broadening the potential market. John Holloran's belief in such progress underpins his faith in what he describes as a very engaging technology – which will lead more and more publishers to 'publish into the technology': i.e. to adapt their publishing to the digital process.

CHINA

There have been a number of developments that will have alerted the British publishing community that China is becoming a market to take seriously, but none closer to home than the announcement that the firm of literary agents, Andrew Nurnberg Associates, had opened a representative office in Beijing in June 2002. This was followed in September by the announcement that HarperCollins, in conjunction with China's leading English language textbook publisher, Foreign Language Teaching and Research Press, is to develop and produce a new range of Chinese-English dictionaries. They are to appear under both publishers'imprints, the first title being due in 2004.

Underlying these and other initiatives is the now abundant evidence of China's acceptance in the international community, notably with its member-ship in 2001 of the World Trade Organization, its successful bid to stage the Olympics in Beijing in 2008, and two years later the World Fair – Expo 2010 – in Shanghai.

From a publishing standpoint, the single most important upshot is China's recognition that ownership of intellectual property (it was a signatory of the Berne Convention and of the Universal Copyright Convention in 1992) must be backed by measures to curb infringements and piracy. Last year's decision to increase the frequency of the Beijing International Book Fair from once every two years to annually (postponed by four months in 2003 because of the Sars virus) is also consistent with this rise in copyright respectability, while the invitation extended to Professor Paul Richardson to give a lecture ahead of the 2003 Book Fair to some two hundred Chinese publishers on the very subject of copyright underlines the change in atmosphere.

Up to now, China cannot be said to have been invisible to British publishers – if that degree of myopia were at all conceivable. Under the auspices of the Publishers Association, numerous missions have been organized since 1978. While there was a ten-year hiatus from 1988 – a case perhaps of publisher fatigue in the face of limited results – the year 1998 saw a resumption and again in 2002. On the production front, many a publisher has had recourse to Chinese (as well as Hong Kong) printers for at least part of their needs. Numerous British and US educational and academic publishers have been developing a Chinese presence. What is new is epitomized in the experience of the late Louis Alexander, Longman's leading English language teaching author, when he noted three years ago with some satisfaction that he was beginning to receive Chinese royalty cheques of some significance.

The statistics are impressive: population 1.3bn (end 2001); gross domestic product US$1210bn (2002); gross domestic product per head $930; annual growth rate of the economy 7-8%; primary students for whom English is a compulsory subject 120m; number of Chinese actively studying English 250m; book sales of 7bn units in 2001 for a retail sales value of £3.4bn; average retail price per book 48.5p; average receipt to the publisher 30p.

Viewed through one set of spectacles, these numbers suggest a dizzying potential for English-language publishers. Viewed through another set of spectacles, the exuberant macro figures at the national level are overshadowed by the more sobering micro statistics at the per caput and per unit level.

The two subject areas that continue to attract the greatest interest – and have done so for a long period of time – are, unsurprisingly, connected with the English language: English language teaching and reference/dictionaries. STM (science, technical, medical) publishing, another sector characterized by strong demand, but one which suffered more than most from piracy, is benefiting considerably from the closure by the government of the main distributor of pirated academic journals. This took place in December 2001 and was directly linked to China's admission to the World Trade Organization.

Within trade publishing, the most promising sector remains children's books, both in English and translation, stimulated in part by English having been made a compulsory subject three years ago for students in the middle of the primary level. Egmont Books, in conjunction with People's Post & Telecommunications Publishing House, has a strong presence. Macmillan, in conjunction with Foreign Language Teaching and Research Press, has been a particularly successful supplier of ELT material to the school market. In recent experience, sport is a subject area that has shown marked strength, a feature that is likely to be well sustained ahead of the Olympics in 2008, while business books are currently enjoying a surge of demand. Other subject areas where interest is developing include life-style titles, how-to books and self-improvement books. Travel guides are a promising sector in line with the progressive granting of 'approved destination status'. Germany is the first country in the European Union to have been so designated, with effect from February 2003. Others will follow. For their part, the German tourist authorities are contemplating overnight stays by Chinese tourists of up to one million within five years.

While the large US and British educational and academic publishers have typically dealt direct with Chinese publishers, trade publishers have up to now usually gone through agencies, notably the two Taiwan-based commercial agencies, Bardon Agency and Big Apple Tuttle-Mori. They in turn have dealt with the Chinese publishers in what is overwhelmingly a rights market, with the Chinese publisher paying an advance against royalties – 10% for the most part – calculated on the retail sale price.

Controls remain extensive. Foreign investment in publishing is not at this stage permitted. Direct imports have to go through some six authorized importers. There are close to six hundred state-owned publishers who hold the licence to publish and, consequently, have access to ISBN numbers supplied to them without charge by the State. At the same time, there are numerous private 'publishers' or distributors who buy from a state publisher a block of ISBNs for a fixed fee. This enables them to create titles which ultimately appear under the state publisher's imprint but in the creation of which the private companies have been wholly responsible. It is this phenomenon, countenanced by the authorities, that prompts Andrew Nurnberg to draw attention to the 'huge wave of entrepreneurial publishing going on in China'.

Measuring the force of this wave presents considerable difficulties, all the more so as the developments in China that are making it into a serious contender for the attention of a wide range of outside publishers, notably US and UK, are still very fresh, and such issues as piracy and corruption are still present, albeit less intense. Nor should the political challenge facing an autocratic government as it guides the country on a growth curve be underestimated.

To cite Andrew Nurnberg again, the Chinese market for trade titles is not as huge as many believe and the sums are not large: advances of $1500 to $3000 are the norm, based on print runs of 7000 to 15,000. To quote specific instances, a Bloomsbury 2002 title *Business, the Ultimate Resource* secured an advance well above average, while Profile Books in its 2002/3 financial year sold translation rights on as many as 26 titles (mainly business books). This experience is not, however, prompting Andrew Franklin at Profile Books to add a Chinese revenue line to his projections, taking as he does a very cautious view – 'but we relish it while it lasts'.

The sale of rights in China currently holds out to the British publisher who is a successful supplier the prospect of incremental revenue benefits, the quality of which, however, is high, given Chinese publishers' good payment record. To set against this there is the Scottish proverb 'many a mickle makes a muckle', while consideration of the speed of change already experienced in the Chinese market is grist to the mill of those such as Ian Taylor of the Publishers Association, who see considerable opportunities for those British publishers who are prepared to seize them.

VENTURE CAPITAL

Venture funds, variously defined, have a long history of supplying finance to publishing businesses at different stages in their development. Family money is the traditional source for a fledgling enterprise. Canongate is a recent case in point, as is Profile. Private individuals acting as angels often feature at an early stage in a company's history. Such equity injections give comfort to the banks who are the time honoured source of short term borrowings.

As an instance of long-term banking support, when Robin Hyman acquired George Bell in 1977, and again when Bell & Hyman merged with Allen & Unwin nine years later, Hambros merchant bank provided the backing, giving it a significant equity holding of 35%. For an example of a corporate angel, there is Guardian Newspapers supplying Fourth Estate with the equity finance that enabled it to advance beyond the nursery stage.

Venture capital groups played, unusually, the main role in two trade publishing start-up companies: Headline and Bloomsbury were each backed by venture capital firms in 1987 and 1986 respectively, the former having Rothschild Ventures as the lead financier, the latter Caledonia Investments.

The more traditional function of venture capital companies - involvement in businesses that have already achieved a degree of maturity - can be illustrated by way of a management buy-in (where top management is supplied from outside the company in question), as at Routledge in 1996, where Cinven provided the finance, with Bob Kiernan appointed executive chairman. A case of a management buy-out (where existing top management remains in place) was the backing given in 1988 by Kleinwort Benson Development Capital to Octopus Publishing Group management.

Finance as described above has often been a prelude to the disposal of the business to another company – Routledge to Taylor & Francis in 1998, Octopus to Hachette in 2001 – or to a stock market quotation – Headline in 1991 and Bloomsbury in 1994. In all such cases, the original backers are given the opportunity of realizing all or part of their investment.

What is new is that recent circumstances have militated strongly against the use of the stock market as a source of funds. This throws into relief the greatly expanded role of venture capital money in filling – temporarily perhaps and only partially – this financial void at a time when the pool of such funds awaiting investment in both the USA and the UK has assumed lake-like proportions: at the start of 2003, some 450 private equity groups had an estimated $190bn uninvested.

The term 'venture capital', which used to be restricted to small start-ups of up to say £20m, is now used more loosely, being interchangeable with 'private equity'. Typically, a private equity group solicits commitments to a specific fund from pension funds, financial firms, university endowments, investment groups; this may have a life of seven to ten years, during the course of which it may make investments in perhaps ten businesses, drawing down the funds as and when needed. The duration of such investments could be of three to five years, and as these are realized the proceeds are distributed to the venture capital investors, the principle being that, within each fund, money is invested only once. Venture capital funds make investments well beyond the sums raised through their ability to borrow heavily: in the late 1990s the ratio of 20% equity 80% debt was achievable; in the current more restrained climate, the ratio is closer to 40% equity 60% debt. The increased equity content serves as an extra filter on projects judged acceptable, given the investors' objective of a 20%+ annual return on equity capital over the life of each investment.

An essential ingredient in venture capital/private equity financing relates to the incentives given to management in the target companies. This will often call for an initial capital commitment on management's part and involve setting aside up to 15% of the company's equity in performance-related share options and allocations as their entitlement to the gains on the eventual sale. As Nigel Stapleton, formerly joint managing director of Reed Elsevier and past chairman of Veronis Suhler International Ltd stresses, 'you should not under-estimate the potential of an existing management team under a new environment freed from corporate bureaucracy and within which a higher risk factor is able to bloom'.

A focus of uncertainty in venture capital financing concerns the finite life of most funds. Should there be a dearth of trade buyers and in the absence of a stock market receptive to flotations, one possibility is the sale of the rump of a fund's investments to another venture capital fund, in what is known as a secondary buy-out. While a discount is to be anticipated, the benefits in terms of liquidity are significant. Another aspect of the present environment is that the life of investments within funds is lengthening: many exits are now taking up to eight years to complete. This in turn has negative implications for profitability: the head of one private equity fund described the assumption of a 20% compound rate of return under present conditions as 'heroic'. Although there are some funds nursing substantial losses on investments made in the heat of the dot com and stock market booms, when compared to the stock market, private equity performance has had the edge in many cases.

Indeed the collapse of share prices has prompted many financial institutions to question the investment weightings, typically heavy, that they have given in the past to quoted equities in their portfolios. Most famously, the Boots pension fund switched entirely into bonds in March 2001. Others have been much less draconian in their reassessment. Private equity as a distinct asset class in its own right, alongside for example property, commodities, hedge funds, has itself been a beneficiary. In March 2003 Foreign & Colonial Investment Trust, the UK's largest investment trust group, decided to invest £150m in private equity. Also in January 2003 Hermes Investment Management, owned by BT Pension Fund, launched its own £200m private equity fund as part of its strategy to develop its alternative investment business. The decision was based on an optimistic view of the growth potential in medium-sized company buy-outs. That this represents a trend that is likely to be sustained received confirmation in a survey among British Venture Capital Association members reported on in February 2003: 40% of institutional investors were proposing to direct more money into private equity over the next two to three years, increasing their asset allocations by one-third.

One consequence of the collapse of share prices and of stock market ratings has been to strengthen greatly private equity's hand in any competitive situations with quoted companies where the latter no longer have the benefits of high share prices and exalted stock market ratings. This is reflected in the number of occasions that a financial buyer has been able to get the better of a trade buyer. An additional advantage is the ability to act speedily, a particularly important feature as in the case of Vivendi's sale of Houghton Mifflin in November 2002, where the seller had an urgent need to pay down his debt. The other, which also makes for speed, is that private equity is much less likely to run into regulatory difficulties. When Wolters Kluwer sold its academic publishing division in October 2002, regulatory considerations effectively ruled out Reed Elsevier as a possible buyer and gave the private equity combination Cinven-Candover the edge. Taylor & Francis, for its part, was at a disadvantage in that it would have needed to secure shareholder approval.

Confrontation between trade buyers and private equity investors (often acting in groups of two to three) can, however, be replaced by co-operation. In the 2003 sale of Bertelsmann-Springer, Apax Partners and Taylor & Francis joined forces to submit a bid. In the March 2003 auction of AOL's Time Warner Books, Cinven undertook to underwrite a W. H. Smith bid, which would have given Hodder Headline a long-desired US presence. This was at a time when W. H. Smith itself was unable to mount a bid on its own, with its share price depressed and its balance sheet stretched by pension fund obligations. In the event they later withdrew from the auction, which in turn was subsequently annulled when nobody came close enough to the asking price.

This leads into a change in the character of private equity, with some funds taking on the role of companies – whose current freedom of action is constrained financially – by themselves assembling businesses with a view to creating specialist or diversified groups. This has to be more than a warehousing exercise, since 'value' has to be added in the process, in order to achieve ultimately the desired investment returns. Some funds are now making of this creative role an explicit objective. As one of two examples affecting publishing companies in 2002, Quad Ventures in the USA bought Troll, the book club and children's publishing business which at one time was owned as to 49% by Pearson, with a view to combining it with other educational companies in Quad's portfolio. In the UK, Providence Equity Partners bought F. & W. Publications, parent company of David & Charles, with a view to using the company as a platform for the acquisition of small special interest publishers, having sales of £5m to £10m. On an altogether different scale, the Cinven-Candover purchase of Wolters Kluwer's academic publishing arm in October 2002 has been followed by their acquisition of Bertelsmann-Springer.

The UK-based venture capital firms that stand out as having a record of past investment in various forms of publishing include Cinven, Candover, Apax, 3i, and Electra. Among the smaller funds operating from a UK base, Botts & Co. (Osprey, Continuum), Veronis Suhler (Blackstone Press), HgCapital (Bertrams), and Dresdner Kleinwort Benson (Octopus) have made investments (as indicated) in the book trade. During the course of the last four to five years, the involvement of some of the major US funds in European investments has increased substantially. One example from the retail trade is the 1998 management buy-out of EMI's HMV operations and W. H. Smith's Waterstones, which was backed by the US group, Advent.

While the absence of takeovers between corporate buyers and sellers has been partly compensated for by private equity activity, this does not mean that companies have ceased to work on their assets. Among numerous instances, since the start of 2002 Penguin has bought the 49% of Rough Guides it did not already own. Hodder Headline has sold Helicon. Macmillan has sold the Grove reference list, including the *New Grove Dictionary of Music and Musicians*, to Oxford University Press. Random House has bought Harvill Press as well as Everyman's Library of republished classics for assimilation into its Alfred Knopf division. Bloomsbury has strengthened its position in the reference, nautical, ornithological, and educational markets with the purchase of Whitaker's Almanack, T. & D. Poyser, Peter Collin, and Thomas Reed. Octopus publishing group, owned by Hachette, has sold Brimax children's book publishing to Autumn Publishing, part of the Swedish Bonnier media group.

Clear beneficiaries of this activity have been media consultants. Veronis Suhler, the longest established, is also itself a source of venture capital. The Van Tulleken Company (set up in 1995 by Kit van Tulleken in succession to the Pofcher Company), has in common with Veronis Suhler strong trans-Atlantic links.

From among the transactions undertaken by the Van Tulleken Company since its inception, 27 have involved book publishing, five directories, thirteen software and databases, typically in a £5m to £100m range in terms of transaction size. Of the thirteen deals completed in year 2002 and the first quarter of 2003, eight involved book publishing, five of them academic/reference, two STM, one trade (Berlitz). In Kit van Tulleken's experience, the publishing entrepreneur of today is likely to be looking to realize his business rather sooner than his predecessors – say after ten to fifteen years – and indeed may have from the start pencilled in an exit date, especially if in the course of its development past financing has included private equity money. The potential buyer is likely to be a division within a global company or one of the growing medium-sized groups, such as Taylor & Francis and Bloomsbury. This in turn implies a distinct publishing profile for the business on offer and tends to point towards non-fiction trade businesses and professional specializations.

These preferences are echoed by private equity fund managers when discussing their investment criteria: they respond to the attraction of cash generative businesses with earnings streams that have a relatively non-cyclical character and where the investor is not exposed to sudden surprises. In publishing, this points in the direction of such sectors as academic, professional, and STM, and within trade publishing those areas that have the more specialized profiles. For the short term, the fact that Dresdner Kleinwort Benson is not believed to have had much of a return on its investment in Octopus may well have acted as a dampener on private equity enthusiasm beyond illustrated non-fiction life-style publishing.

The absence of fiction in this want list cannot come as a surprise: it is notoriously cash absorbent and subject to unpredictable successes/failures. Nor do lenders rank it high when assessing cover. Fiction is properly the domain of the private investor. This has been demonstrated in the earlier accounts of Octopus, Hodder Headline, William Collins, and Penguin.

To conclude, those currently in search of funds can derive comfort from the certain knowledge of the weight of money seeking investment. Secondly, private equity investors will not all subscribe to the criteria listed above. 'Tired franchises', for example, are included in one such investor's desiderata. And to the lament that the independent publisher no longer exists, Kit Van Tulleken points to the number of young start-ups that are often specialized in their business - and known within their sectors but not outside.

But beyond the near term, the private equity industry cannot live in-definitely by creating its own liquidity. A resumption in the not too distant future of healthy financial markets is the underlying assumption beneath much of the current activity within private equity funds.

VALUATIONS

Throughout this account of postwar publishing, valuations have been a recurrent theme. The measures most frequently used in assessing what company X has paid for company Y is to relate the consideration to sales and profits. This immediately raises a number of questions.

(a) What is meant by consideration? The most frequently used definition is the value of the cash and/or shares being issued. Increasingly, this is being replaced by 'the enterprise value'; this includes, where known, the debt being assumed less the cash in the target company's balance sheet. The valuation attributed to a predator's shares, where these form part of the payment, should logically be that prevailing at completion, but in practice it usually relates to the share price at the time of the bid announcement. That a substantial gap can emerge was illustrated in AOL's acquisition of Time Warner: on the announcement in January 2000 the bid was worth $156bn; a year later when the deal closed it was worth $106bn.

(b) The sales figure, assuming properly audited accounts, presents perhaps the fewest difficulties.

(c) Profits require in the first instance differentiation: are they operating profits before interest (and any exceptional charges or credits), or are they pre-tax profits and in that case what if any are the exceptionals? In the case of private companies, which are run in a way that maximizes the benefits to the proprietor(s), a wide range of adjustments may well have to be made to put them on a comparable basis to those presented by public companies.

(d) Publishers' balance sheets are notoriously opaque in respect of debtors, which may be shielding unearnable advances, and stocks, which can be housing unsaleable books, both of which have a direct bearing on the quality of reported profits.

An enumeration of this kind highlights the difficulties of obtaining an exact picture of a company's financial position as a prelude to a takeover or merger. Indeed, where the transaction is conducted at speed (Reed's purchase of Octopus) or involves a hostile approach, the purchaser may only secure this information after the event – hence the number of occasions that surprises are a feature of chairmen's statements in the aftermath of takeovers.

A more fundamental reservation in assessing takeover valuations is that company trading statistics, such as they exist, tell one what has occurred in the past. Onto these must be grafted an appreciation of existing trends, forthcoming synergies, prospective economies. A seemingly high purchase price for a business may prove a hugely rewarding investment in one company's hands, in the same way that a seemingly inexpensive purchase may contain the seeds of disaster. In the light of these complexities, there is little surprise that the most widely used valuation yardstick for takeovers is also the simplest: the multiple of revenues that a purchase price represents. In the Statistical Appendix, a selection has been made of transactions dating from the 1980s, broken down into five main divisions.

In the educational sector, the first point that emerges is the consistency shown, with valuations seemingly centred on a multiple of two, plus or minus one fifth. The major exception, the curriculum assessment and data management group, National Computer Systems, bought by Pearson in August 2000, falls more readily into the category of a software company than an educational publisher. The purchase of Addison-Wesley by Pearson in March 1988 is noteworthy for the apparent absence of scars from the October 1987 stock market crash. More topically, Houghton Mifflin provides an unusual example of a major group bought and sold within the space of 18 months. Vivendi's purchase price in June 2001 of $2.2bn gave a multiple of 2.2× on revenues of $1bn. Vivendi's sale price in November 2002, now expressed in euros, of €1.7bn in relation to revenues of €1bn gave a multiple of 1.7×. With the euro close to par against the dollar, the attrition in value was of the order of 23%. What is impressive is that a forced seller, seeking to restore health to a heavily indebted balance sheet in the wake of the puncturing of Jean-Marie Messier's global ambitions – and in the light of the dramatic falls in equity markets throughout the world – should have achieved the price it did. On a much smaller scale, the purchase of John Murray by Hodder Headline in June 2002 on a multiple of revenues of 2.1× was confirmation that desirable educational assets continue to command substantial prices – even when accompanied by a trade publishing arm (one quarter of turnover) that was indifferently profitable, albeit high in reputation.

Legal publishing has the distinction of having attracted the highest multiples. This has had much to do with the strength of the publishers' positions within their national markets and the 'monopoly' characteristics that this implies. The point has to be made, however, that legal publishing valuations have not been tested on any significant scale since the end of the 1990s. The five intervening years have been particularly marked by the impact of information technology on the publishing process, the companies' response to which has been far from uniform. This has led to sharp differences in stock market valuations – with for example Thomson Corporation holding on to its high rating and Wolters Kluwer suffering a major downgrading. Significantly, 53% of Thomson's revenues in 2002 were derived from products and services delivered electronically (over the internet, through dedicated transmission lines, on compact discs, and even hand-held wireless devices). The comparable figure for Wolters Kluwer was 32%. With the economies of scale of electronic publishing that much higher than those of hard-copy publishing because of the lower variable costs, a gap of this size is magnified at the level of operating margins. In turn, this suggests that in any future transactions involving legal publishers, valuations are likely to be more discriminating than seemed necessary in the past.

The STM sector covers a gamut of publishing specializations. Medical publishers' multiples have ranged from less than two to close to three. Scientific multiples have also been variable extending up to 4.8× for Plenum Publishing, the academic publishing group; this was bought by Wolters Kluwer in 1998 at a time of market buoyancy. Four years later, the decision by Cinven and Candover to pay in October 2002 four times sales for the whole of Wolters Kluwer's academic publishing arm – with 700 scientific and journal titles and 1200 new book titles a year – owes nothing to euphoria in financial markets. Quite the reverse. Instead it is a vindication of the attractions of a business that is cash generative, judged to be relatively immune to economic fluctuations, and was seen as a stepping-stone in the creation of what would become an important publishing group supplying a growing international market. Less than eight months later, Cinven-Candover won the auction for Bertelsmann-Springer on an apparently modest multiple of turnover of 1.4× (reflecting in part the inclusion of less attractive business-to-business operations - 35% of sales). Taking the two together, they paid 1.9× turnover.

Routledge, whose exposure to such 'soft' areas as humanities and social sciences secures it a lower rating than the 'harder' fields, provides an interesting illustration of value creation. In June 1996 it was the object of a management buy-in from the Thomson Corporation, when the consideration of £28m was broadly equal to sales. In 1997, with the continued backing of Cinven, Routledge acquired Carfax for £25m. In relation to sales of £9m, the multiple of 2.8× was high – justified by Carfax's concentration on journals, in both the hard and soft sciences, and of the strong attendant cash flow. Also in 1997, E. & F. N. Spon, the specialist architecture publisher, was bought for £4m. These acquisitions were a means of giving balance to the business and, as it were, fattening up Routledge ahead of market day. In November 1998, Routledge was acquired by Taylor & Francis, which paid £90m for a business with sales of £47m, a multiple of 1.9×. This indicated a surplus of £33m over acquisition costs of £57m, achieved within a period of a little less than two and a half years.

The diversified groups classification is undoubtedly arbitrary. It could well have been expanded since few companies are so focussed as to exclude all diversifications. But it happens to have the merit of including the two publishing events that epitomize acquisitive euphoria: Reed International's purchase of Octopus in July 1987 and America On Line's acquisition of Time Warner in January 2000. These events immediately preceded the two collapses of financial markets that have an unassailable place in business history books – the stock market meltdown of October 1987 and the dot com bubble burst that dates from March 2000.

Trade publishing covers a great diversity of businesses. It does seem, however, that a valuation of 1× revenues has served as a point of departure in a number of trade publishing transactions. Valuations significantly below that figure can be accounted for by reference to an indifferent record and poor profitability. For those where the multiple is richer than 1×, the explanations may cover such matters as prevailing economic conditions and the state of financial markets. But usually circumstances peculiar to individual transactions turn out to be the determining considerations. In other words, it is very hard to engage in the generalizations to which educational, legal, and to some extent STM transactions appear to lend themselves.

Random House paid in 1989 what looked like a full price for Century Hutchinson, but then they were acquiring a vigorously managed vertically integrated publishing house. Chatto, Virago, Bodley Head & Jonathan Cape and the Reed Trade Division (William Heinemann and Secker & Warburg), both bought for around 1× turnover in 1987 and 1997 respectively, were acknowledged repositories of exceptional literary copyrights; they suffered, however, from being hardback businesses without a credible paperback arm and this was duly reflected in the prices paid.

Where an auction is held (News Corporation's purchase of Harper & Row) or the bid is contested (News Corporation's takeover of William Collins) the valuations are, unsurprisingly, inflated. This leaves unexplained the apparently generous prices paid by HarperCollins for Fourth Estate and by W. H. Smith for Hodder Headline on multiples of turnover of 1.2× and 1.8× respectively. One was barely profitable, though the other convincingly so. As already explained, the Fourth Estate transaction had much to do with the decision by News Corporation to recruit Victoria Barnsley to run the UK business. That involving Hodder Headline had echoes of Reed's purchase of Octopus: the diversification looked bizarre, while the vendor had a solidly based reputation for financial astuteness. The difference with Octopus is that Hodder Headline, under its new ownership, has performed strongly, while the broadened responsibilities of Tim Hely Hutchinson within the parent company, where he has also been put in charge of news distribution, brings one closer to the rationale for HarperCollins's purchase of Fourth Estate.

The major acquisition that remains to be discussed is Penguin's purchase of Dorling Kindersley. This took place in April 2000, on the eve of the recession in financial markets. It was opportunistic in the sense that Dorling Kindersley had just reported a miscalculation that had involved an over-printing of some ten million copies of Star Wars books, requiring a provision of £14m against profits. More fundamentally, it involved the addition of a genuine consumer brand to the portfolio of the UK publisher best qualified to recognize the benefits that flow from consumer recognition of this kind. In addition, there was the lure of advantageous links with Pearson's educational interests in both the UK and the USA. The price paid of £311m was judged at the time to be generous at 1.6× turnover (and 25.7× operating profits). Adding in the £51m of debt that Penguin assumed, brings the enterprise value to £362m, indicating a multiple of turnover of 1.8×. Had the analysis been taken one step further by recognizing Penguin's resolve, once successful in its bid, to close the loss-making electronic and direct-selling activities which accounted for some £50m of turnover, the multiple would have been lifted to a spectacular 2.4× – but the multiple of profits stood to be reduced. The purchase has been followed by three years of hard labour, gradually moving Dorling Kindersley into profit and meshing it in to the Pearson book interests. Perhaps the unsung motivation for the purchase was its sheer size as an independent within UK trade publishing and the distaste with which Penguin would have viewed its being bought by a rival publisher.

A curiosity was the acquisition of the literary agency Peters Fraser & Dunlop by CSSStellar, the sports and entertainment agency, for an initial consideration

Table 35: *Flotation valuations*

Date	Company	Valuation	Sales†	Multiple	Pre-tax profits†	Multiple	EPS	P/E
April 1961	Penguin‡	£1.5m	£2.0m	0.8×	£0.20m	7.5×	3.8p	15.8×
April 1983	Octopus	£55.0m	£30.8m	1.8×	£4.80m	11.5×	21.2p§	16.5×
April 1991	Headline	£11.1m	£8.3m	1.3×	£1.10×*	10.1×	6.9p	14.5×
Oct. 1992	D.K.	£101.7m	£70.9m	1.4×	£7.50m	13.6×	13.0p	12.7×
June 1994	Cassell	£10.5m	£20.1m	0.5×	£1.20m	8.8×	11.0p	13.0×
June 1994	Bloomsbury	£9.0m	£8.5m	1.1×	£0.75m	12.0×	7.5p	14.0×
May 1998	Taylor & Fs	£129.3m	£30.0m	4.3×	£7.15m	18.1×	8.2p	24.4×
May 2002	HMV	£773m	£1.7bn	0.5×	£53.6m	14.4×	14.5p	13.2×

* Pro forma.
† Historic.
‡ Company profits and earning forecasts for 1961; sales are estimated. Earning per share of 3.8p (equivalent to 9.1d) are after tax of 52.5%.
§ On a full tax charge, EPS = 14.8p. The valuation and price earnings ratio are calculated on the striking price of 350p.

of £11.6m. In relation to turnover of £6.6m, the purchase multiple was a lofty 1.8×. Since November 2001 the shares of CSSStellar have fallen dramatically from over 300p. While much of this can be laid at the door of the stock market slide, it may also suggest that the concept of a totally comprehensive agency is easier to expound but harder to implement.

Underlying trade publishing is insecurity. This makes it, every so often, a cherished home for private stock market investors. If an Australian depression in the ground can generate expectations of a rich diamond pipe, what could be more natural than that they should support a type of publishing in which the role of luck can also play a major part? Table 35 lists the principal new issues of British trade publishers in the postwar period, starting with Penguin in 1960. In addition, the contrasting statistics for Taylor & Francis, the academic publisher, and HMV, which houses Waterstones as well as EMI's music and video retailing, are included for comparative purposes.

Within the trade publishers, the flotations of Headline, Cassell, and Bloomsbury were by means of placings, where the shares are bought by clients of the sponsoring underwriter and broker. This has the merit of reducing the risks in an issue, but at the cost of restricting demand. The three other flotations were by public offerings, that of Octopus by tender, as described in Chapter 6. With flotations, the multiples of pre-tax profits as well as price earnings ratios are the preferred valuation measures. The low ratio for Cassell is largely explained by an indifferent profits performance in the three or so years leading up to the stock market debut. In all the other cases, the preceding period had witnessed adequate growth (Bloomsbury, Penguin) to rapid growth (Octopus, Headline, Dorling Kindersley). The Taylor & Francis valuation underlines the perceived quality of academic publishing cash flows and profits reliability.

All the publishing flotations, barring those of Cassell and Bloomsbury (both supported by venture capital funds) came at times of strong investor interest in

Table 36: *Stock market price performance on day one*

	Penguin	Octopus	Headline	DK	Cassell	Bloomsbury	T. & F.	HMV
Price at start	12s	275p*	100p	165p	143p	105p	200p	192p
Price at close	17s 3d	350p†	122p	213p	151p	110p	240p	177½p
Change %	+44	+27	+22	+29	+6	+5	+20	−8

* Minimum subscription price. † Actual striking price.

new issues. Taylor & Francis came to the market on a wave of stock market buoyancy, while HMV's flotation, the timing of which was governed by the needs of its two investors, EMI and Advent, came in the midst of a market slide.

A look (table 36) at the performance of these shares at the end of the first day of dealings establishes first of all that in every case, barring HMV, the issues were judged to be 'a success' from the point of view of their pricing. More interestingly, they convey some of the excitement that flotations of a handful of trade publishers have provided investors in the past.

This glowing picture has to be adjusted, however, to take account of the fact that trade publishing is by no means a sure route to financial success. Even in the case of a company, such as Fourth Estate, where the sale price to HarperCollins of £13.55 a share compares favourably with the range of £5 to £8 which the majority of investors had paid for their shares, this does not spell untold riches. There have, furthermore, been those launches that have disappointed their founders, such as Sinclair-Stevenson Publishers and Collins & Brown. The Harvill Press management buyout and refinancing in 1995, amounting to £1m, which then required periodic further injections of capital before its purchase by Random House, led to a total write-off for its backers. But thanks to four consecutive years of substantial losses, Harvill reached Random House endowed with a valuable lump of tax losses to set against future profits – as well as its thoroughly desirable backlist.

But the lure of trade publishing, particularly literary publishing, is not simply to be equated with financial aspirations, whether it be on the part of the publishers themselves or those who invest in their businesses. There is a newsworthiness about trade publishing which sets it apart from all other parts of the industry. This is stimulated by high-profile book prizes, which provide excellent press copy and, in the case of the Man Booker Prize for fiction, television coverage, plus the attention of the William Hill betting shops. When in January 2003, Random House dismissed Ann Godoff, head of their trade group, and Penguin recruited her eight days later – what in any other industry would have qualified as a very small earthquake - this made the headlines in the *New York Times* media section and was widely reported and commented upon in the UK. For many, the recurrent surveys of the public's favourite fiction writers, or better still the nation's hundred favourite books, are compulsive reading and form part of the seductive appeal that trade publishing can exert. In short, trade publishing is likely to remain in competition with the ocean-going yacht or the thoroughbred racehorse for the savings of the wealthy individual or even the company considering an uplifting diversification. As this book has demonstrated, it has, nonetheless, also been the occasional medium for the creation of substantial wealth.

STATISTICAL APPENDIX TO MERGERS AND ACQUISITIONS

Date	Target	Predator	Bid	Revenues	Multiple
Diversified Groups					
July 1985	Heinemann	Octopus	£100m	£41m	2.4×
July 1987	Octopus	Reed Intl	£535m	£159m	3.4×
Nov. 1993	Macmillan Inc.	Paramount	$553m	$285m	1.9×
Feb. 1994	Paramount	Viacom	$9.7bn	$4.3bn	2.3×
April 1995	Macmillan*	Holtzbrinck	£374m	£248m	1.5×
Jan. 2000	Time Warner	AOL	$156bn	$27bn	5.8×
May 2000	A. & C. Black	Bloomsbury	£16.4m	£7.9m	2.1×
Trade Publishing					
Mar. 1987	Harper & Row	News Corp.	$300m	$202m	1.5×
May 1987	CVBH & Cape	Random House	£20m	£17m	1.2×
June 1989	Century Hutchinson	Random House	£64m	£39m	1.6×
Jan. 1989	Wm. Collins	News Corp.	£403m	£230m	1.8×
June 1993	Hodder & Stoughton	Headline	£49m	£56m	0.9×
Dec. 1996	Putnam Berkley	Pearson	$336m	$276m	1.2×
Feb. 1997	Reed Trade Div.	Random House	£17.5m	£20m	0.9×
Mar. 1998	Random House	Bertelsmann	$1.3bn	$1.2bn	1.1×
July 1998	Orion (70%)*	Hachette	£36m	£37m	1.0×
Aug. 1998	Reed Illustrated	Management	£33m	£45m	0.7×
May 1999	Hodder Headline	W. H. Smith	£185m	£102m	1.8×
April 2000	Dorling Kindersley	Pearson	£362m	£199m	1.8×
July 2000	Fourth Estate	HarperCollins	£9.0m	£7.3m	1.2×
Oct. 2001	Octopus	Hachette	£35m	£40m	0.9×
Oct. 2002	Vivendi Europe ‡	Lagardere	€1.25bn	€1.1bn	1.1×
Education					
Jan. 1988	Rich. D. Irwin	Times Mirror	$135m	$62m	2.2×
Mar. 1988	Addison-Wesley	Pearson	$283m	$167m	1.7×
Dec. 1989	Scott-Foresman	Harper & Row	$455m	$249m	1.8×
Oct. 1995	D. C. Heath	Houghton Mifflin	$455m	$180m	2.5×
Feb. 1996	HarperCollins Educ.	Pearson	$580m	$316m	1.8×
Nov. 1998	Simon & Sch. Educ.	Pearson	$4.6bn	$1.9bn	2.4×
Aug. 2000	Ntl. Comp. Systems	Pearson	$2.5bn	$630m	4.0×
June 2001	Houghton Mifflin	Vivendi	$2.2bn	$1.0bn	2.2×
June 2002	John Murray	Hodder Headline	£17.0m	£8.0m	2.1×
Nov. 2002	Houghton Mifflin	T. H. Lee & Bain Capital	€1.7bn	€1.0bn	1.7×
Legal Publishing					
July 1987	Associated Book Pub.	Thomson	£210m	£85m	2.5×
May 1989	Lawyers Coop.	Thomson	$810m	$200m	4.1×
Oct. 1994	Mead Data Central	Reed Elsevier	$1.5bn	$551m	2.7×
Dec 1995	CCH Inc.	Wolters Kluwer	$1.9bn	$579m	3.3×
Mar. 1996	West Publishing	Thomson	$3.5bn	$827m	4.2×
Mar. 1998	FTLaw & Tax	Thomson	£70m	£21.5m	3.3×

STATISTICAL APPENDIX *continued*

Date	Target	Predator	Bid	Revenues	Multiple
Scientific, Technical & Medical					
June 1990	J. B. Lippincott	Wolters Kluwer	$280m	$100m	2.8×
Aug. 1997	Churchill Livingstone	Harcourt General	$92.5m	$47.8m	1.9×
Feb. 1998	Waverley Inc.	Wolters Kluwer	$375m	$172m	2.2×
May 1998	Mosby	Harcourt General	$415m	$225m	1.8×
June 1998	Plenum Pub.	Wolters Kluwer	$258m	$54m	4.8×
Oct. 2000	Harcourt General†	Reed Elsevier	$4.5bn	$1.4bn	3.2×
Oct. 2002	Wolters Kluwer Acad.	Cinven, Candover	€600m	€150m	4.0×
May 2003	Bertels. Springer	Cinven, Candover	€1.05bn	€730m	1.4×

* Partial bid grossed up to 100%.

† Total cost of Harcourt General (before disposal to Thomson Corporation of higher education and professional services businesses): $5.7bn (of which debt $1.2bn). On total revenues of $2.14bn, bid multiple = 2.7×.

‡ Subject to approval by the European Commission.

Note: Where known, the value of the bid includes debt. In a number of cases, it has been necessary to rely on trade estimates. See also *Who Owns Whom in British Book Publishing*, Christopher Gasson (Bookseller Publications, 2002).

INDEX

INDEX

INDEX